JOSH HOWARD
BLACK
HARVEST

BLACK HARVEST

written & illustrated
by

JOSH HOWARD

layout
by

PATRICK BUSSEY

www.joshhoward.net

IMAGE COMICS, INC. - WWW.IMAGECOMICS.COM

ROBERT KIRKMAN - CHIEF OPERATING OFFICER
ERIK LARSEN - CHIEF FINANCIAL OFFICER
TODD McFARLANE - PRESIDENT
MARC SILVESTRI - CHIEF EXECUTIVE OFFICER
JIM VALENTINO - VICE-PRESIDENT

ERIC STEPHENSON - PUBLISHER
TODD MARTINEZ - SALES &LICENSING COORDINATOR
BETSY GOMEZ - PR & MARKETING COORDINATOR
BRANWYN BIGGLESTONE - ACCOUNTS MANAGER
SARAH deLAINE - ADMINISTRATIVE ASSISTANT

TYLER SHAINLINE - PRODUCTION MANAGER
DREW GILL - ART DIRECTOR
JONATHAN CHAN - PRODUCTION ARTIST
MONICA HOWARD - PRODUCTION ARTIST
VINCENT KUKUA - PRODUCTION ARTIST
KEVIN YUEN - PRODUCTION ARTIST

BLACK HARVEST
ISBN: 978-1-60706-315-5
First Printing

Published by Image Comics, Inc. Office of publication: 2134 Allston Way, 2nd Floor, Berkeley, CA 94704. Copyright © 2010 Josh Howard. Originally
published in single magazine form as BLACK HARVEST #1-6 by Devil's Due Publishing. All rights reserved. BLACK HARVEST ™ (including all
prominent characters featured herein), its logo and all character likenesses are trademarks of Josh Howard, unless otherwise noted. Image Comics®
and its logos are registered trademarks and copyright of Image Comics, Inc. All rights reserved. No part of this publication may be reproduced or
transmitted, in any form or by any means (except for short excerpts for review purposes) without the express written permission of Image Comics,
Inc. All names, characters, events and locales in this publication are entirely fictional. Any resemblance to actual persons (living or dead), events or
places, without satiric intent, is coincidental.

PRINTED IN SOUTH KOREA

Also from Josh Howard
and Image Comics:

DEAD@17: ULTIMATE EDITION
(vol. 1 - 4)

DEAD@17: AFTERBIRTH
(vol. 5)

chapter 1

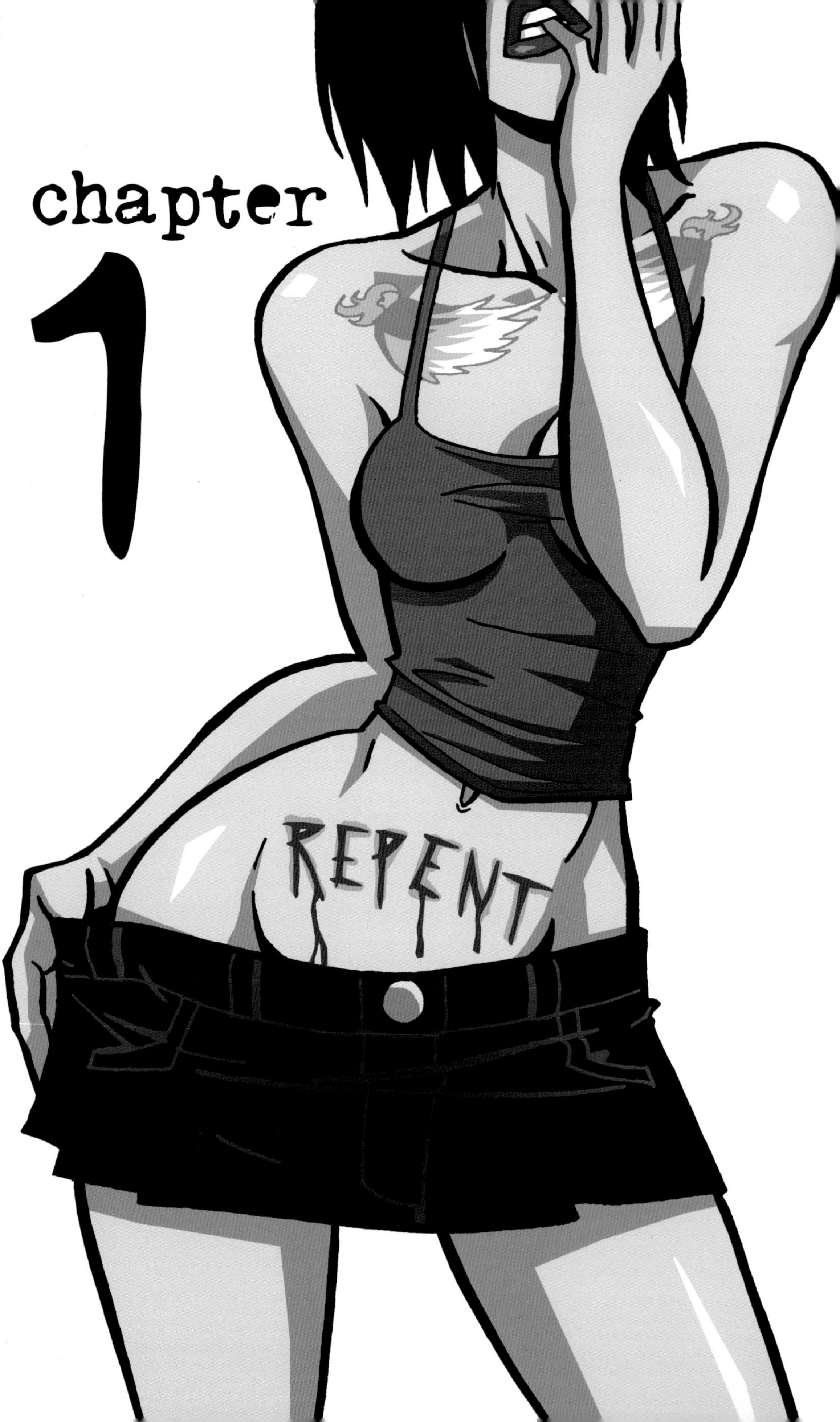
REPENT

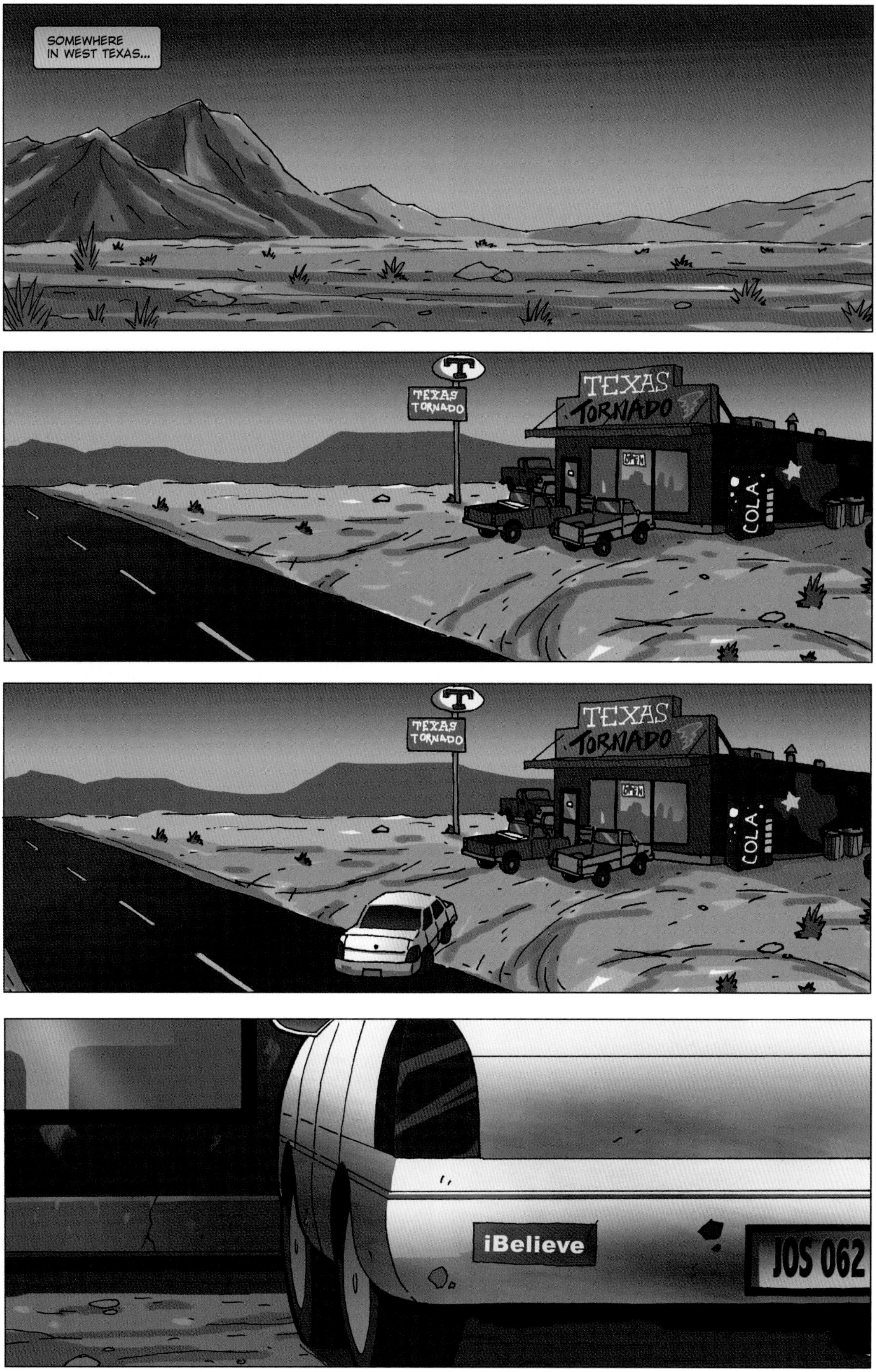
SOMEWHERE IN WEST TEXAS...
TEXAS TORNADO
TEXAS TORNADO
OPEN
COLA
TEXAS TORNADO
TEXAS TORNADO
OPEN
COLA
iBelieve
JOS 062

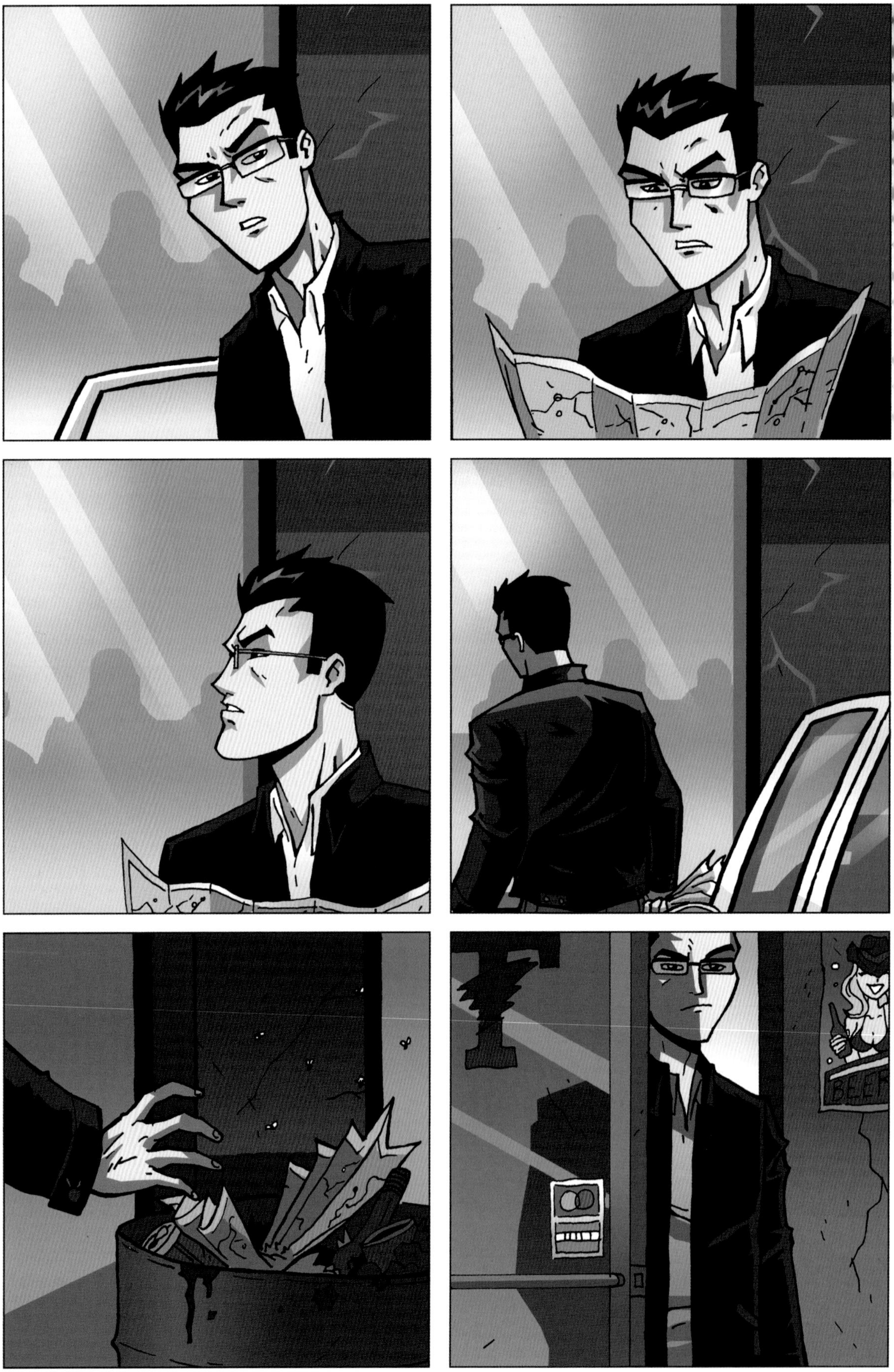

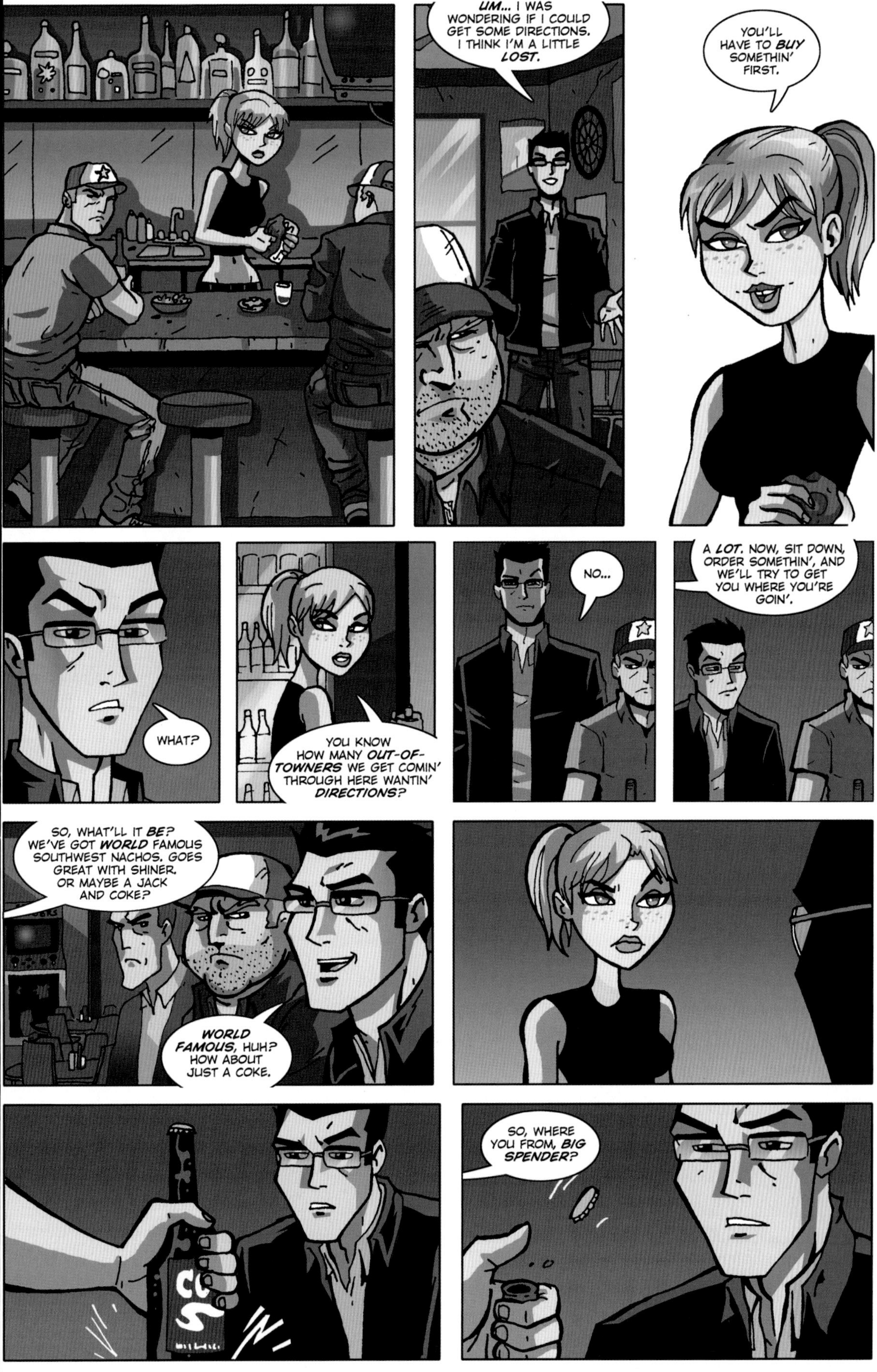
UM... I WAS WONDERING IF I COULD GET SOME DIRECTIONS. I THINK I'M A LITTLE LOST.
YOU'LL HAVE TO BUY SOMETHIN' FIRST.
WHAT?
YOU KNOW HOW MANY OUT-OF-TOWNERS WE GET COMIN' THROUGH HERE WANTIN' DIRECTIONS?
NO...
A LOT. NOW, SIT DOWN, ORDER SOMETHIN', AND WE'LL TRY TO GET YOU WHERE YOU'RE GOIN'.
SO, WHAT'LL IT BE? WE'VE GOT WORLD FAMOUS SOUTHWEST NACHOS. GOES GREAT WITH SHINER. OR MAYBE A JACK AND COKE?
WORLD FAMOUS, HUH? HOW ABOUT JUST A COKE.
SO, WHERE YOU FROM, BIG SPENDER?

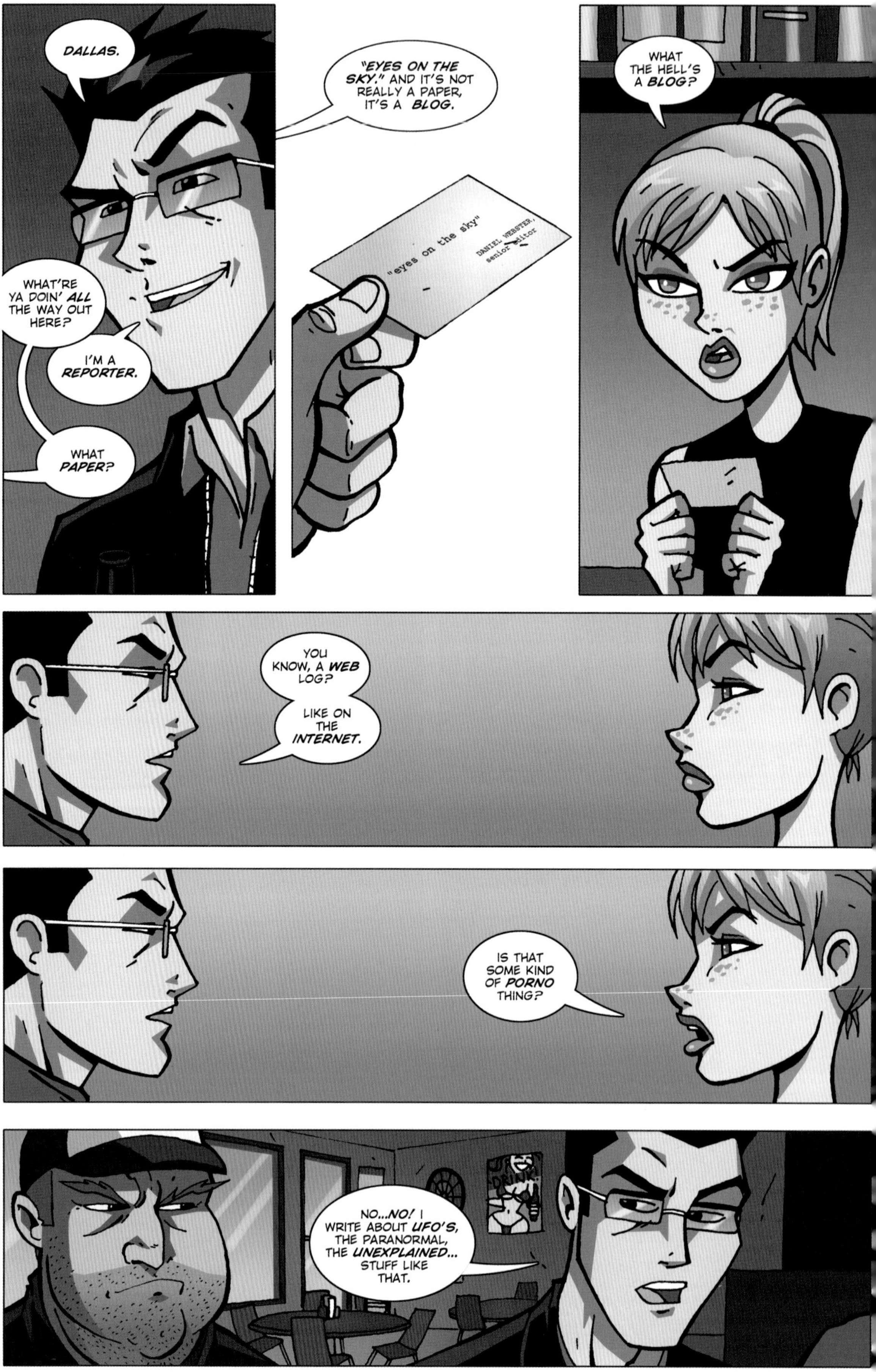
DALLAS.
WHAT'RE YA DOIN' ALL THE WAY OUT HERE?
I'M A REPORTER.
WHAT PAPER?
"EYES ON THE SKY." AND IT'S NOT REALLY A PAPER, IT'S A BLOG.
"eyes on the sky"
DANIEL WEBSTER, senior editor
WHAT THE HELL'S A BLOG?
YOU KNOW, A WEB LOG?
LIKE ON THE INTERNET.
IS THAT SOME KIND OF PORNO THING?
NO...NO! I WRITE ABOUT UFO'S, THE PARANORMAL, THE UNEXPLAINED... STUFF LIKE THAT.

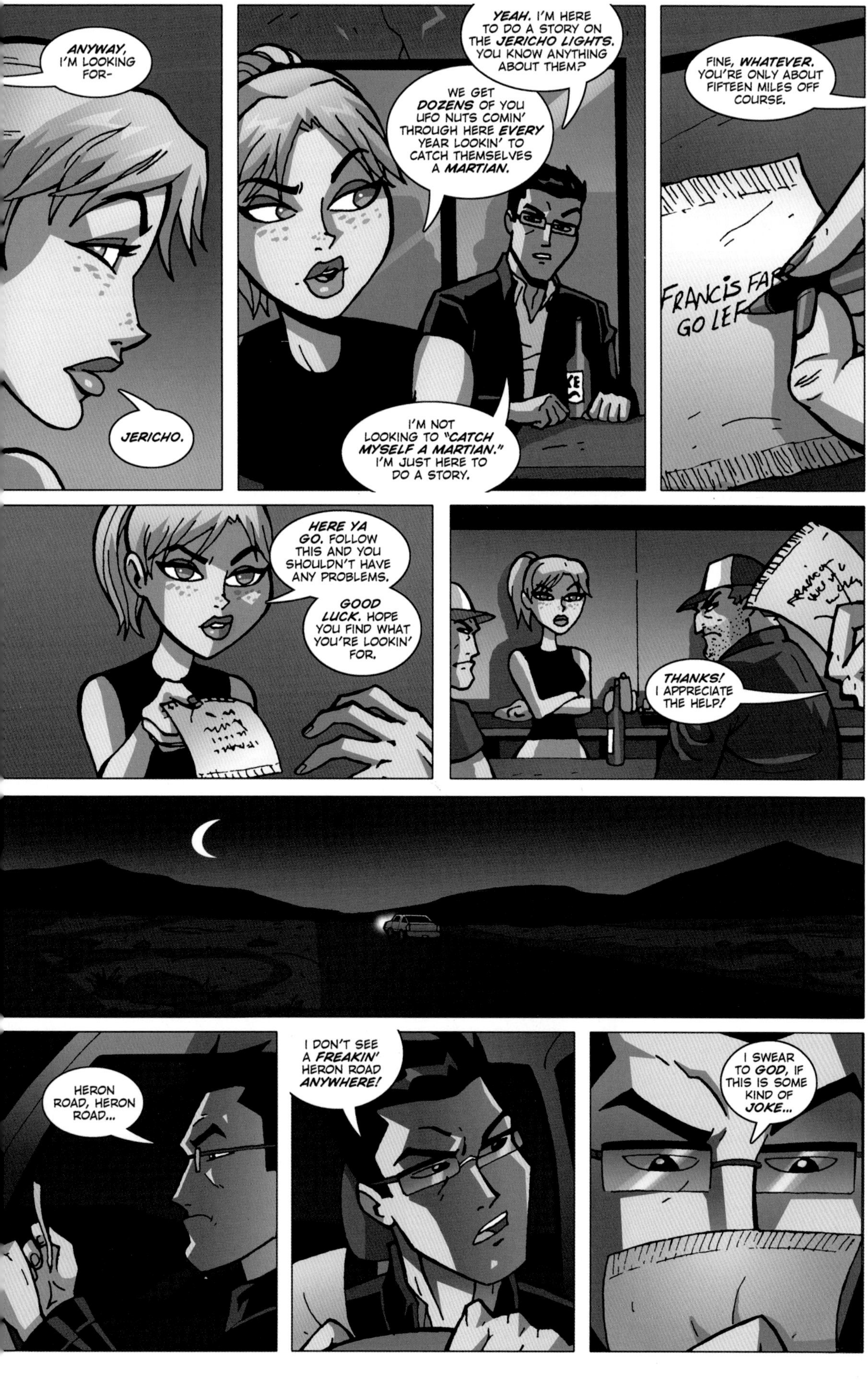
ANYWAY, I'M LOOKING FOR-
JERICHO.
YEAH. I'M HERE TO DO A STORY ON THE JERICHO LIGHTS. YOU KNOW ANYTHING ABOUT THEM?
WE GET DOZENS OF YOU UFO NUTS COMIN' THROUGH HERE EVERY YEAR LOOKIN' TO CATCH THEMSELVES A MARTIAN.
I'M NOT LOOKING TO "CATCH MYSELF A MARTIAN." I'M JUST HERE TO DO A STORY.
FINE, WHATEVER. YOU'RE ONLY ABOUT FIFTEEN MILES OFF COURSE.
FRANCIS FAR
GO LEF
HERE YA GO. FOLLOW THIS AND YOU SHOULDN'T HAVE ANY PROBLEMS.
GOOD LUCK. HOPE YOU FIND WHAT YOU'RE LOOKIN' FOR.
THANKS! I APPRECIATE THE HELP!
HERON ROAD, HERON ROAD...
I DON'T SEE A FREAKIN' HERON ROAD ANYWHERE!
I SWEAR TO GOD, IF THIS IS SOME KIND OF JOKE...

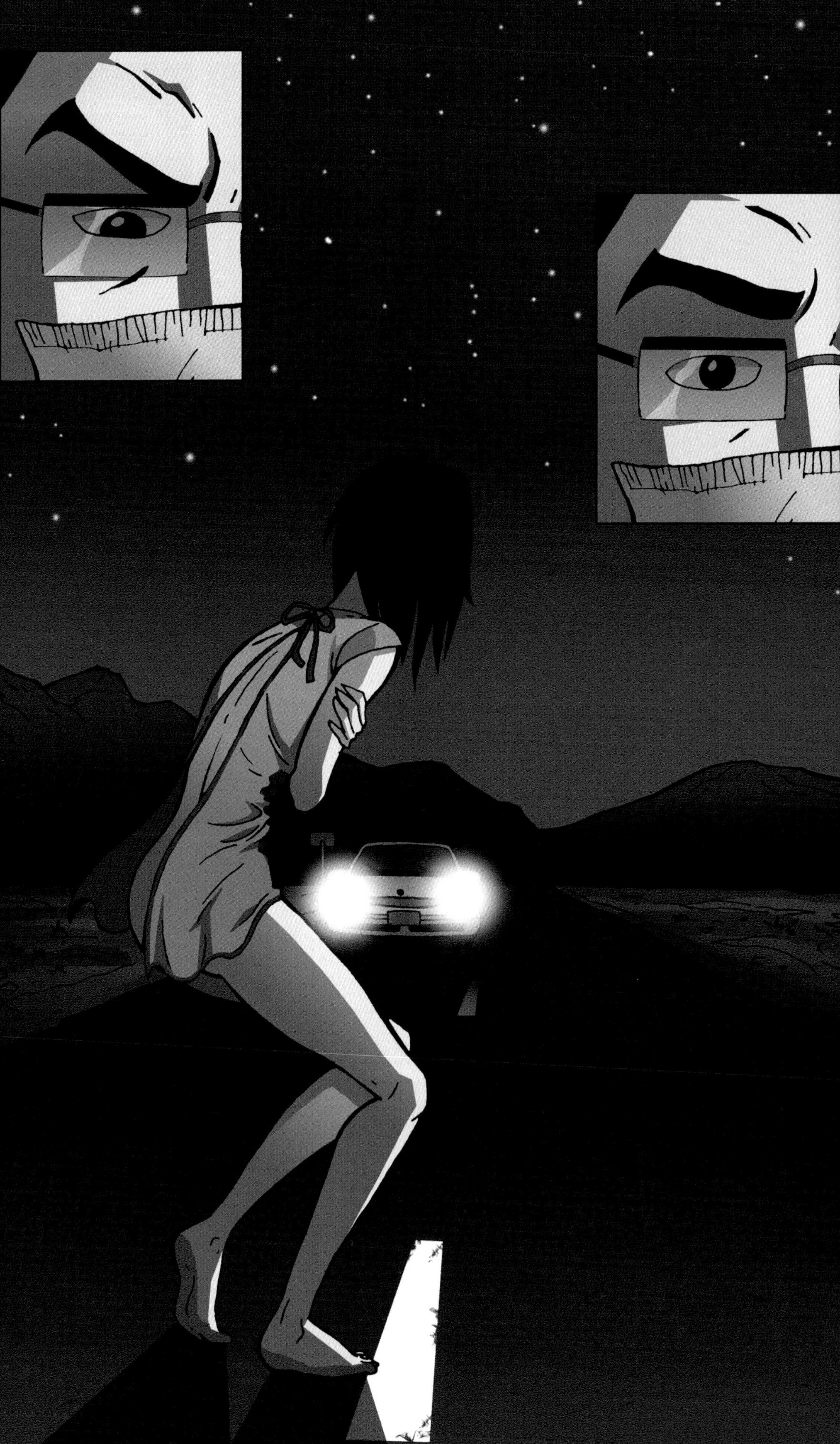

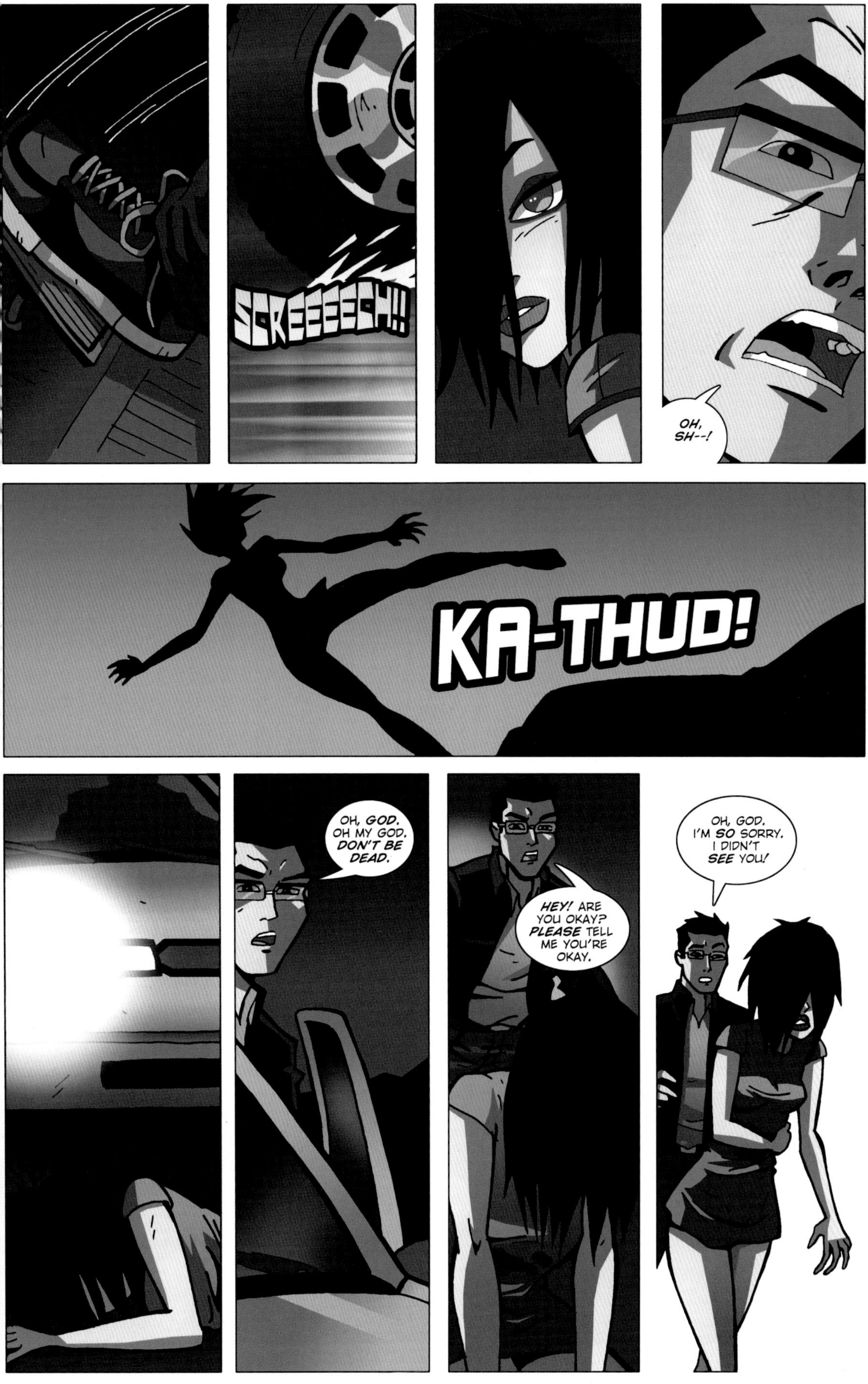
SCREEEECH!!
OH, SH--!
KA-THUD!
OH, GOD. OH MY GOD. DON'T BE DEAD.
HEY! ARE YOU OKAY? PLEASE TELL ME YOU'RE OKAY.
OH, GOD. I'M SO SORRY. I DIDN'T SEE YOU!

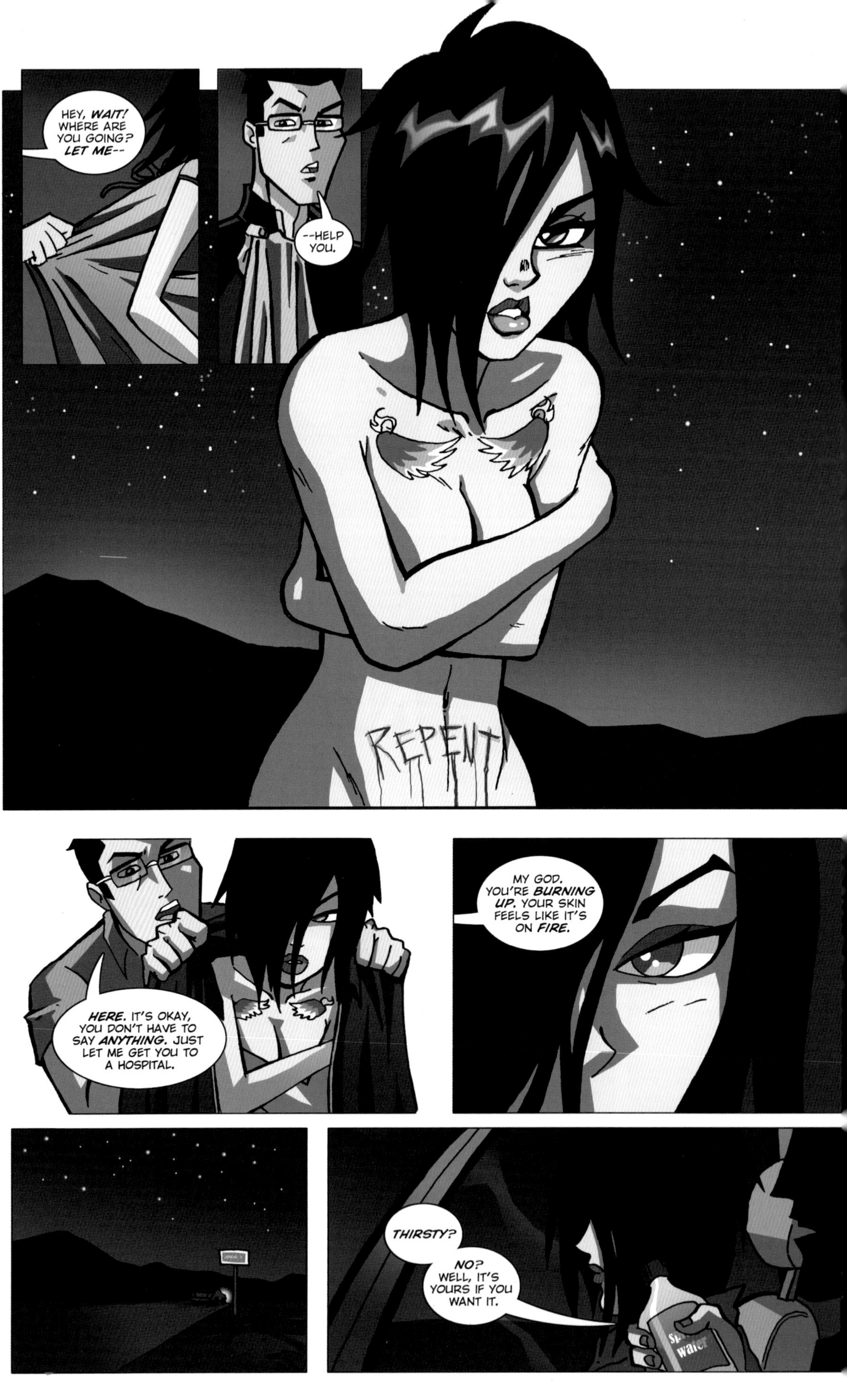
HEY, WAIT! WHERE ARE YOU GOING? LET ME--
--HELP YOU.
REPENT
HERE. IT'S OKAY, YOU DON'T HAVE TO SAY ANYTHING. JUST LET ME GET YOU TO A HOSPITAL.
MY GOD. YOU'RE BURNING UP. YOUR SKIN FEELS LIKE IT'S ON FIRE.
THIRSTY?
NO? WELL, IT'S YOURS IF YOU WANT IT.

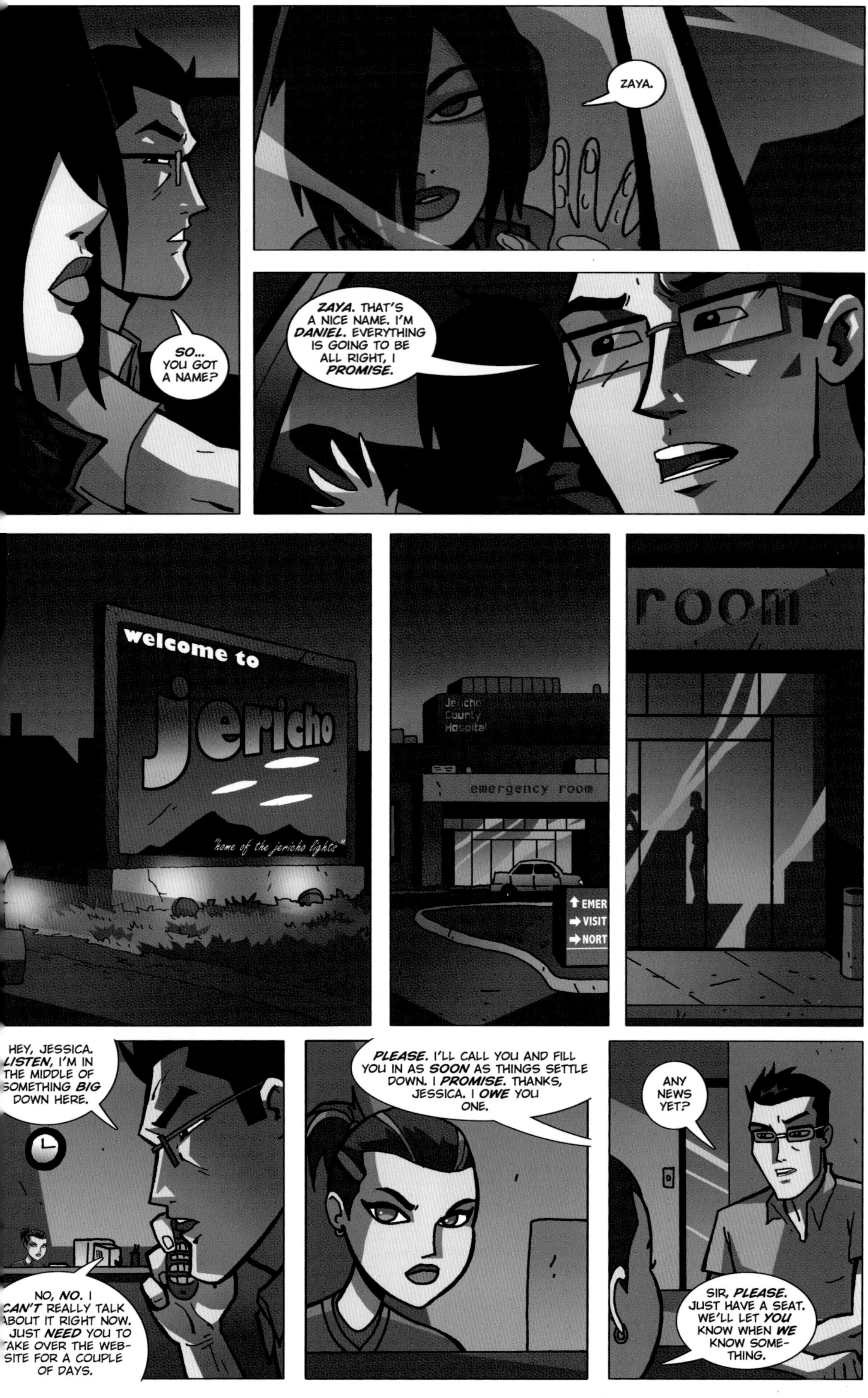
SO... YOU GOT A NAME?
ZAYA.
ZAYA. THAT'S A NICE NAME. I'M DANIEL. EVERYTHING IS GOING TO BE ALL RIGHT, I PROMISE.
welcome to jericho
"home of the jericho lights"
Jericho County Hospital
emergency room
EMER
VISIT
NORT
room
HEY, JESSICA. LISTEN, I'M IN THE MIDDLE OF SOMETHING BIG DOWN HERE.
NO, NO. I CAN'T REALLY TALK ABOUT IT RIGHT NOW. JUST NEED YOU TO TAKE OVER THE WEB-SITE FOR A COUPLE OF DAYS.
PLEASE. I'LL CALL YOU AND FILL YOU IN AS SOON AS THINGS SETTLE DOWN. I PROMISE. THANKS, JESSICA. I OWE YOU ONE.
ANY NEWS YET?
SIR, PLEASE. JUST HAVE A SEAT. WE'LL LET YOU KNOW WHEN WE KNOW SOME-THING.

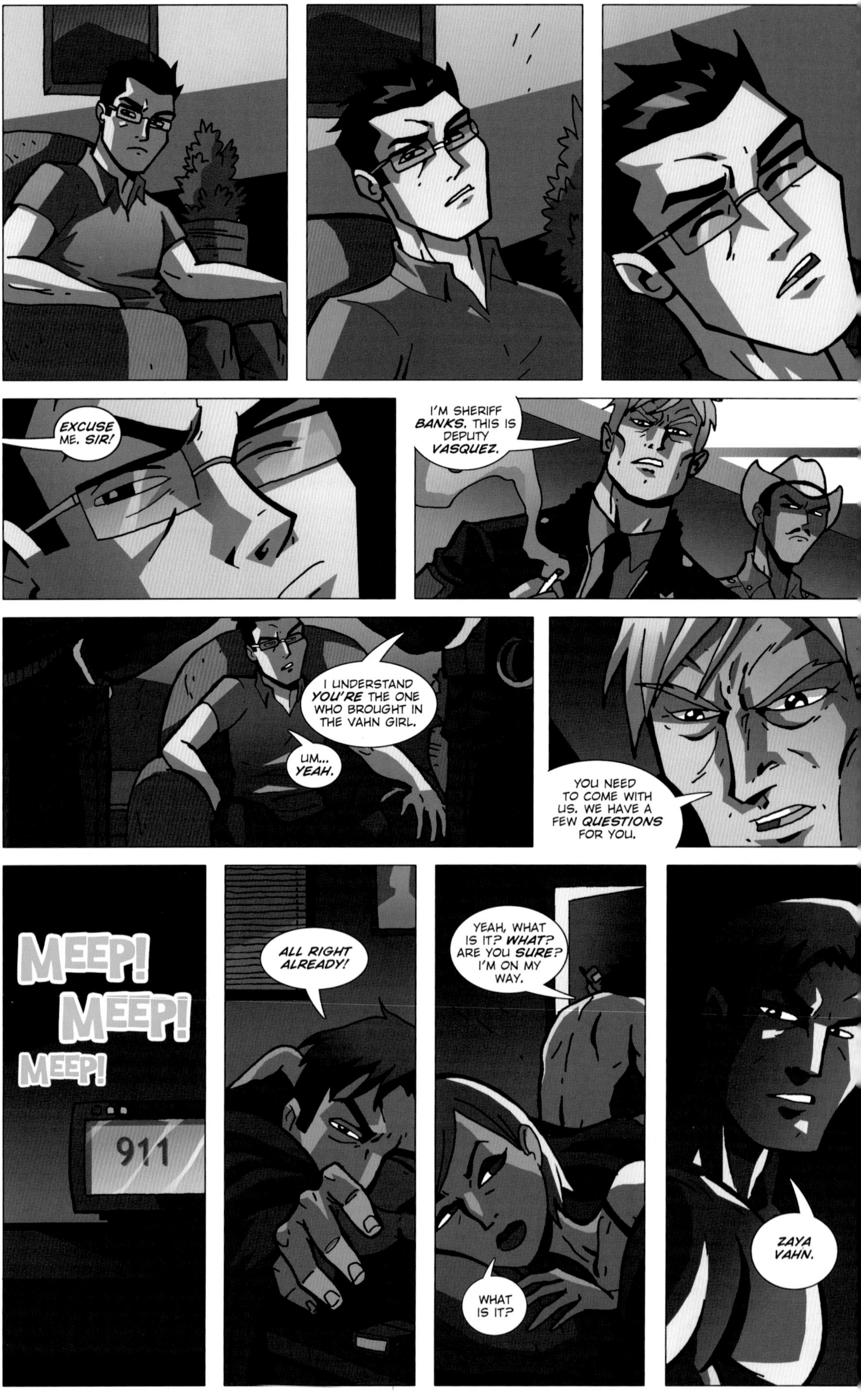
EXCUSE ME. SIR!
I'M SHERIFF BANKS. THIS IS DEPUTY VASQUEZ.
I UNDERSTAND YOU'RE THE ONE WHO BROUGHT IN THE VAHN GIRL.
UM... YEAH.
YOU NEED TO COME WITH US. WE HAVE A FEW QUESTIONS FOR YOU.
MEEP! MEEP! MEEP!
911
ALL RIGHT ALREADY!
YEAH, WHAT IS IT? WHAT? ARE YOU SURE? I'M ON MY WAY.
WHAT IS IT?
ZAYA VAHN.

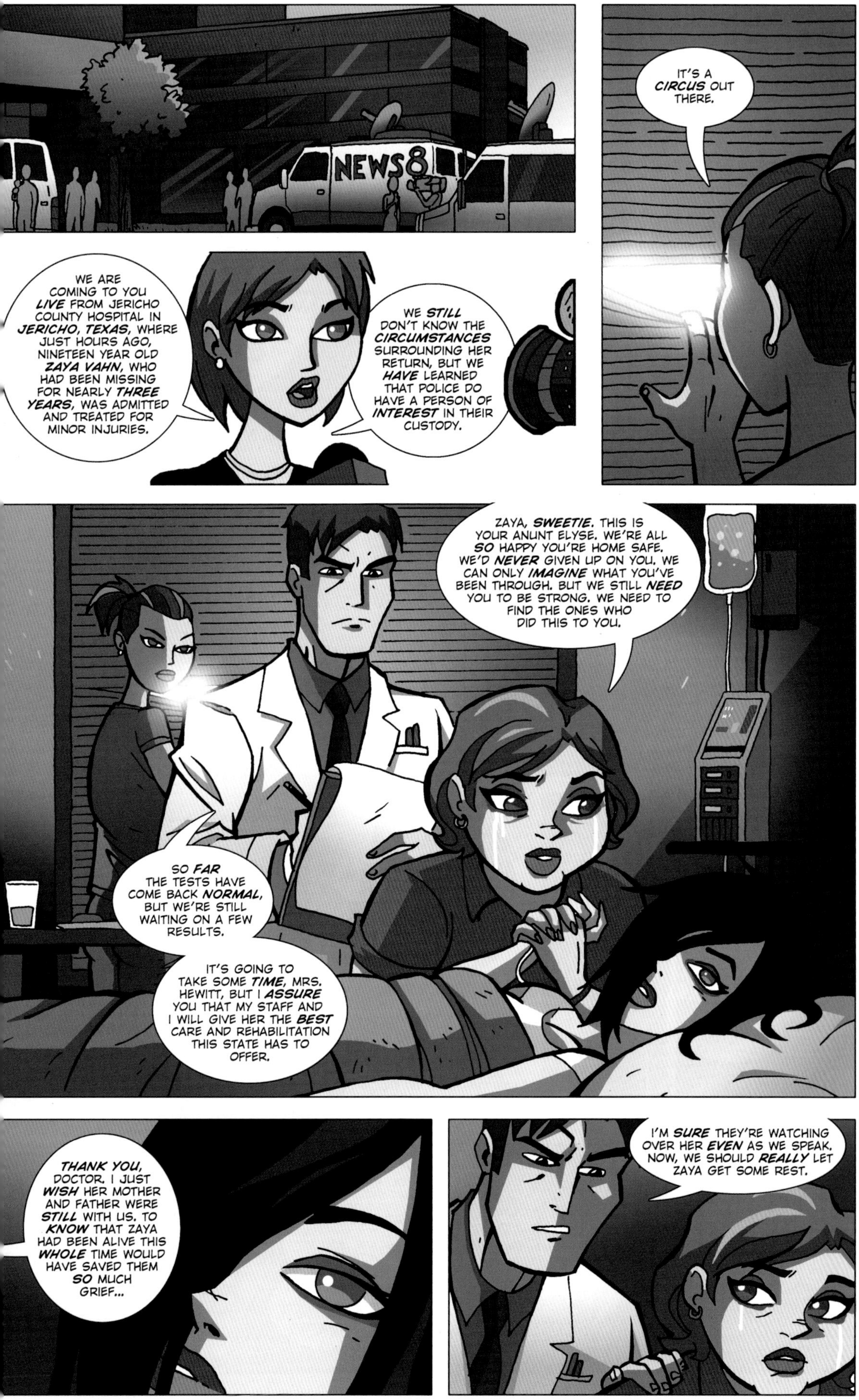

NEWS 8
IT'S A CIRCUS OUT THERE.
WE ARE COMING TO YOU LIVE FROM JERICHO COUNTY HOSPITAL IN JERICHO, TEXAS, WHERE JUST HOURS AGO, NINETEEN YEAR OLD ZAYA VAHN, WHO HAD BEEN MISSING FOR NEARLY THREE YEARS, WAS ADMITTED AND TREATED FOR MINOR INJURIES.
WE STILL DON'T KNOW THE CIRCUMSTANCES SURROUNDING HER RETURN, BUT WE HAVE LEARNED THAT POLICE DO HAVE A PERSON OF INTEREST IN THEIR CUSTODY.
ZAYA, SWEETIE. THIS IS YOUR ANUNT ELYSE. WE'RE ALL SO HAPPY YOU'RE HOME SAFE. WE'D NEVER GIVEN UP ON YOU. WE CAN ONLY IMAGINE WHAT YOU'VE BEEN THROUGH. BUT WE STILL NEED YOU TO BE STRONG. WE NEED TO FIND THE ONES WHO DID THIS TO YOU.
SO FAR THE TESTS HAVE COME BACK NORMAL, BUT WE'RE STILL WAITING ON A FEW RESULTS.
IT'S GOING TO TAKE SOME TIME, MRS. HEWITT, BUT I ASSURE YOU THAT MY STAFF AND I WILL GIVE HER THE BEST CARE AND REHABILITATION THIS STATE HAS TO OFFER.
THANK YOU, DOCTOR. I JUST WISH HER MOTHER AND FATHER WERE STILL WITH US. TO KNOW THAT ZAYA HAD BEEN ALIVE THIS WHOLE TIME WOULD HAVE SAVED THEM SO MUCH GRIEF...
I'M SURE THEY'RE WATCHING OVER HER EVEN AS WE SPEAK. NOW, WE SHOULD REALLY LET ZAYA GET SOME REST.

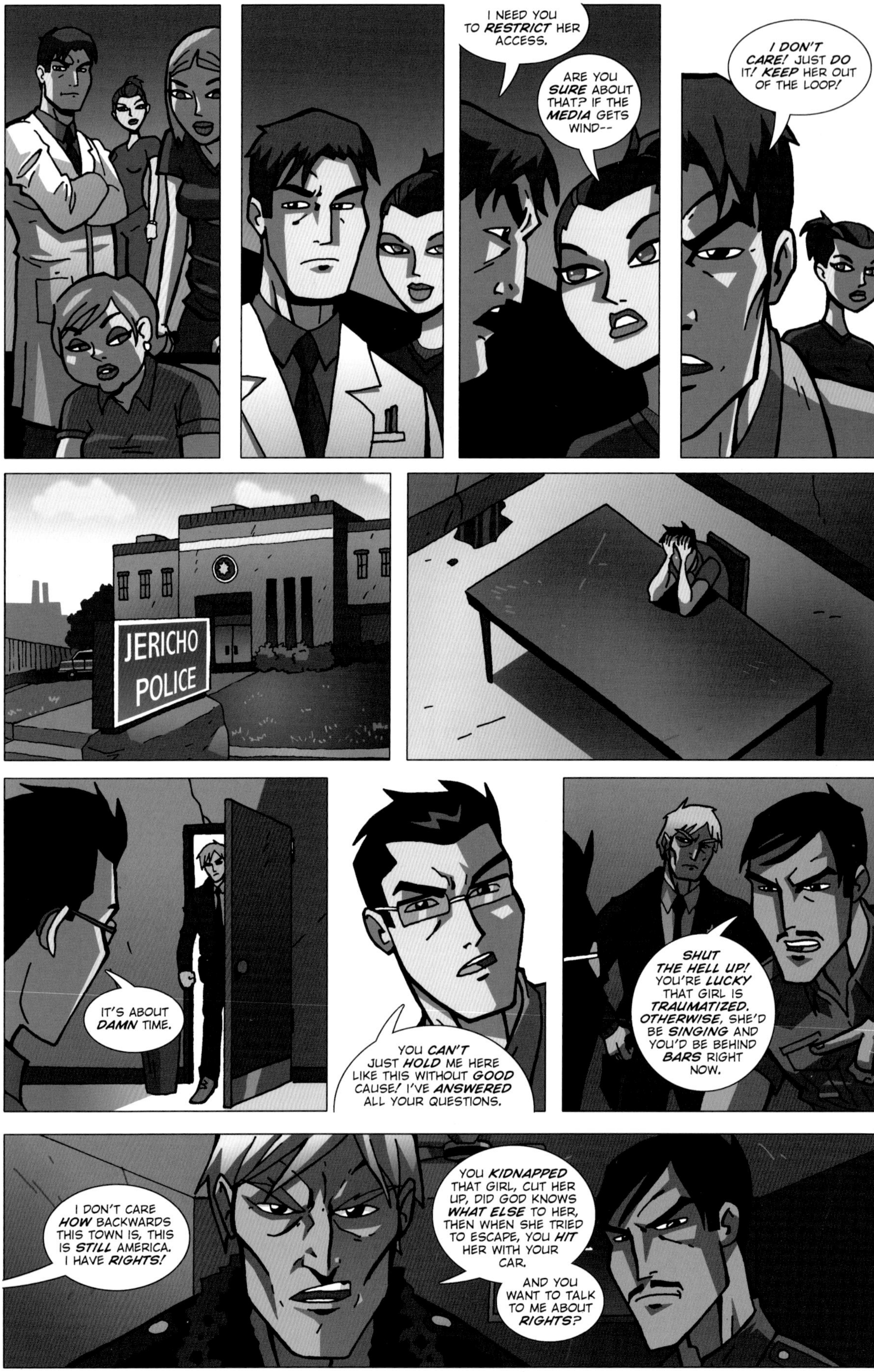
I NEED YOU TO RESTRICT HER ACCESS.
ARE YOU SURE ABOUT THAT? IF THE MEDIA GETS WIND--
I DON'T CARE! JUST DO IT! KEEP HER OUT OF THE LOOP!
JERICHO POLICE
IT'S ABOUT DAMN TIME.
YOU CAN'T JUST HOLD ME HERE LIKE THIS WITHOUT GOOD CAUSE! I'VE ANSWERED ALL YOUR QUESTIONS.
SHUT THE HELL UP! YOU'RE LUCKY THAT GIRL IS TRAUMATIZED. OTHERWISE, SHE'D BE SINGING AND YOU'D BE BEHIND BARS RIGHT NOW.
I DON'T CARE HOW BACKWARDS THIS TOWN IS, THIS IS STILL AMERICA. I HAVE RIGHTS!
YOU KIDNAPPED THAT GIRL, CUT HER UP, DID GOD KNOWS WHAT ELSE TO HER, THEN WHEN SHE TRIED TO ESCAPE, YOU HIT HER WITH YOUR CAR.
AND YOU WANT TO TALK TO ME ABOUT RIGHTS?

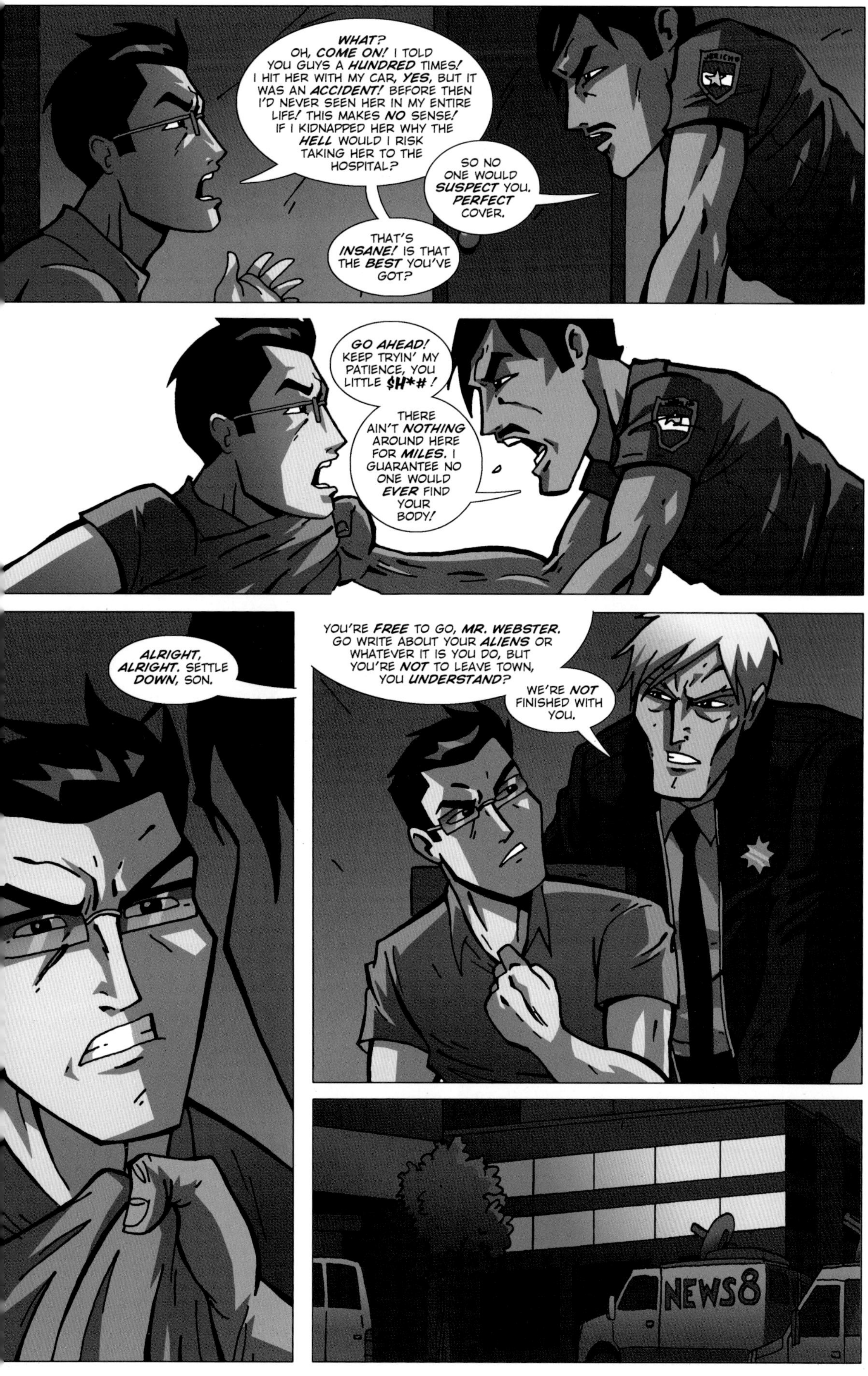
WHAT? OH, COME ON! I TOLD YOU GUYS A HUNDRED TIMES! I HIT HER WITH MY CAR, YES, BUT IT WAS AN ACCIDENT! BEFORE THEN I'D NEVER SEEN HER IN MY ENTIRE LIFE! THIS MAKES NO SENSE! IF I KIDNAPPED HER WHY THE HELL WOULD I RISK TAKING HER TO THE HOSPITAL?
SO NO ONE WOULD SUSPECT YOU. PERFECT COVER.
THAT'S INSANE! IS THAT THE BEST YOU'VE GOT?
GO AHEAD! KEEP TRYIN' MY PATIENCE, YOU LITTLE $H*#!
THERE AIN'T NOTHING AROUND HERE FOR MILES. I GUARANTEE NO ONE WOULD EVER FIND YOUR BODY!
ALRIGHT, ALRIGHT. SETTLE DOWN, SON.
YOU'RE FREE TO GO, MR. WEBSTER. GO WRITE ABOUT YOUR ALIENS OR WHATEVER IT IS YOU DO, BUT YOU'RE NOT TO LEAVE TOWN, YOU UNDERSTAND?
WE'RE NOT FINISHED WITH YOU.
NEWS8

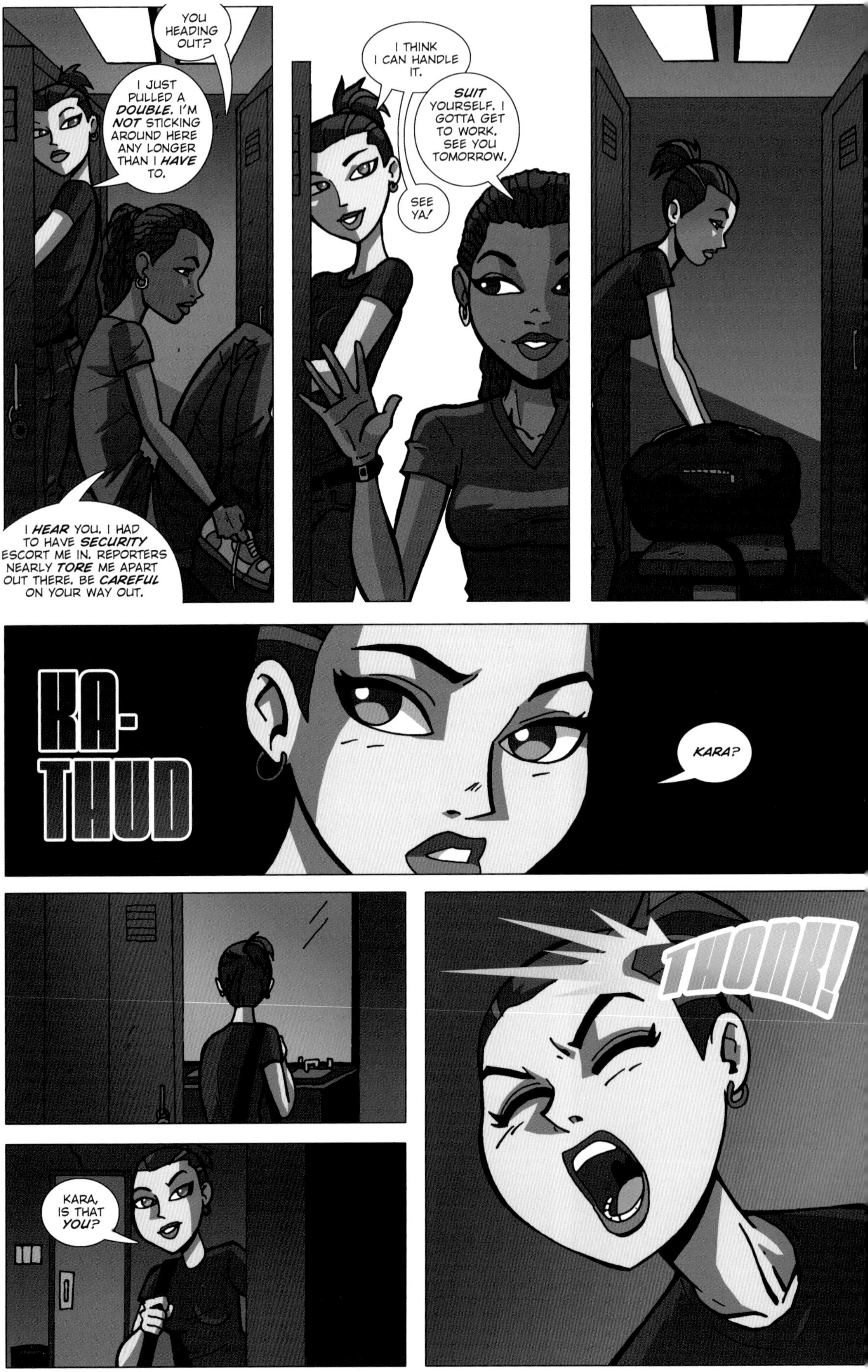
YOU HEADING OUT?
I JUST PULLED A DOUBLE. I'M NOT STICKING AROUND HERE ANY LONGER THAN I HAVE TO.
I HEAR YOU. I HAD TO HAVE SECURITY ESCORT ME IN. REPORTERS NEARLY TORE ME APART OUT THERE. BE CAREFUL ON YOUR WAY OUT.
I THINK I CAN HANDLE IT.
SUIT YOURSELF. I GOTTA GET TO WORK. SEE YOU TOMORROW.
SEE YA!
KA-THUD
KARA?
KARA, IS THAT YOU?
THONK!

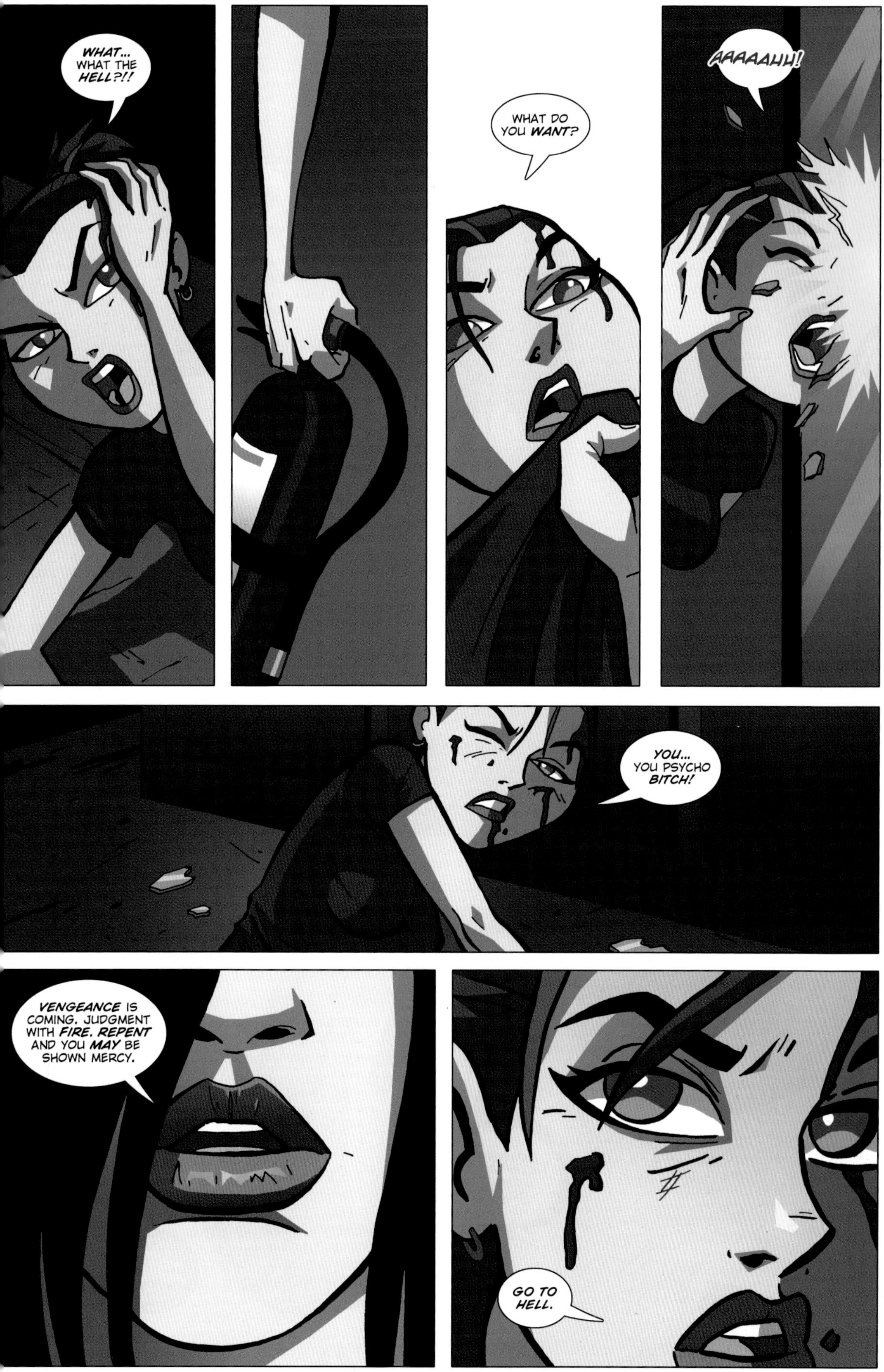
WHAT... WHAT THE HELL?!!
WHAT DO YOU WANT?
AAAAAHH!
YOU... YOU PSYCHO BITCH!
VENGEANCE IS COMING. JUDGMENT WITH FIRE. REPENT AND YOU MAY BE SHOWN MERCY.
GO TO HELL.

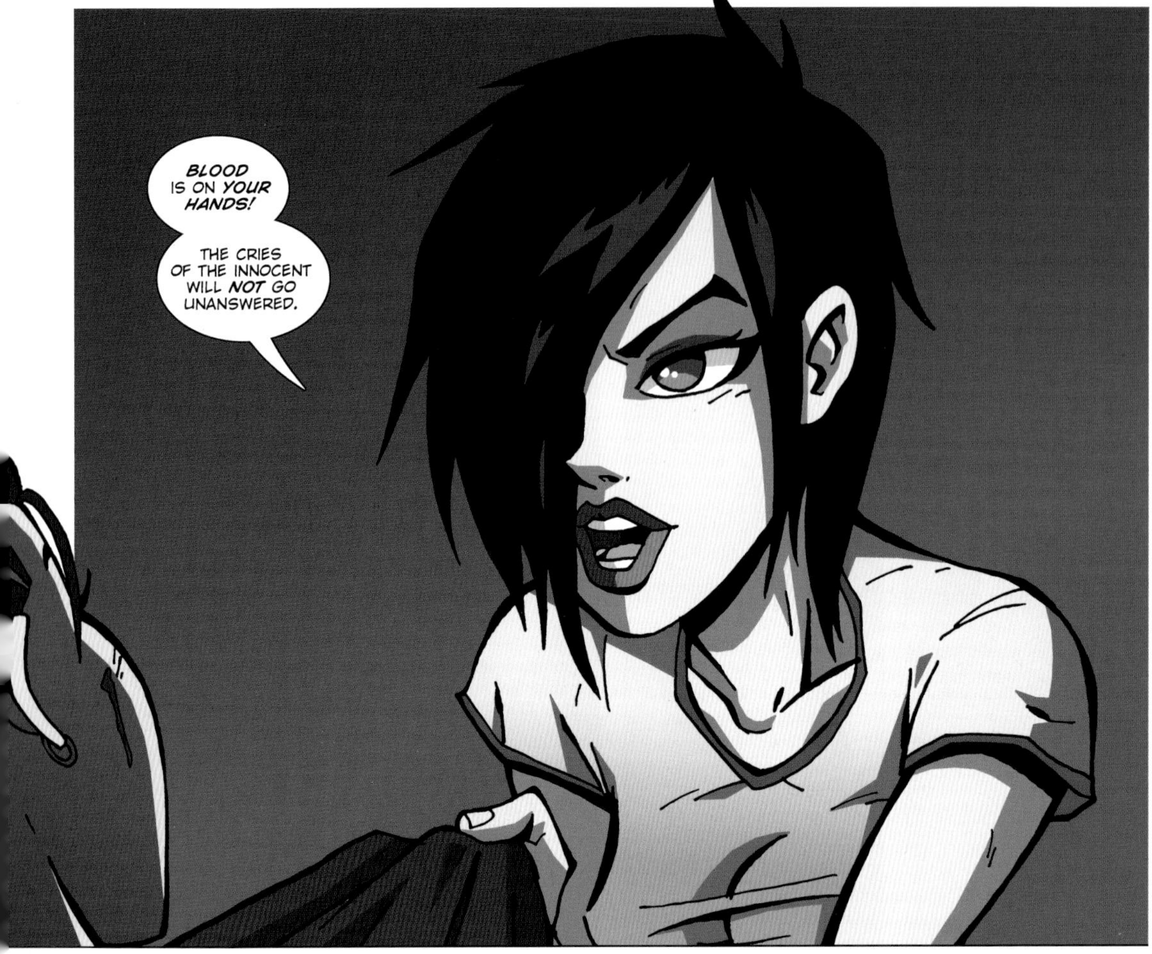
BLOOD IS ON YOUR HANDS!
THE CRIES OF THE INNOCENT WILL NOT GO UNANSWERED.

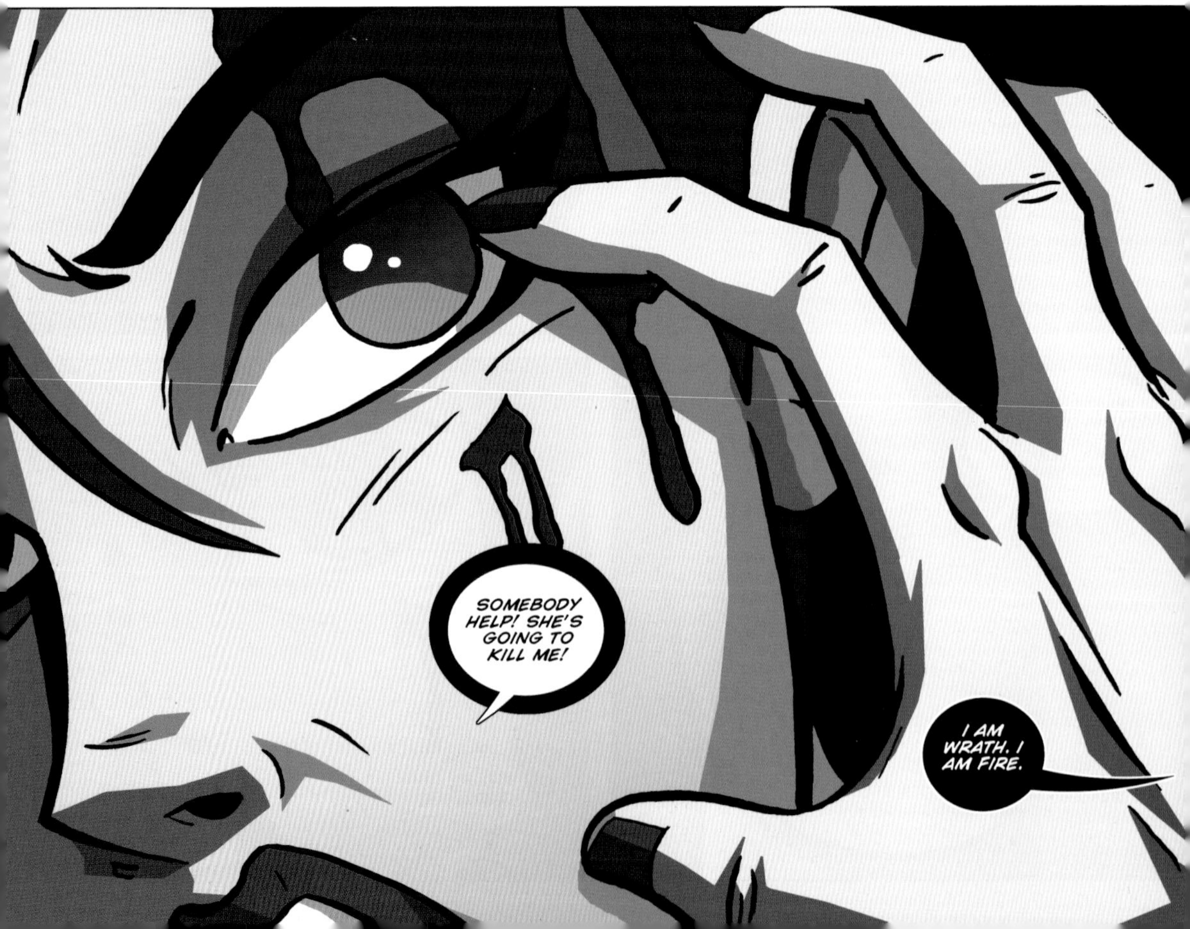
SOMEBODY HELP! SHE'S GOING TO KILL ME!
I AM WRATH. I AM FIRE.

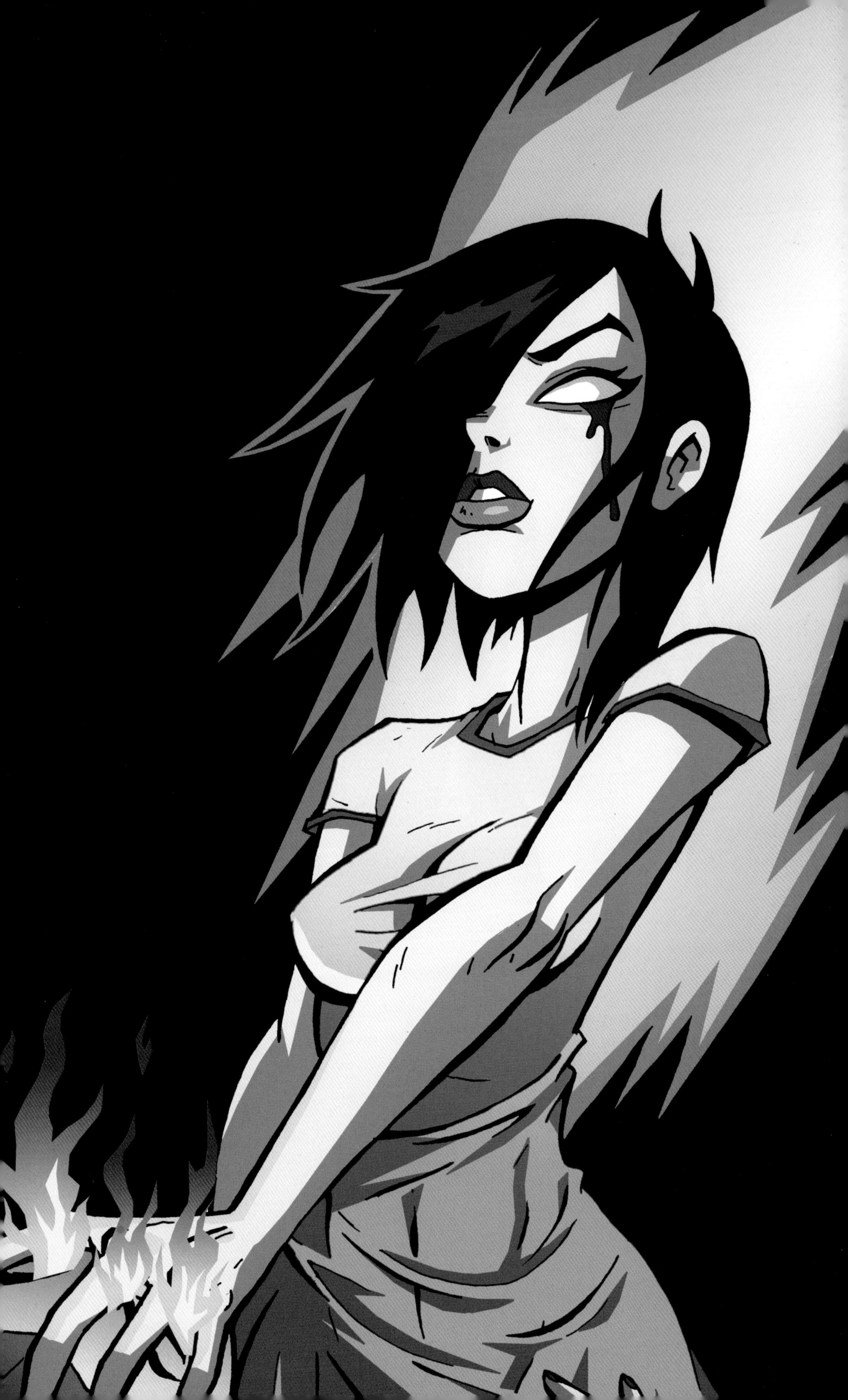

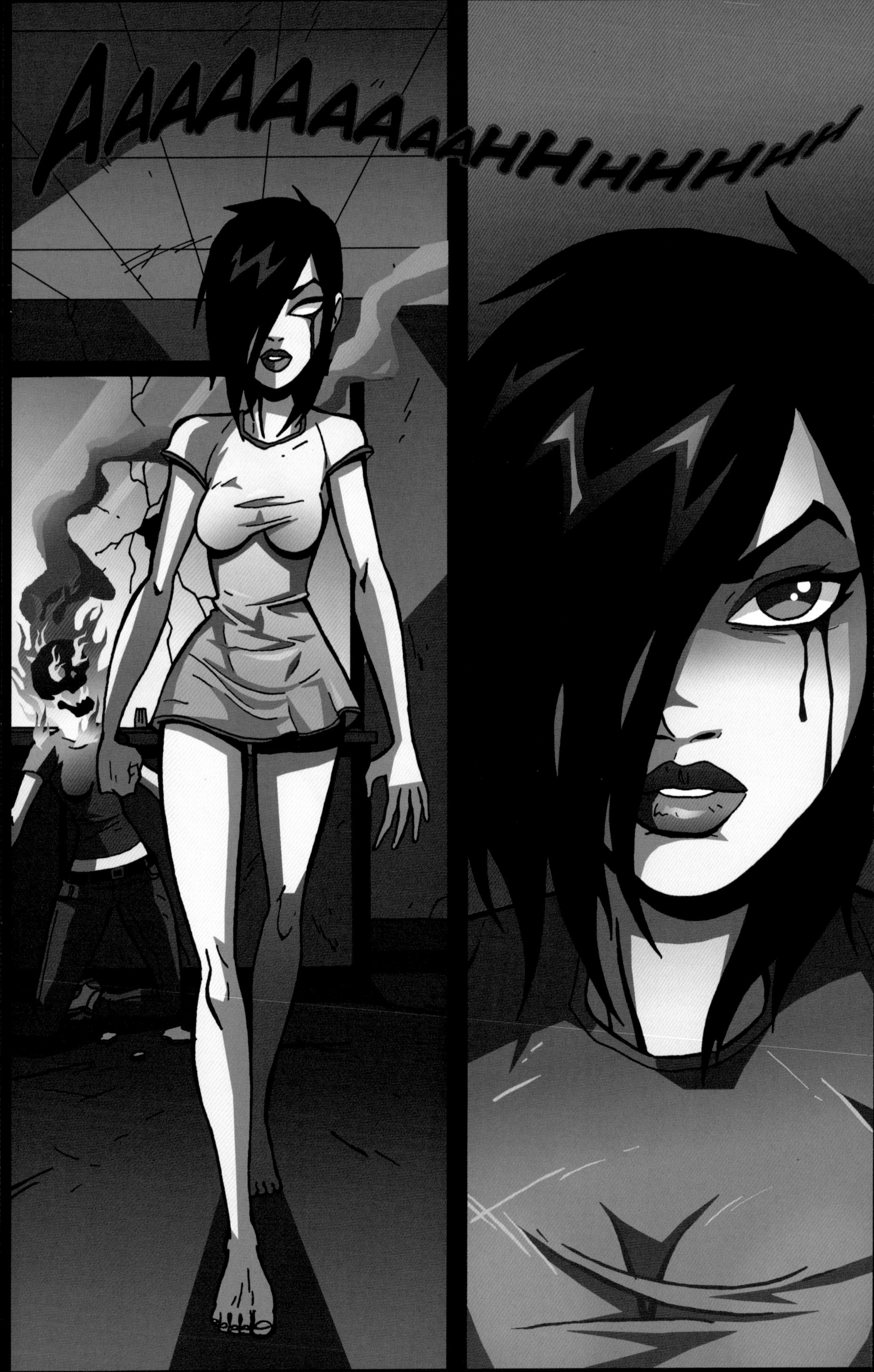
AAAAAAAAAHHHHHHH

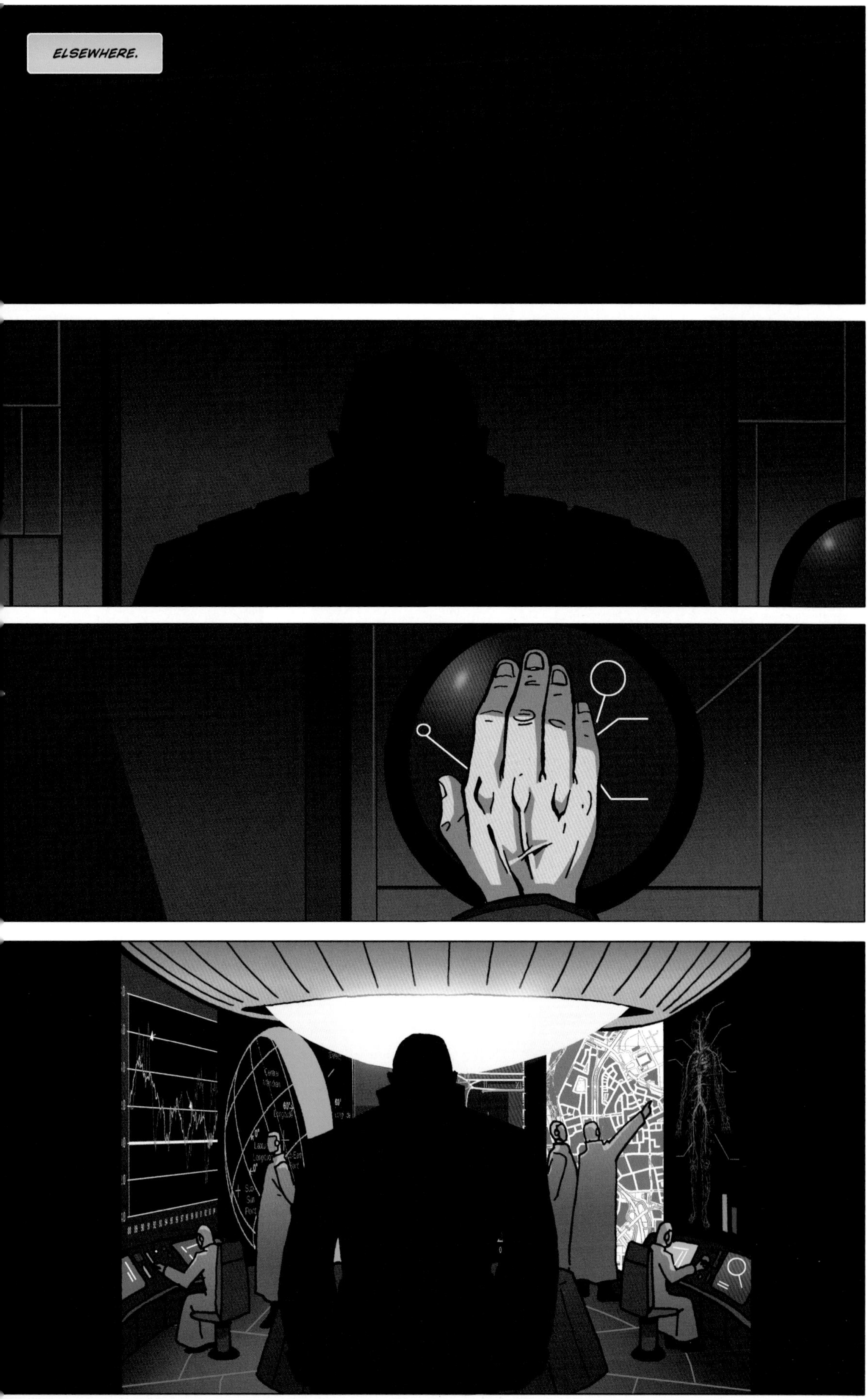
ELSEWHERE.

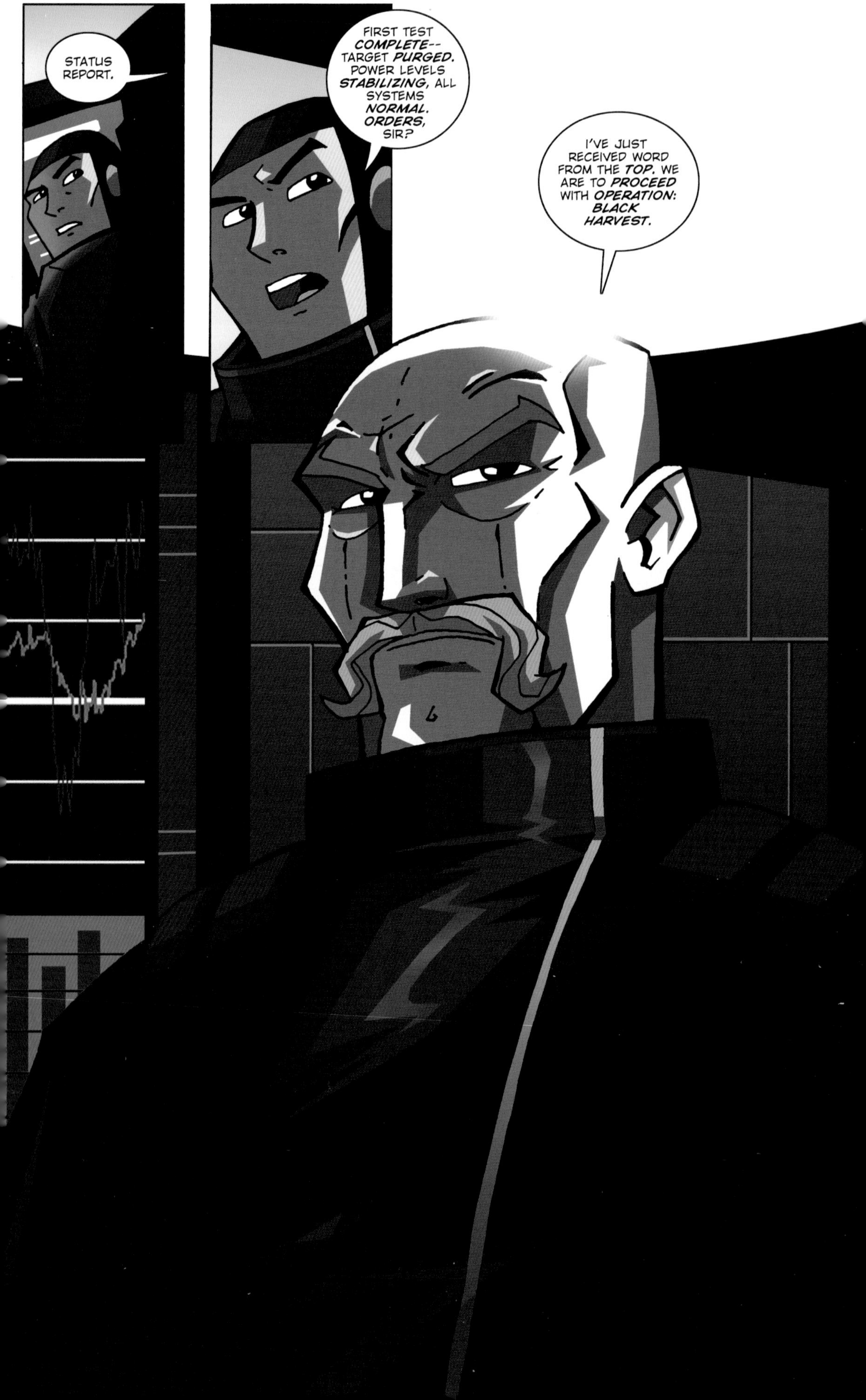
STATUS REPORT.
FIRST TEST COMPLETE-- TARGET PURGED. POWER LEVELS STABILIZING, ALL SYSTEMS NORMAL. ORDERS, SIR?
I'VE JUST RECEIVED WORD FROM THE TOP. WE ARE TO PROCEED WITH OPERATION: BLACK HARVEST.

chapter 2

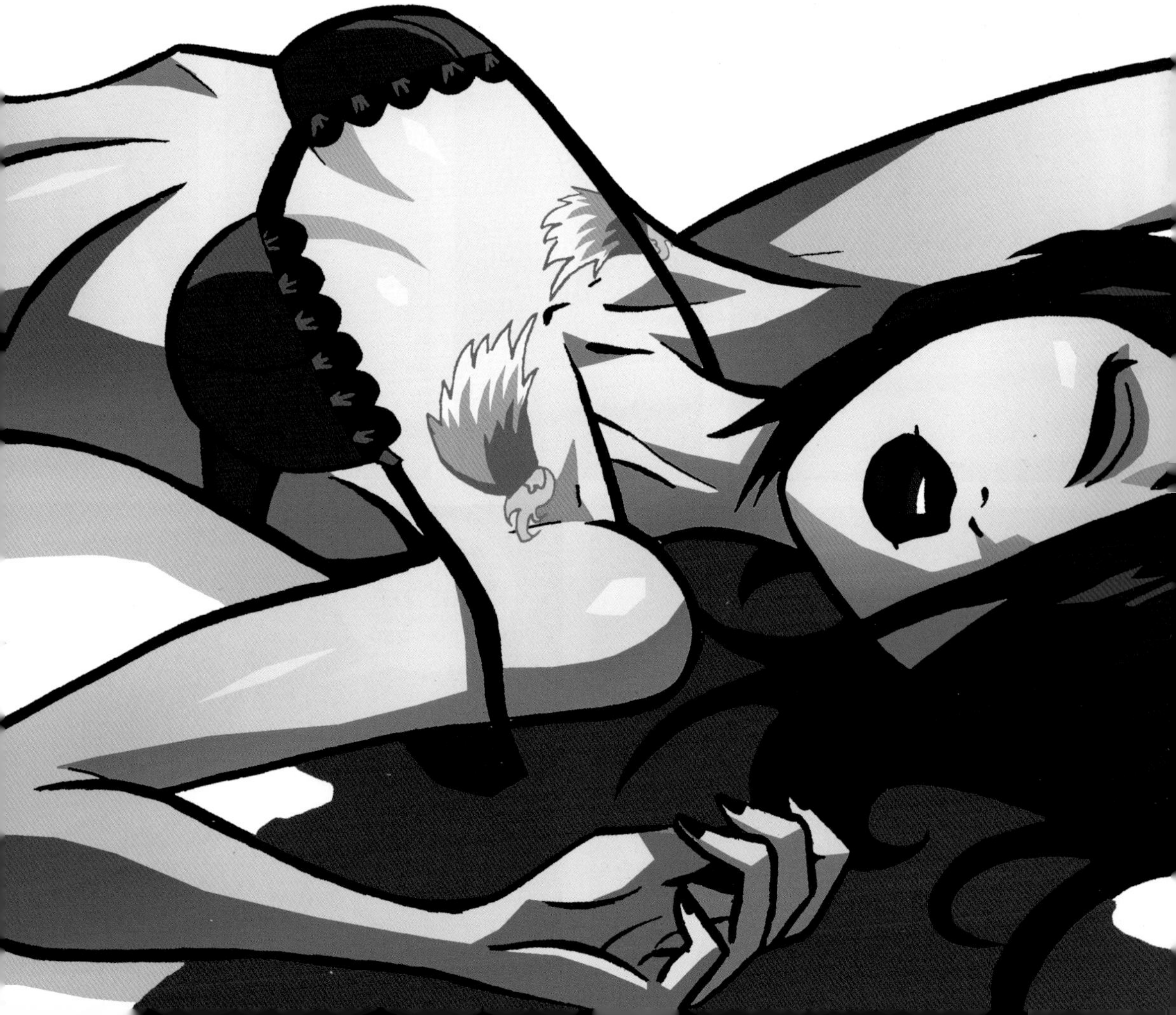

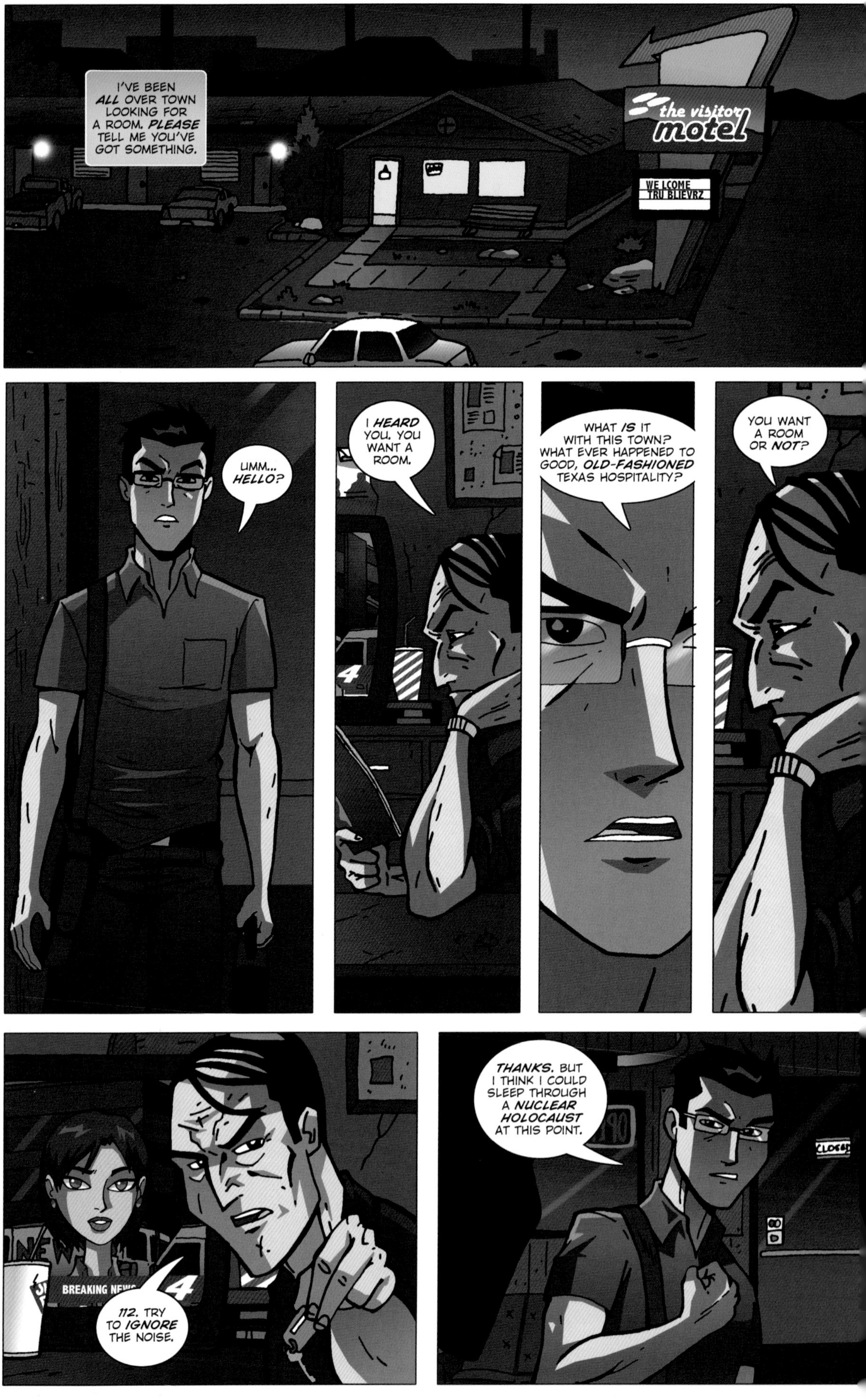
the visitor motel
WE LCOME TRU BLIEVRZ
I'VE BEEN *ALL* OVER TOWN LOOKING FOR A ROOM. *PLEASE* TELL ME YOU'VE GOT SOMETHING.
UMM... *HELLO?*
I *HEARD* YOU. YOU WANT A ROOM.
WHAT *IS* IT WITH THIS TOWN? WHAT EVER HAPPENED TO GOOD, *OLD-FASHIONED* TEXAS HOSPITALITY?
YOU WANT A ROOM OR *NOT?*
BREAKING NEWS
112. TRY TO *IGNORE* THE NOISE.
THANKS. BUT I THINK I COULD SLEEP THROUGH A *NUCLEAR HOLOCAUST* AT THIS POINT.

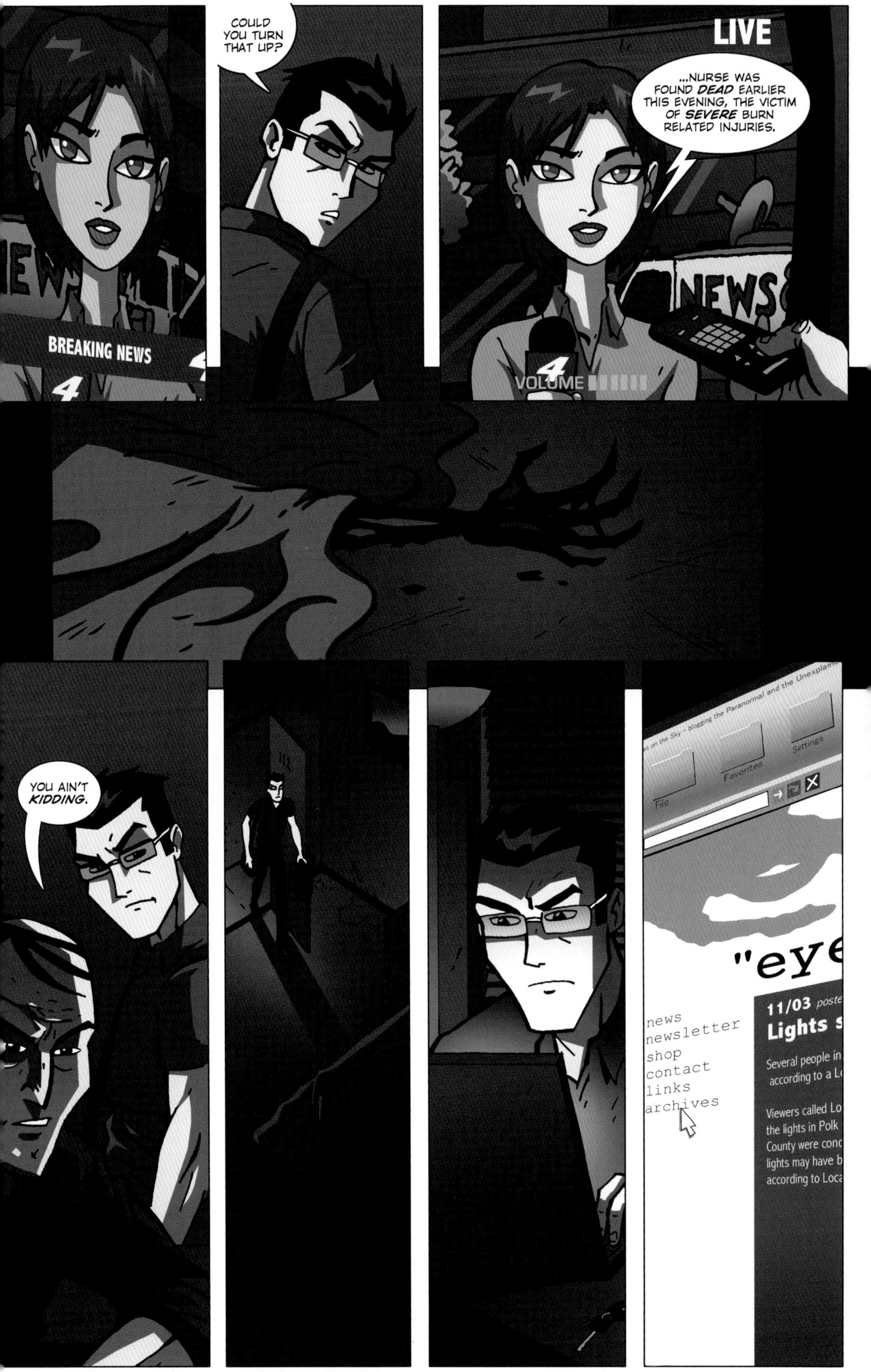
BREAKING NEWS
COULD YOU TURN THAT UP?
LIVE
...NURSE WAS FOUND DEAD EARLIER THIS EVENING, THE VICTIM OF SEVERE BURN RELATED INJURIES.
VOLUME
YOU AIN'T KIDDING.
File
Favorites
Settings
"eye
news
newsletter
shop
contact
links
archives
11/03
Lights s
Several people in
according to a Lo
Viewers called Lo
the lights in Polk
County were conc
lights may have b
according to Loca

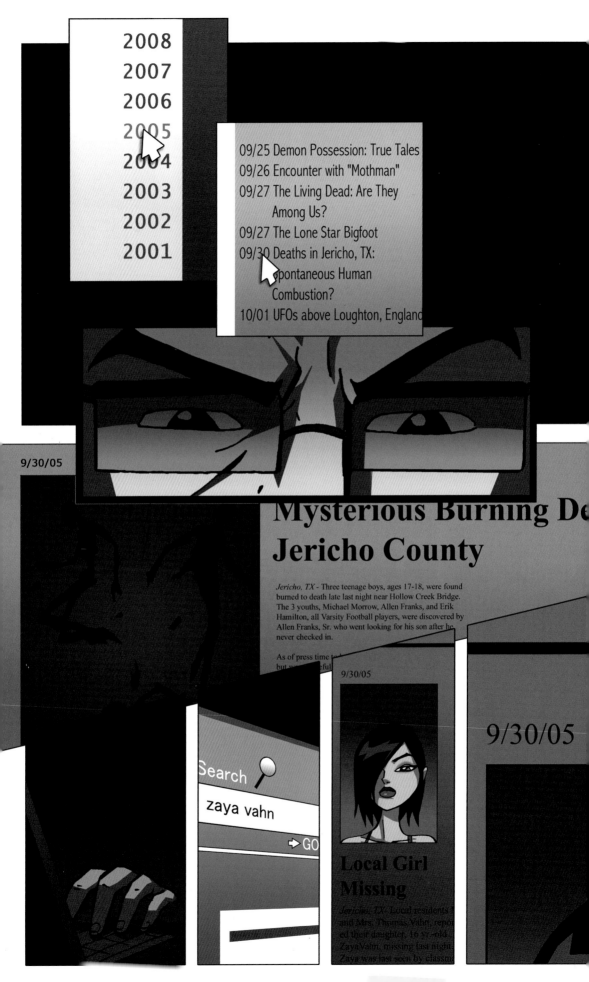

2008
2007
2006
2005
2004
2003
2002
2001

09/25 Demon Possession: True Tales
09/26 Encounter with "Mothman"
09/27 The Living Dead: Are They
Among Us?
09/27 The Lone Star Bigfoot
09/30 Deaths in Jericho, TX:
Spontaneous Human
Combustion?
10/01 UFOs above Loughton, England

9/30/05

Mysterious Burning De
Jericho County

Jericho, TX - Three teenage boys, ages 17-18, were found burned to death late last night near Hollow Creek Bridge. The 3 youths, Michael Morrow, Allen Franks, and Erik Hamilton, all Varsity Football players, were discovered by Allen Franks, Sr. who went looking for his son after he never checked in.

As of press time to b
but w   eful

9/30/05

9/30/05

Search

zaya vahn

➡ GO

Local Girl
Missing

Jericho, TX- Local residents
and Mrs. Thomas Vahn, repor
ed their daughter, 16-yr.-old
Zaya Vahn, missing last night.
Zaya was last seen by classm

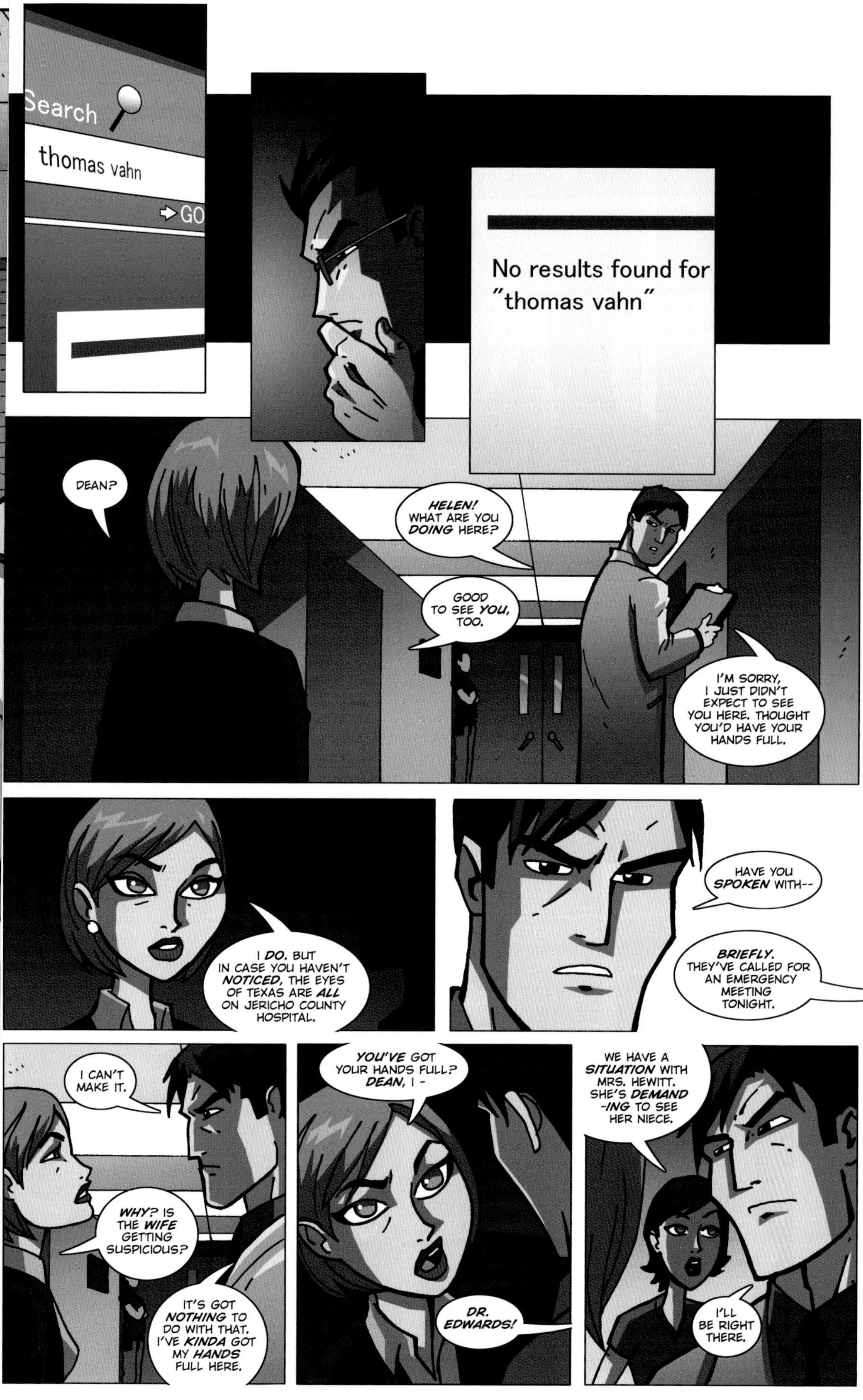
Search
thomas vahn
GO
No results found for "thomas vahn"
DEAN?
HELEN! WHAT ARE YOU DOING HERE?
GOOD TO SEE YOU, TOO.
I'M SORRY, I JUST DIDN'T EXPECT TO SEE YOU HERE. THOUGHT YOU'D HAVE YOUR HANDS FULL.
I DO. BUT IN CASE YOU HAVEN'T NOTICED, THE EYES OF TEXAS ARE ALL ON JERICHO COUNTY HOSPITAL.
HAVE YOU SPOKEN WITH--
BRIEFLY. THEY'VE CALLED FOR AN EMERGENCY MEETING TONIGHT.
I CAN'T MAKE IT.
WHY? IS THE WIFE GETTING SUSPICIOUS?
IT'S GOT NOTHING TO DO WITH THAT. I'VE KINDA GOT MY HANDS FULL HERE.
YOU'VE GOT YOUR HANDS FULL? DEAN, I -
DR. EDWARDS!
WE HAVE A SITUATION WITH MRS. HEWITT. SHE'S DEMAND -ING TO SEE HER NIECE.
I'LL BE RIGHT THERE.

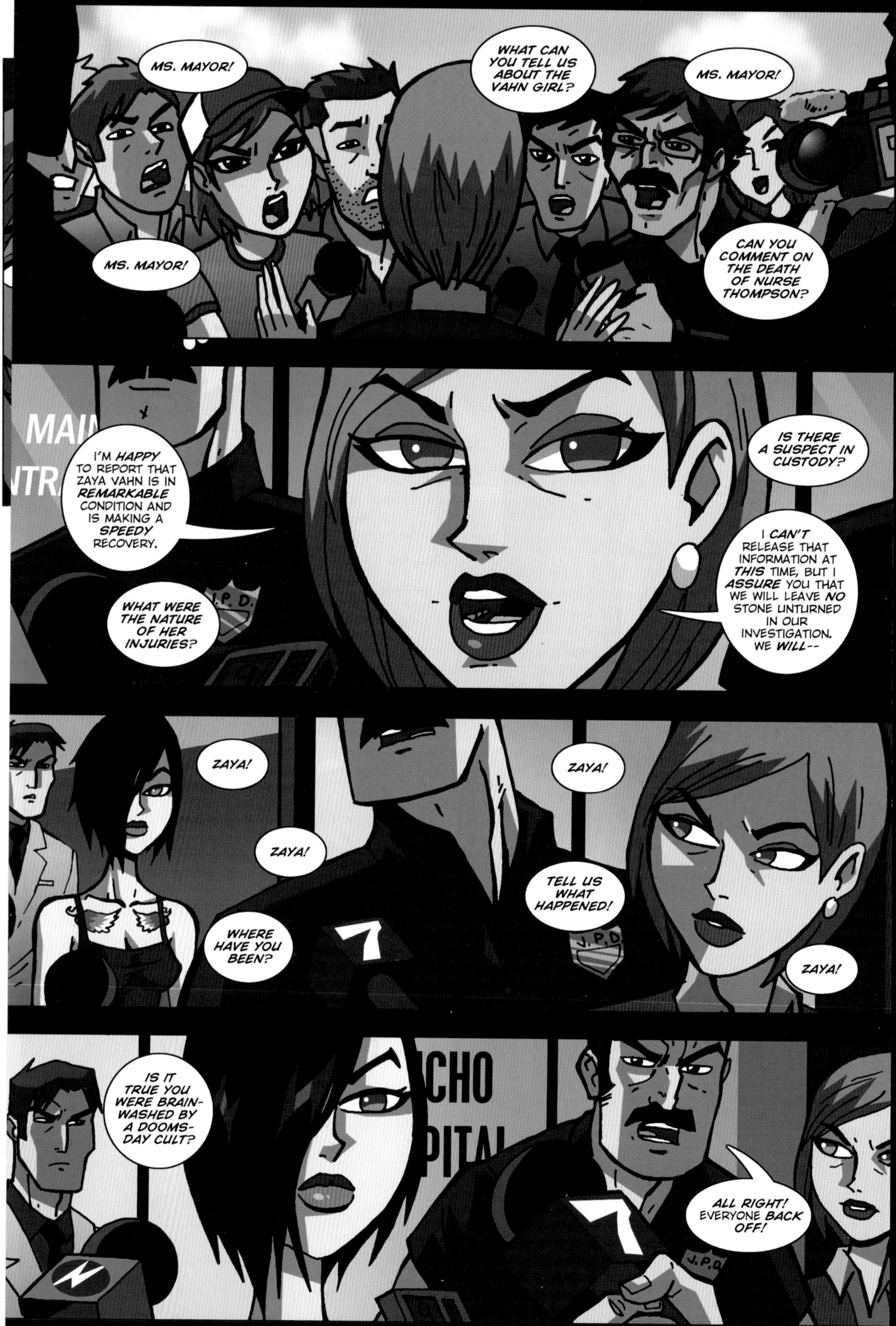

MS. MAYOR!
WHAT CAN YOU TELL US ABOUT THE VAHN GIRL?
MS. MAYOR!
MS. MAYOR!
CAN YOU COMMENT ON THE DEATH OF NURSE THOMPSON?
I'M HAPPY TO REPORT THAT ZAYA VAHN IS IN REMARKABLE CONDITION AND IS MAKING A SPEEDY RECOVERY.
IS THERE A SUSPECT IN CUSTODY?
WHAT WERE THE NATURE OF HER INJURIES?
I CAN'T RELEASE THAT INFORMATION AT THIS TIME, BUT I ASSURE YOU THAT WE WILL LEAVE NO STONE UNTURNED IN OUR INVESTIGATION. WE WILL--
ZAYA!
ZAYA!
ZAYA!
TELL US WHAT HAPPENED!
WHERE HAVE YOU BEEN?
ZAYA!
IS IT TRUE YOU WERE BRAIN-WASHED BY A DOOMS-DAY CULT?
ALL RIGHT! EVERYONE BACK OFF!

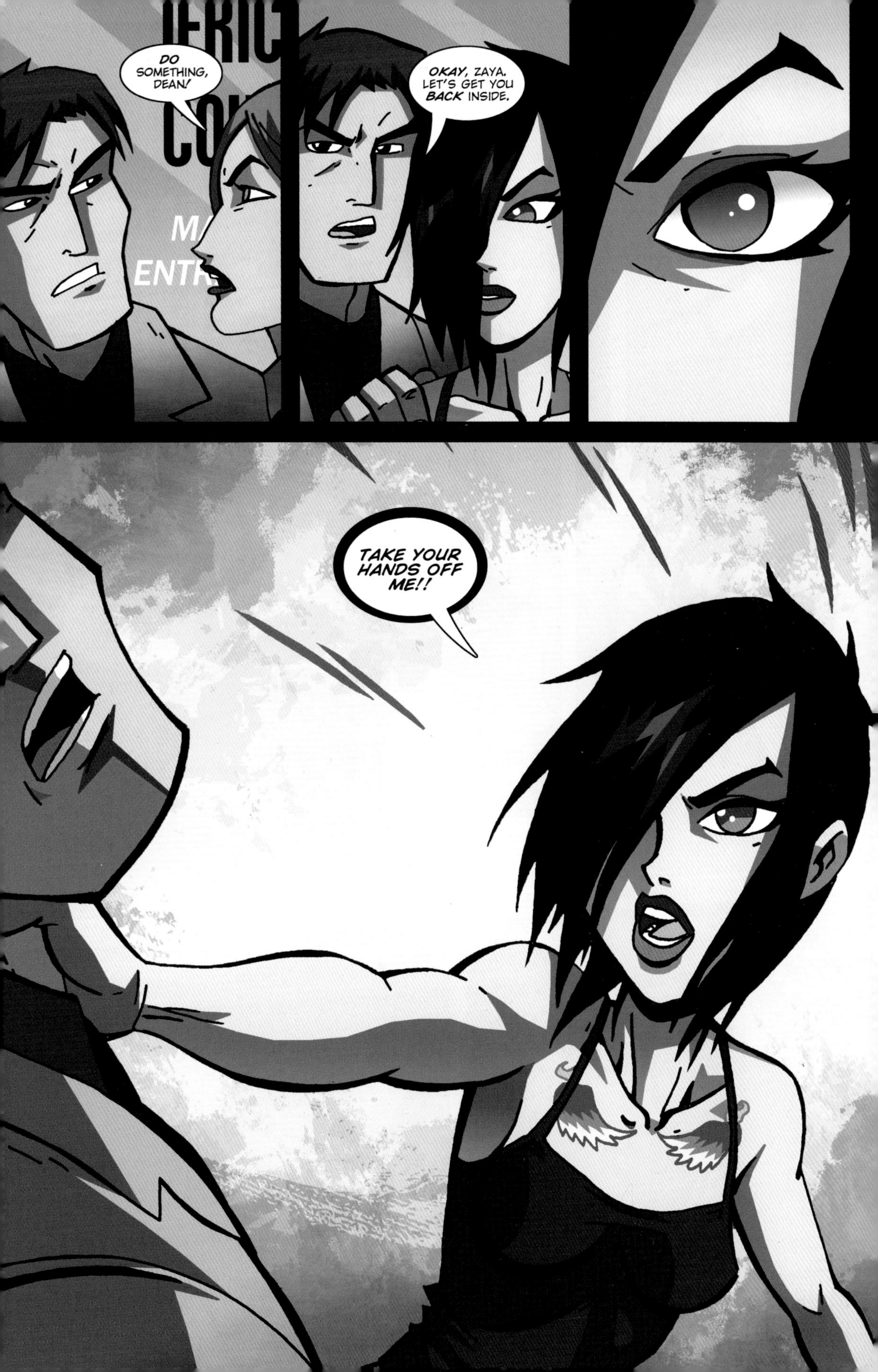
DO SOMETHING, DEAN!
OKAY, ZAYA. LET'S GET YOU BACK INSIDE.
TAKE YOUR HANDS OFF ME!!

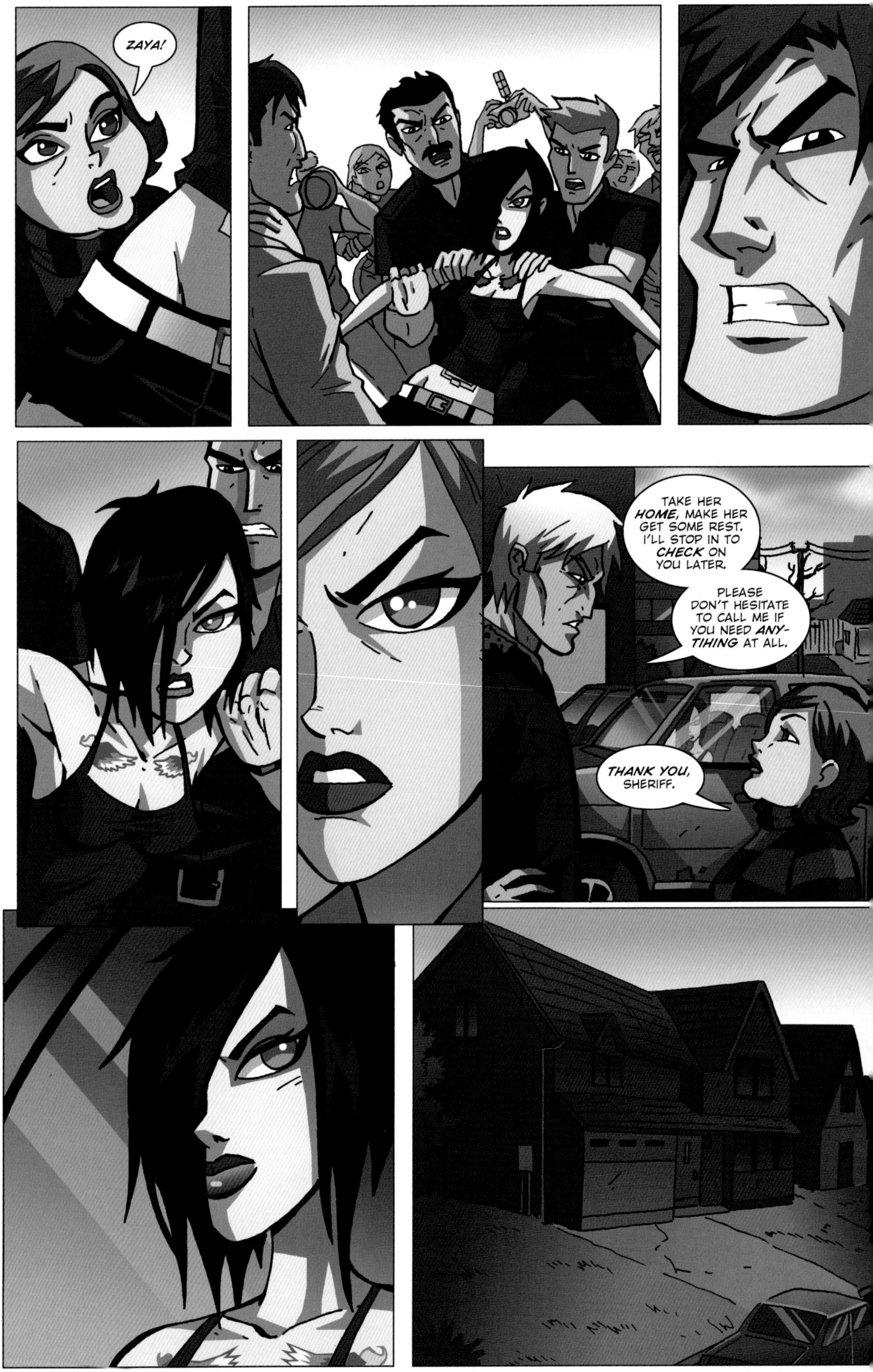
ZAYA!
TAKE HER HOME, MAKE HER GET SOME REST. I'LL STOP IN TO CHECK ON YOU LATER.
PLEASE DON'T HESITATE TO CALL ME IF YOU NEED ANY-TIHING AT ALL.
THANK YOU, SHERIFF.

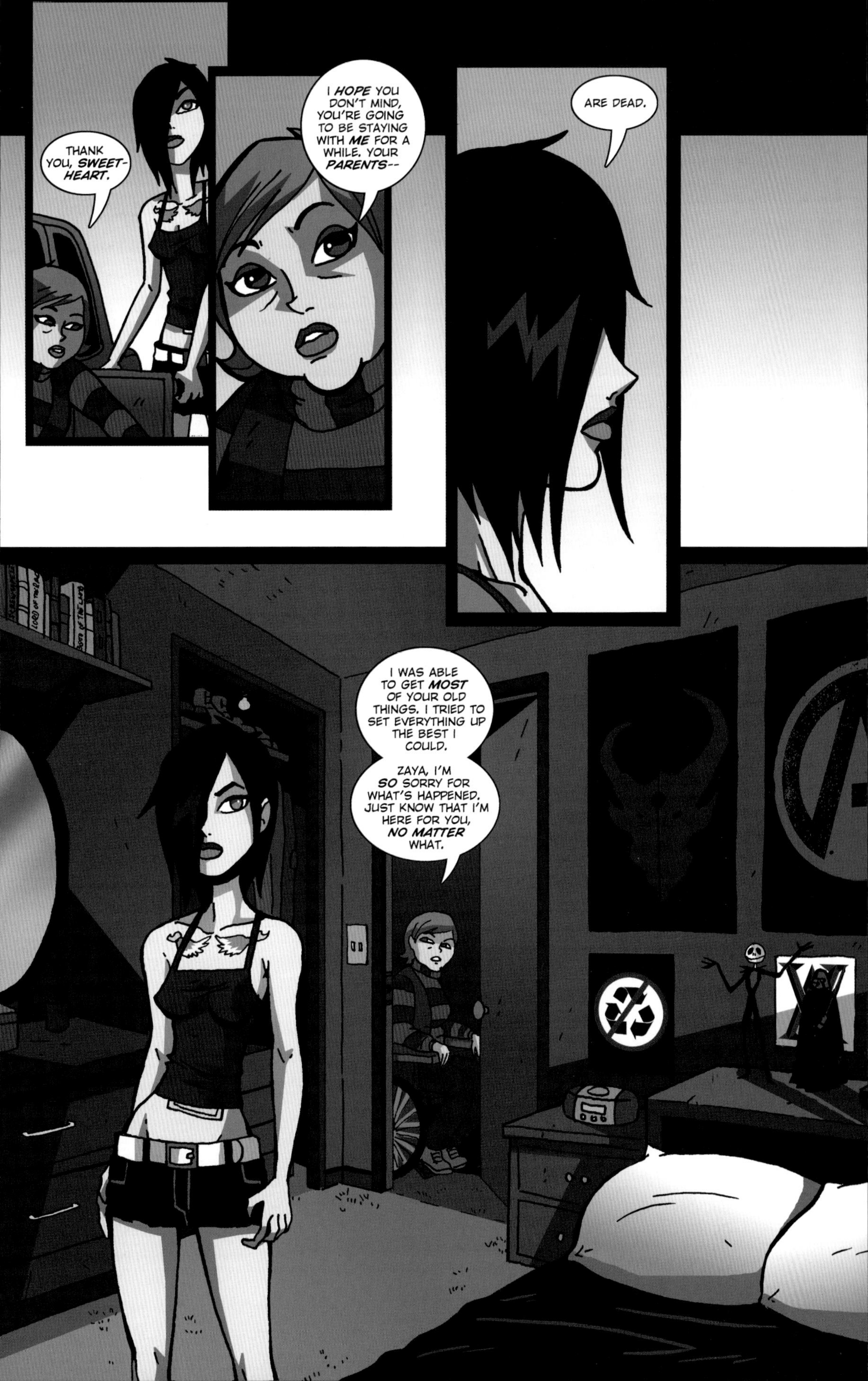
THANK YOU, SWEET-HEART.
I HOPE YOU DON'T MIND, YOU'RE GOING TO BE STAYING WITH ME FOR A WHILE. YOUR PARENTS--
ARE DEAD.
I WAS ABLE TO GET MOST OF YOUR OLD THINGS. I TRIED TO SET EVERYTHING UP THE BEST I COULD.
ZAYA, I'M SO SORRY FOR WHAT'S HAPPENED. JUST KNOW THAT I'M HERE FOR YOU, NO MATTER WHAT.

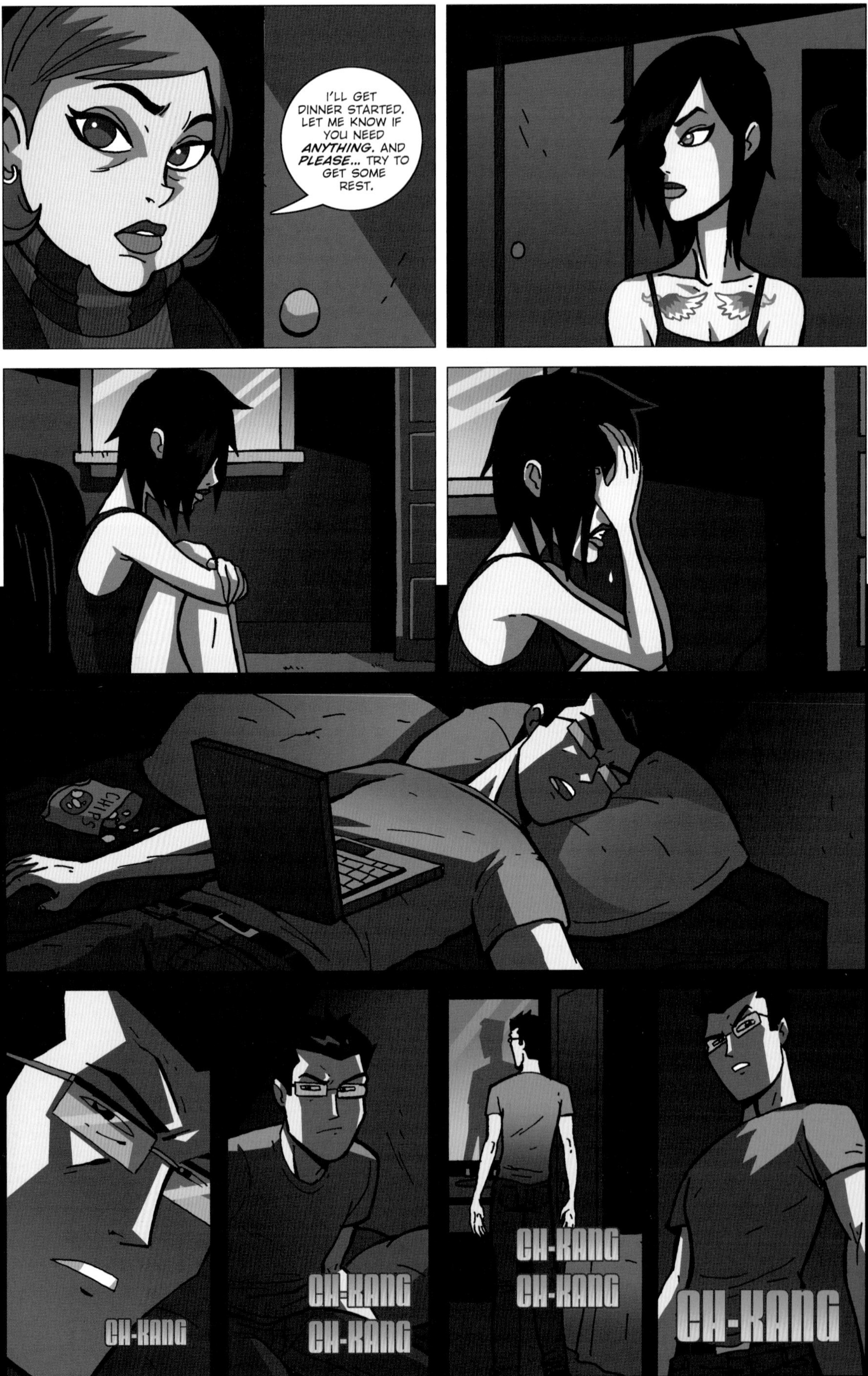
I'LL GET DINNER STARTED. LET ME KNOW IF YOU NEED ANYTHING. AND PLEASE... TRY TO GET SOME REST.
CHIPS
CH-KANG
CH-KANG
CH-KANG
CH-KANG
CH-KANG
CH-KANG

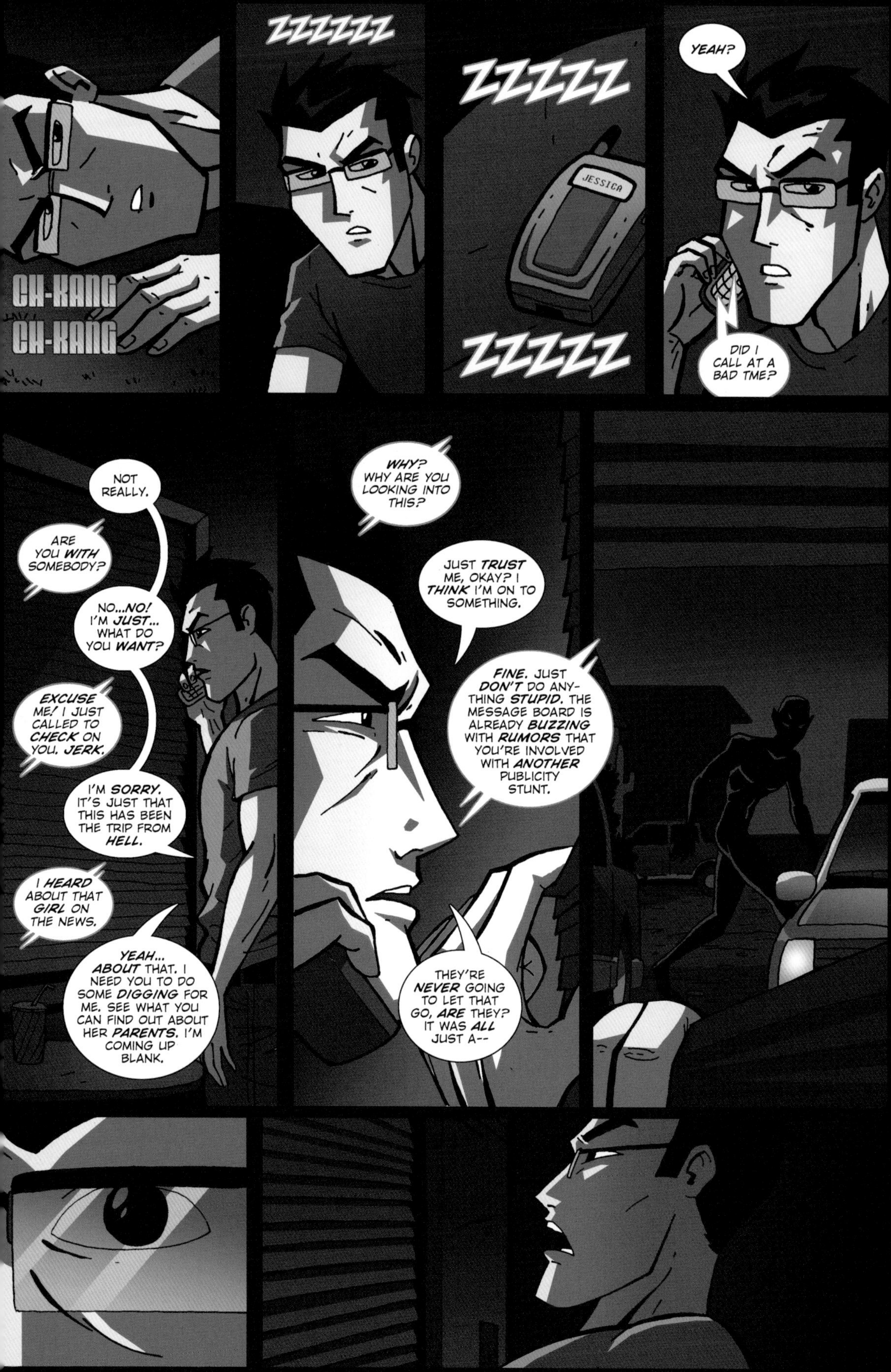
CH-KANG
CH-KANG
ZZZZZZ
ZZZZZ
JESSICA
ZZZZZ
YEAH?
DID I CALL AT A BAD TME?
NOT REALLY.
ARE YOU WITH SOMEBODY?
NO...NO! I'M JUST... WHAT DO YOU WANT?
EXCUSE ME! I JUST CALLED TO CHECK ON YOU. JERK.
I'M SORRY. IT'S JUST THAT THIS HAS BEEN THE TRIP FROM HELL.
I HEARD ABOUT THAT GIRL ON THE NEWS.
YEAH... ABOUT THAT. I NEED YOU TO DO SOME DIGGING FOR ME. SEE WHAT YOU CAN FIND OUT ABOUT HER PARENTS. I'M COMING UP BLANK.
WHY? WHY ARE YOU LOOKING INTO THIS?
JUST TRUST ME, OKAY? I THINK I'M ON TO SOMETHING.
FINE. JUST DON'T DO ANYTHING STUPID. THE MESSAGE BOARD IS ALREADY BUZZING WITH RUMORS THAT YOU'RE INVOLVED WITH ANOTHER PUBLICITY STUNT.
THEY'RE NEVER GOING TO LET THAT GO, ARE THEY? IT WAS ALL JUST A--

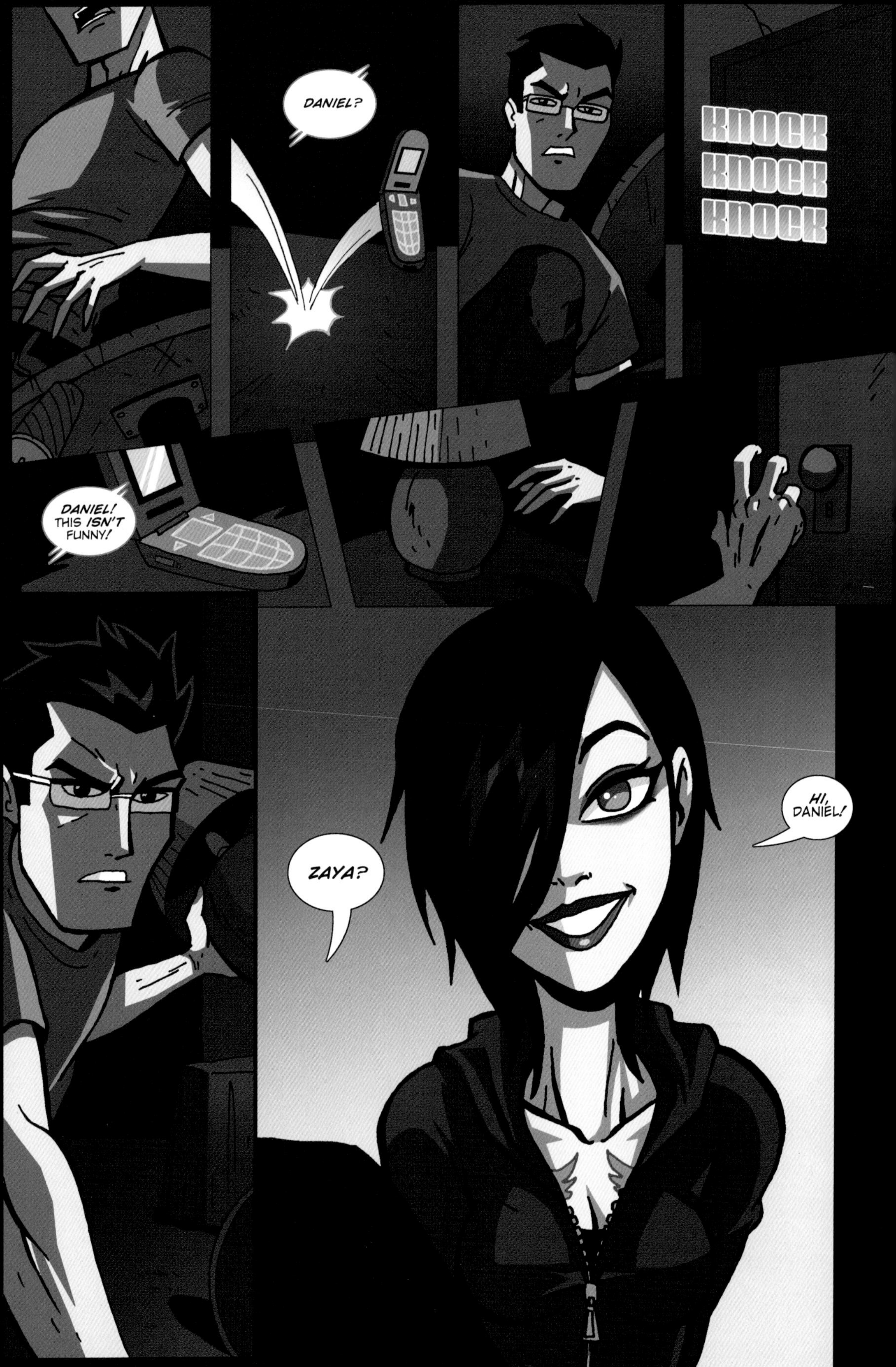
DANIEL?
KNOCK
KNOCK
KNOCK
DANIEL! THIS ISN'T FUNNY!
ZAYA?
HI, DANIEL!

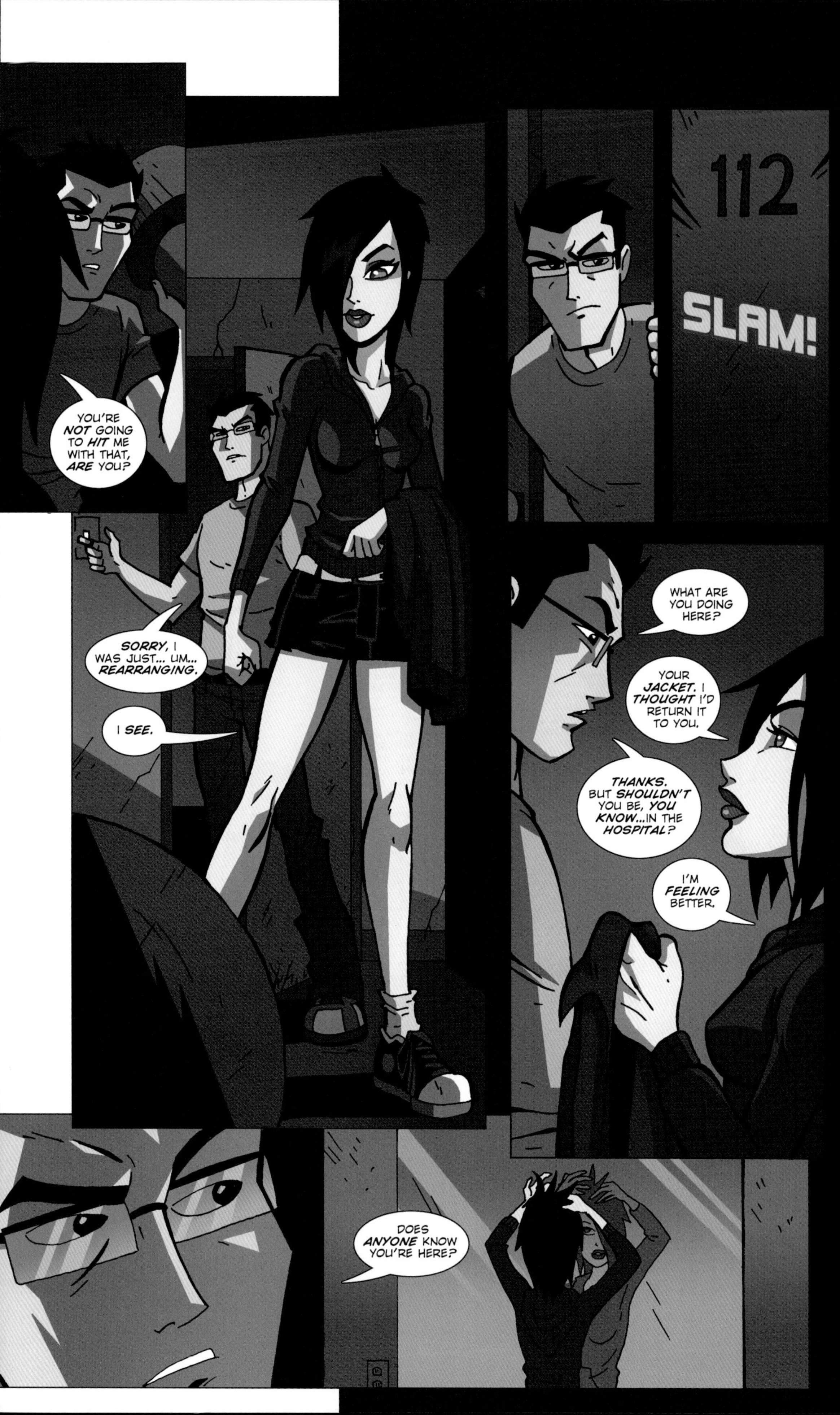
YOU'RE NOT GOING TO HIT ME WITH THAT, ARE YOU?
SORRY, I WAS JUST... UM... REARRANGING.
I SEE.
112
SLAM!
WHAT ARE YOU DOING HERE?
YOUR JACKET. I THOUGHT I'D RETURN IT TO YOU.
THANKS. BUT SHOULDN'T YOU BE, YOU KNOW...IN THE HOSPITAL?
I'M FEELING BETTER.
DOES ANYONE KNOW YOU'RE HERE?

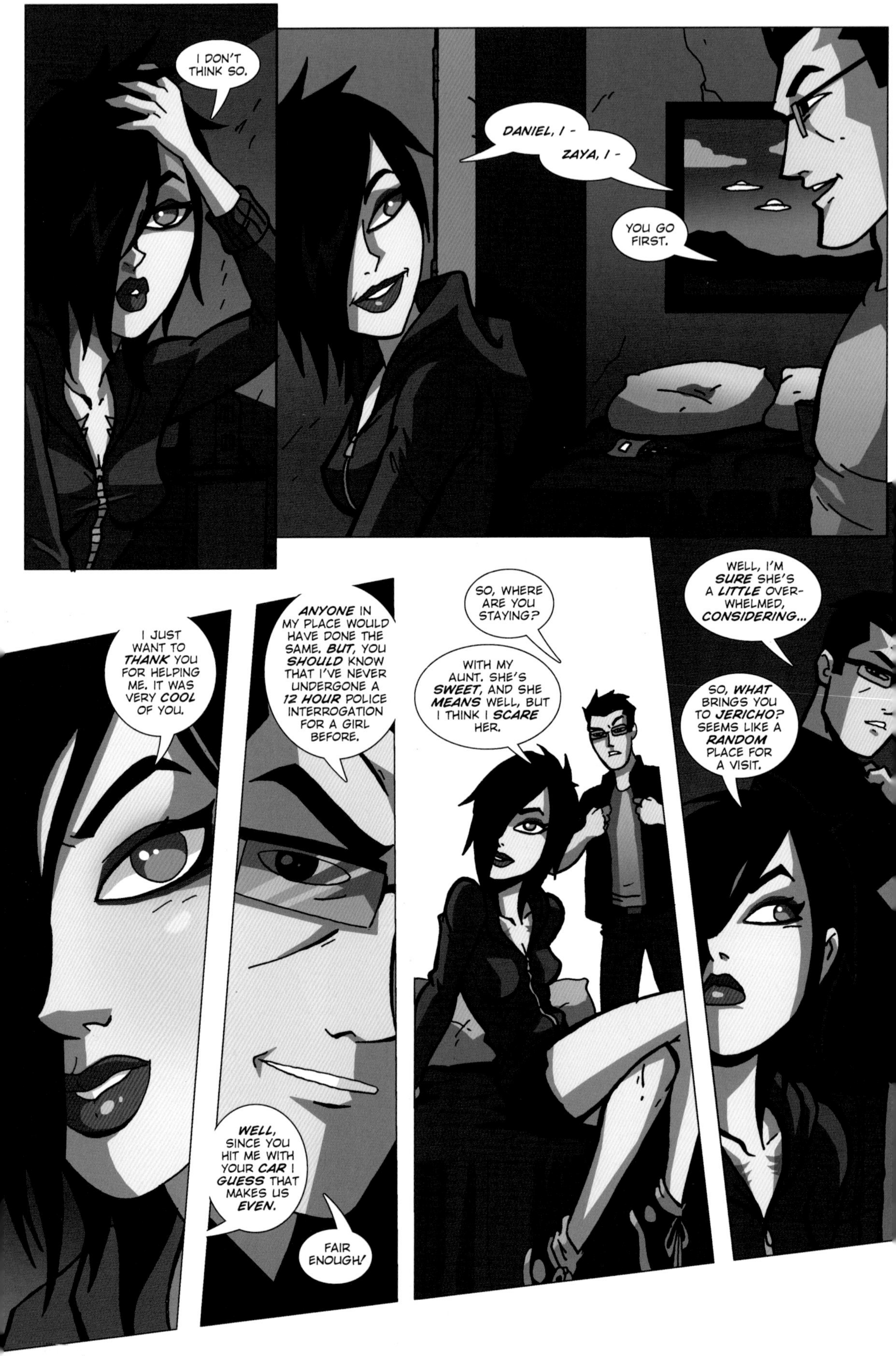
I DON'T THINK SO.
DANIEL, I -
ZAYA, I -
YOU GO FIRST.
I JUST WANT TO THANK YOU FOR HELPING ME. IT WAS VERY COOL OF YOU.
ANYONE IN MY PLACE WOULD HAVE DONE THE SAME. BUT, YOU SHOULD KNOW THAT I'VE NEVER UNDERGONE A 12 HOUR POLICE INTERROGATION FOR A GIRL BEFORE.
WELL, SINCE YOU HIT ME WITH YOUR CAR I GUESS THAT MAKES US EVEN.
FAIR ENOUGH!
SO, WHERE ARE YOU STAYING?
WITH MY AUNT. SHE'S SWEET, AND SHE MEANS WELL, BUT I THINK I SCARE HER.
WELL, I'M SURE SHE'S A LITTLE OVER-WHELMED, CONSIDERING...
SO, WHAT BRINGS YOU TO JERICHO? SEEMS LIKE A RANDOM PLACE FOR A VISIT.

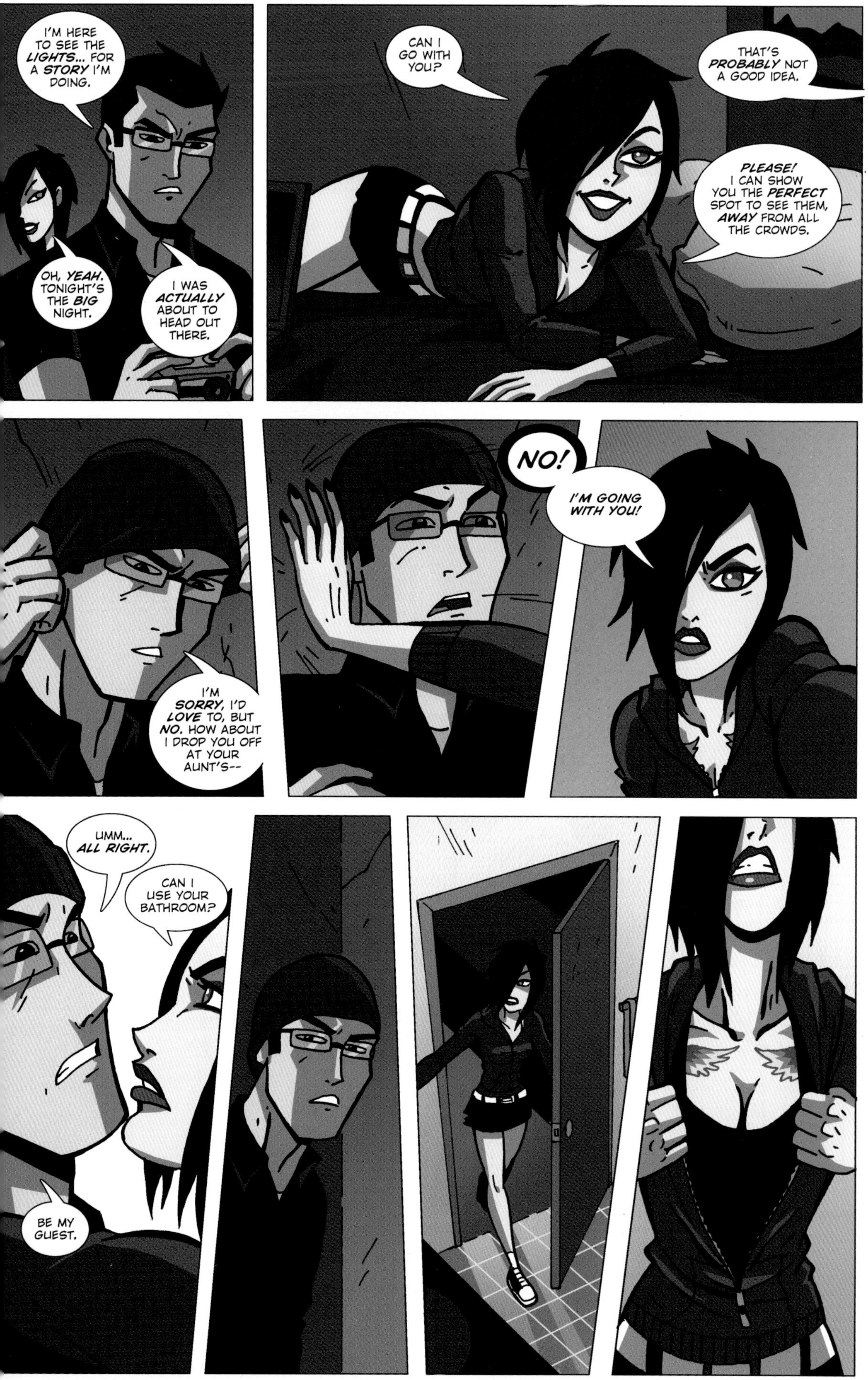

I'M HERE TO SEE THE LIGHTS... FOR A STORY I'M DOING.
OH, YEAH. TONIGHT'S THE BIG NIGHT.
I WAS ACTUALLY ABOUT TO HEAD OUT THERE.
CAN I GO WITH YOU?
THAT'S PROBABLY NOT A GOOD IDEA.
PLEASE! I CAN SHOW YOU THE PERFECT SPOT TO SEE THEM, AWAY FROM ALL THE CROWDS.
I'M SORRY, I'D LOVE TO, BUT NO. HOW ABOUT I DROP YOU OFF AT YOUR AUNT'S--
NO!
I'M GOING WITH YOU!
UMM... ALL RIGHT.
CAN I USE YOUR BATHROOM?
BE MY GUEST.

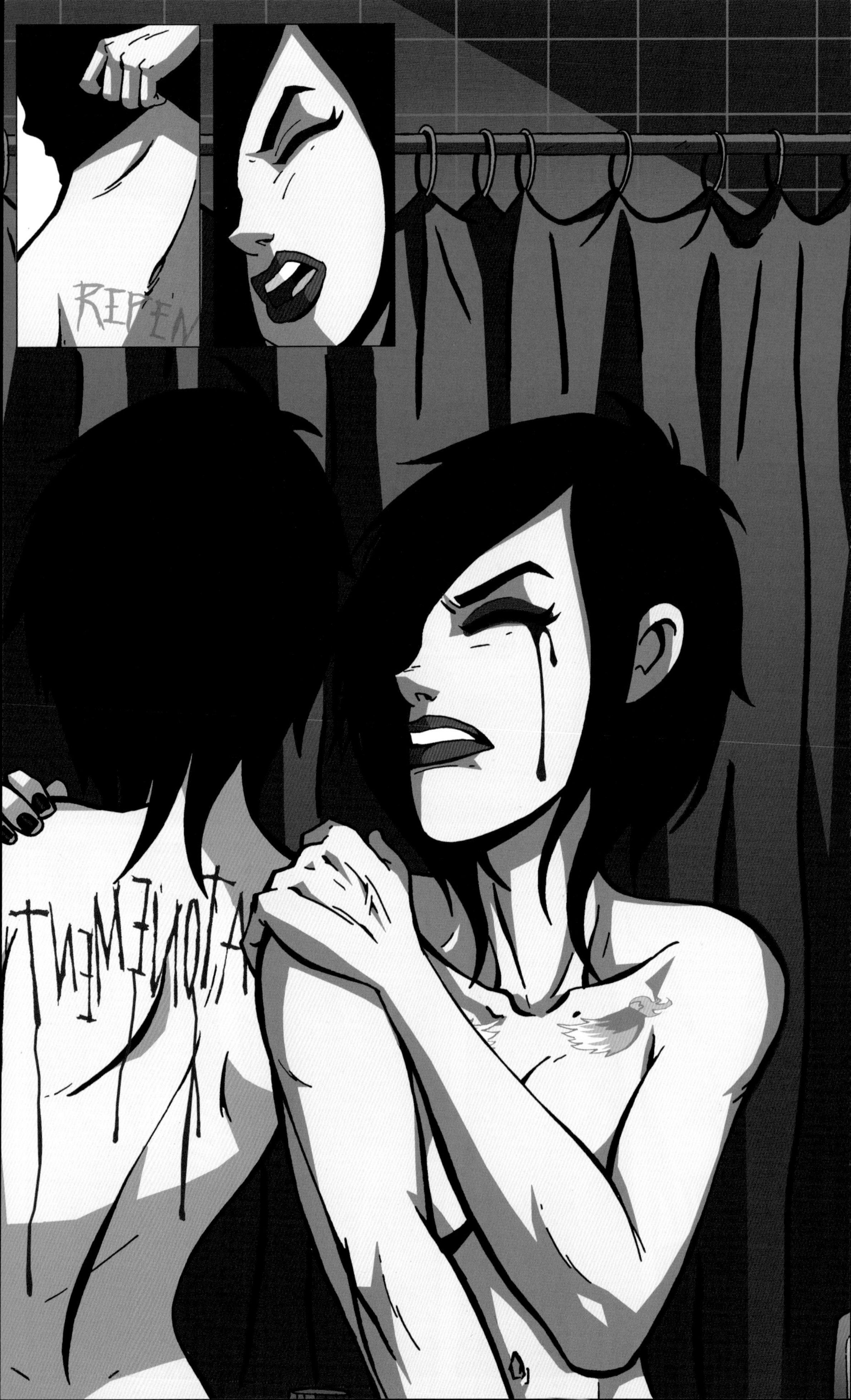

REPEN

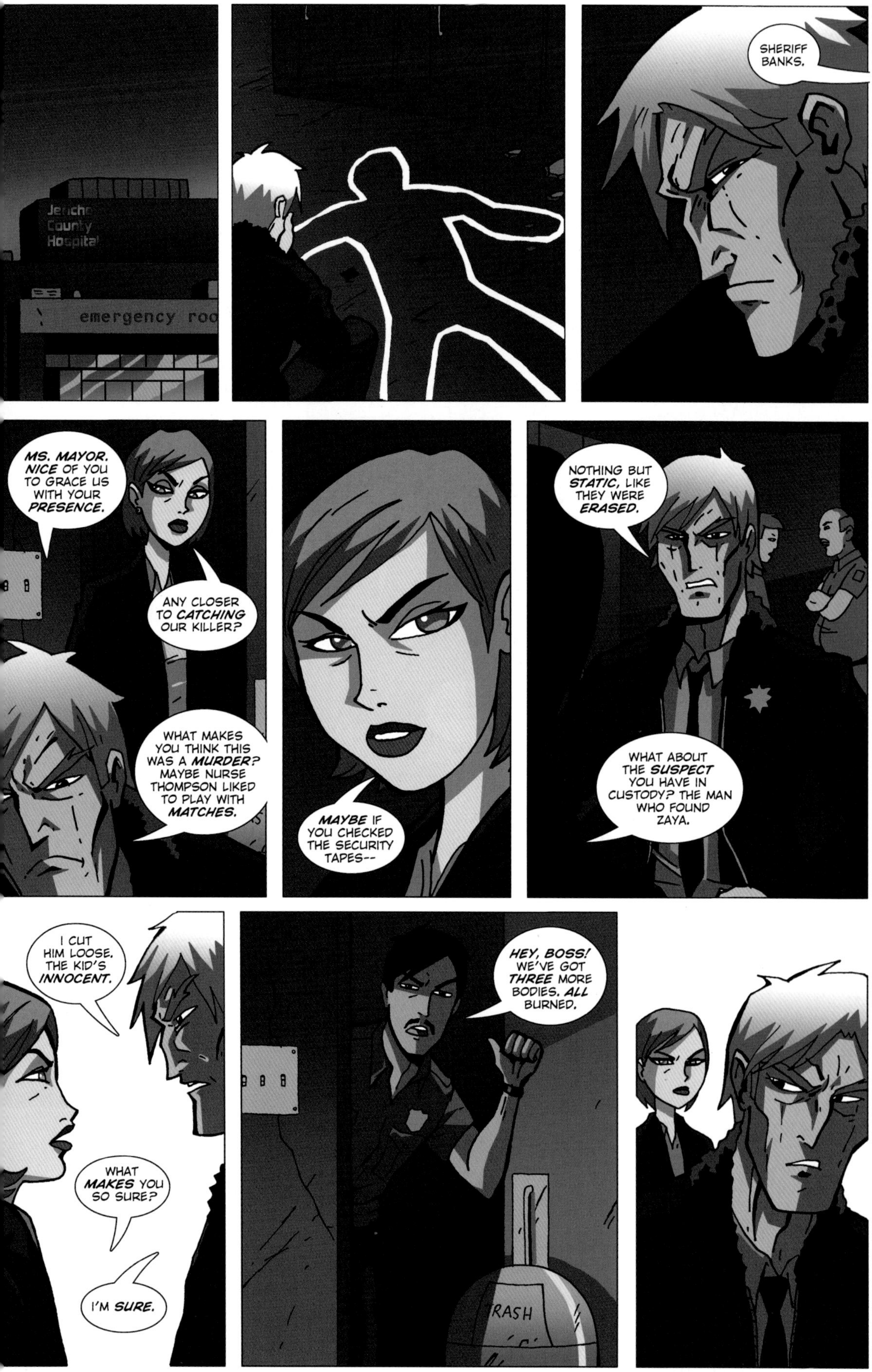
Jericho County Hospital
emergency roo
SHERIFF BANKS.
MS. MAYOR. NICE OF YOU TO GRACE US WITH YOUR PRESENCE.
ANY CLOSER TO CATCHING OUR KILLER?
WHAT MAKES YOU THINK THIS WAS A MURDER? MAYBE NURSE THOMPSON LIKED TO PLAY WITH MATCHES.
MAYBE IF YOU CHECKED THE SECURITY TAPES--
NOTHING BUT STATIC, LIKE THEY WERE ERASED.
WHAT ABOUT THE SUSPECT YOU HAVE IN CUSTODY? THE MAN WHO FOUND ZAYA.
I CUT HIM LOOSE. THE KID'S INNOCENT.
WHAT MAKES YOU SO SURE?
I'M SURE.
HEY, BOSS! WE'VE GOT THREE MORE BODIES. ALL BURNED.
TRASH

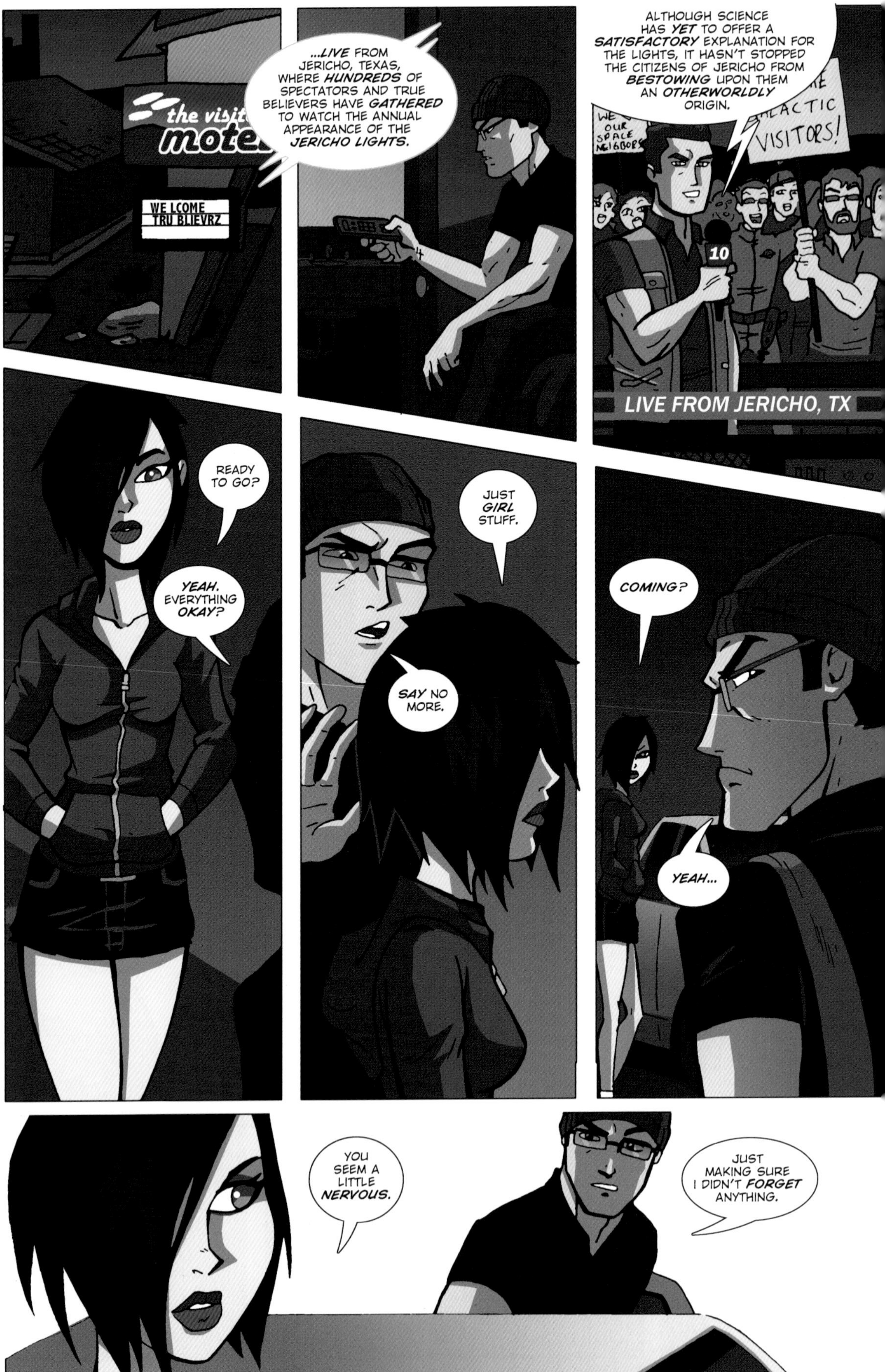
WE LCOME
TRU BLIEVRZ
...LIVE FROM JERICHO, TEXAS, WHERE HUNDREDS OF SPECTATORS AND TRUE BELIEVERS HAVE GATHERED TO WATCH THE ANNUAL APPEARANCE OF THE JERICHO LIGHTS.
ALTHOUGH SCIENCE HAS YET TO OFFER A SATISFACTORY EXPLANATION FOR THE LIGHTS, IT HASN'T STOPPED THE CITIZENS OF JERICHO FROM BESTOWING UPON THEM AN OTHERWORLDLY ORIGIN.
OUR SPACE NEIGBORS
VISITORS!
10
LIVE FROM JERICHO, TX
READY TO GO?
YEAH. EVERYTHING OKAY?
JUST GIRL STUFF.
SAY NO MORE.
COMING?
YEAH...
YOU SEEM A LITTLE NERVOUS.
JUST MAKING SURE I DIDN'T FORGET ANYTHING.

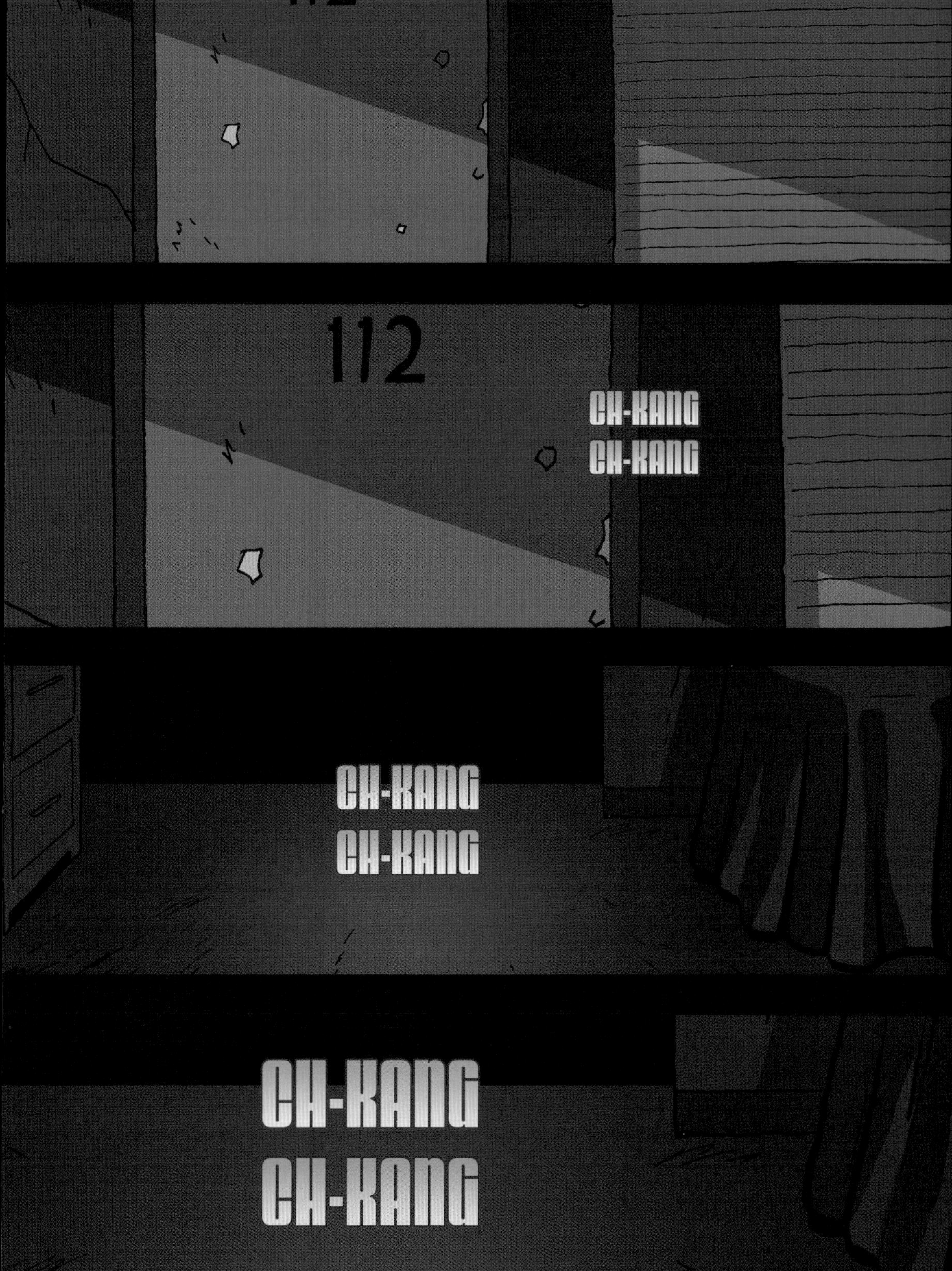
112
CH-KANG
CH-KANG
CH-KANG
CH-KANG
CH-KANG
CH-KANG

chapter
3

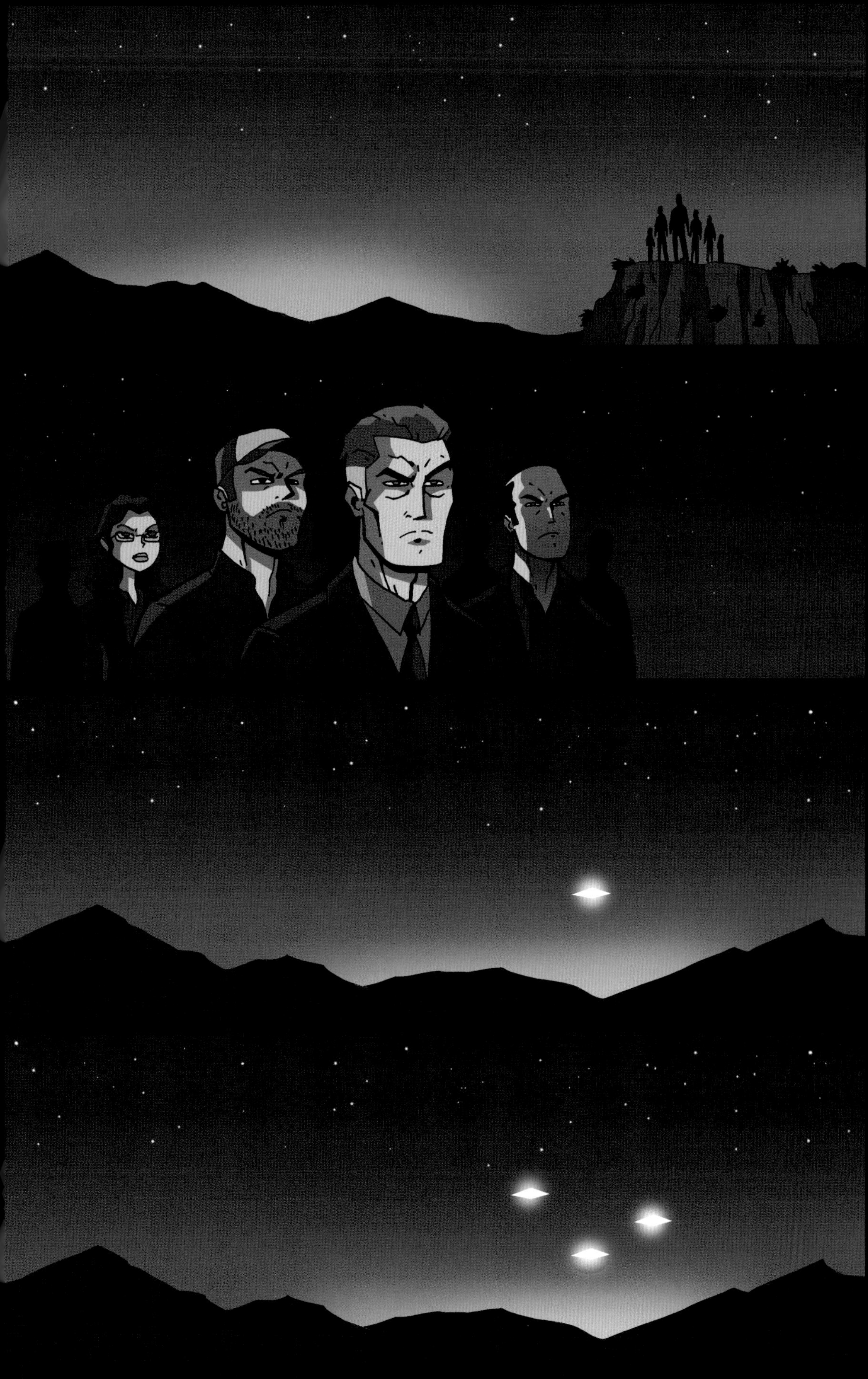

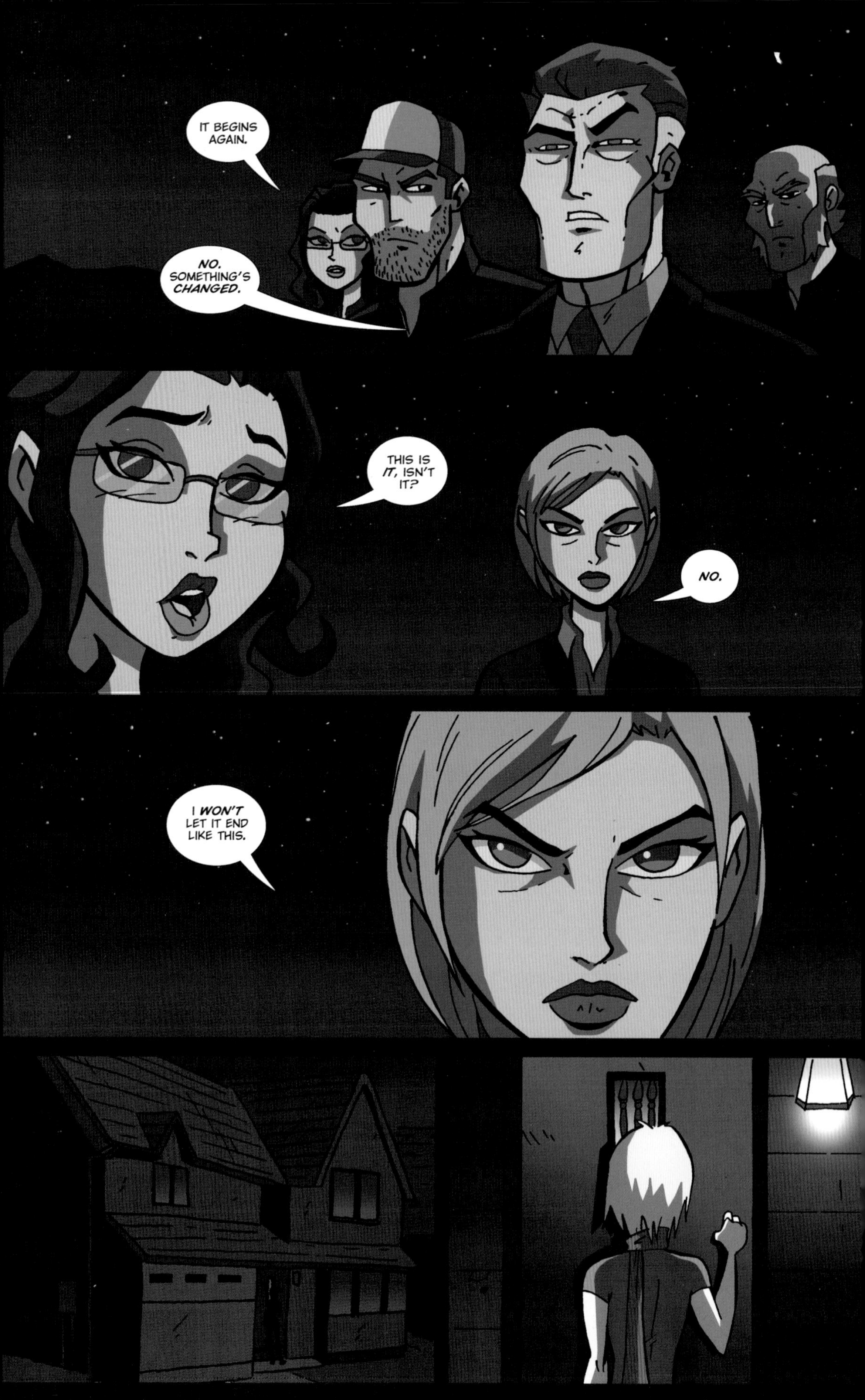
IT BEGINS AGAIN.
NO. SOMETHING'S CHANGED.
THIS IS IT, ISN'T IT?
NO.
I WON'T LET IT END LIKE THIS.

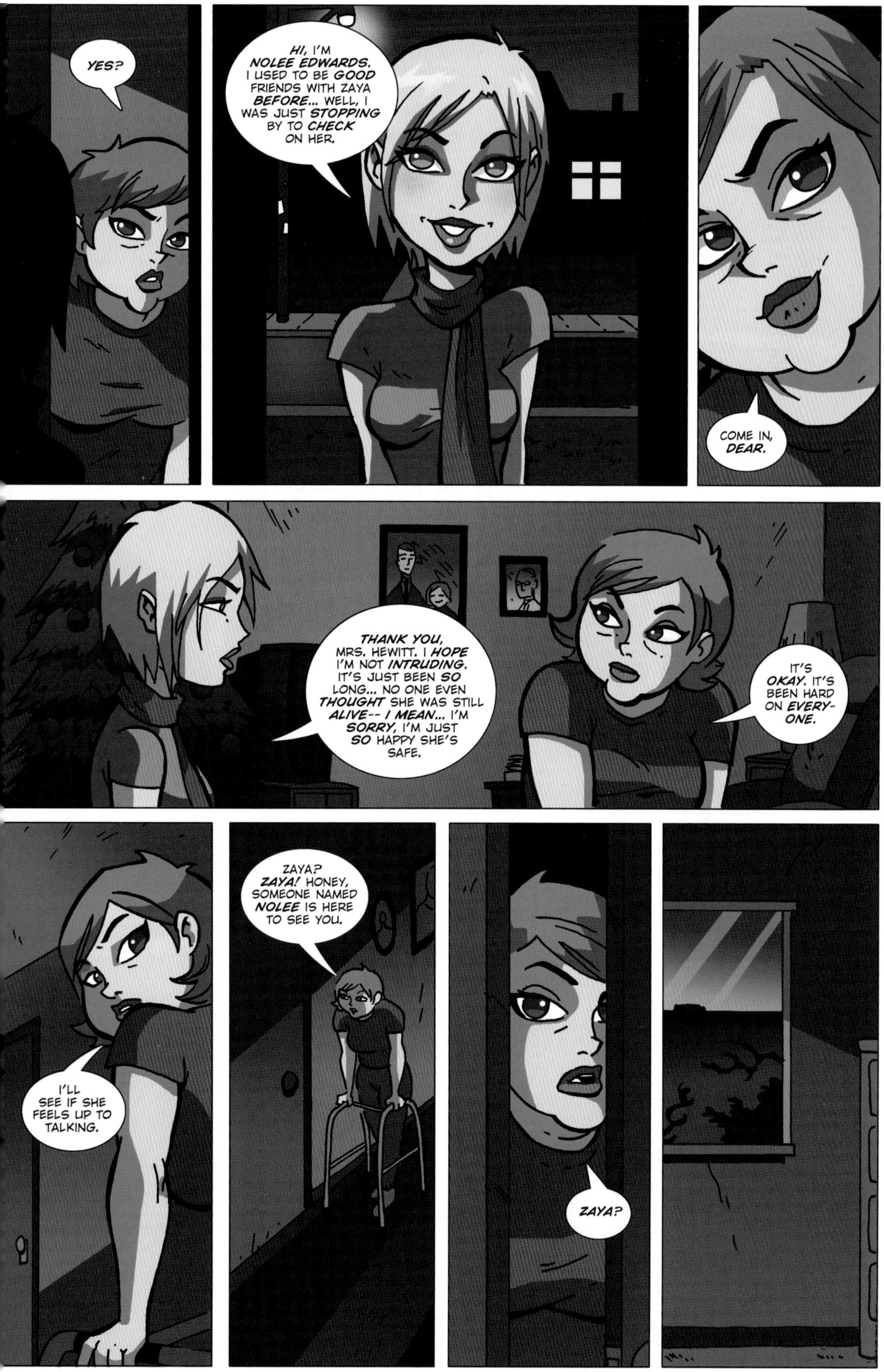
YES?
HI, I'M NOLEE EDWARDS. I USED TO BE GOOD FRIENDS WITH ZAYA BEFORE... WELL, I WAS JUST STOPPING BY TO CHECK ON HER.
COME IN, DEAR.
THANK YOU, MRS. HEWITT. I HOPE I'M NOT INTRUDING. IT'S JUST BEEN SO LONG... NO ONE EVEN THOUGHT SHE WAS STILL ALIVE-- I MEAN... I'M SORRY, I'M JUST SO HAPPY SHE'S SAFE.
IT'S OKAY. IT'S BEEN HARD ON EVERY-ONE.
I'LL SEE IF SHE FEELS UP TO TALKING.
ZAYA? ZAYA! HONEY, SOMEONE NAMED NOLEE IS HERE TO SEE YOU.
ZAYA?

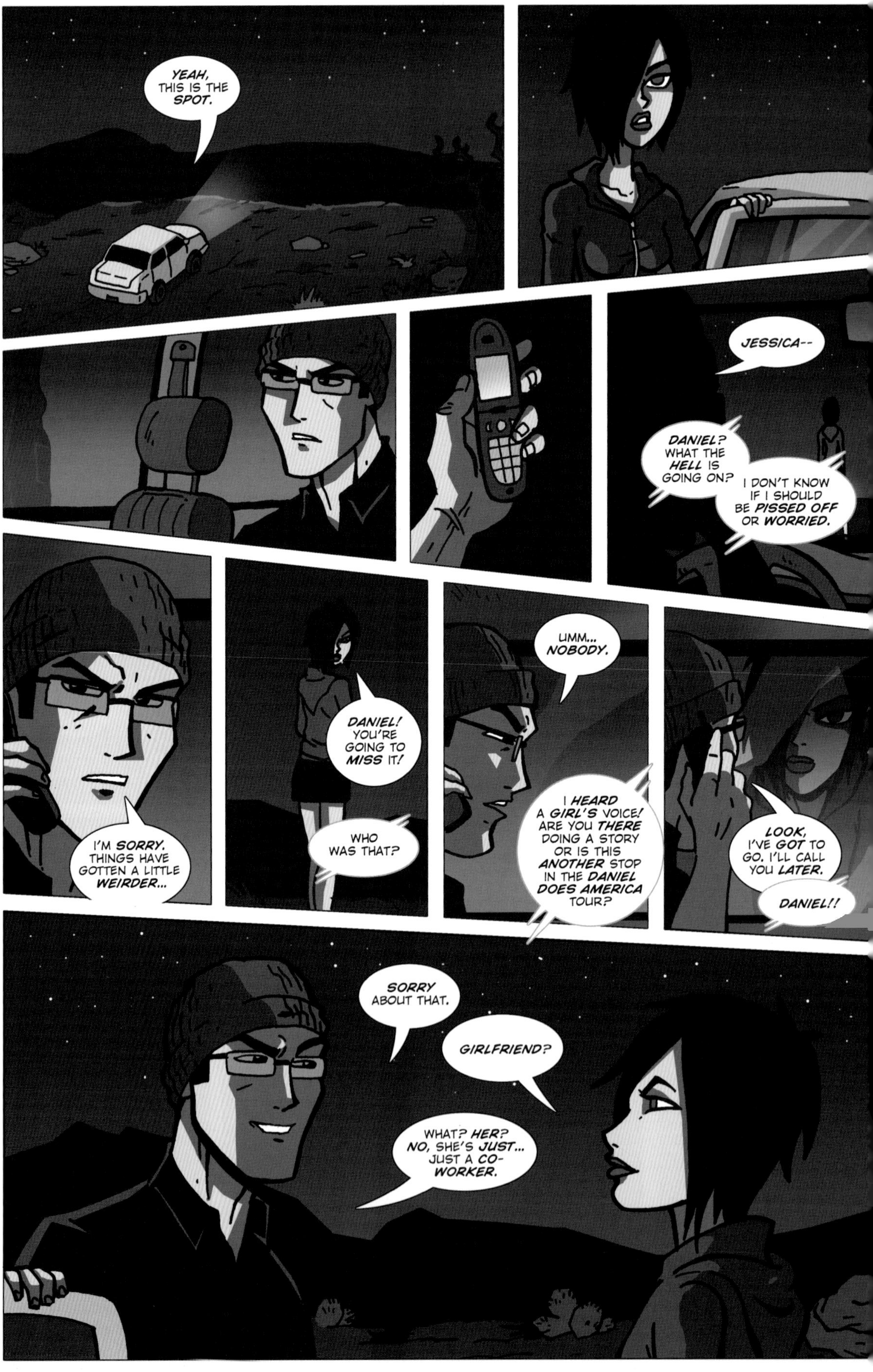
YEAH, THIS IS THE SPOT.
JESSICA--
DANIEL? WHAT THE HELL IS GOING ON?
I DON'T KNOW IF I SHOULD BE PISSED OFF OR WORRIED.
I'M SORRY. THINGS HAVE GOTTEN A LITTLE WEIRDER...
DANIEL! YOU'RE GOING TO MISS IT!
WHO WAS THAT?
UMM... NOBODY.
I HEARD A GIRL'S VOICE! ARE YOU THERE DOING A STORY OR IS THIS ANOTHER STOP IN THE DANIEL DOES AMERICA TOUR?
LOOK, I'VE GOT TO GO. I'LL CALL YOU LATER.
DANIEL!!
SORRY ABOUT THAT.
GIRLFRIEND?
WHAT? HER? NO, SHE'S JUST... JUST A CO-WORKER.

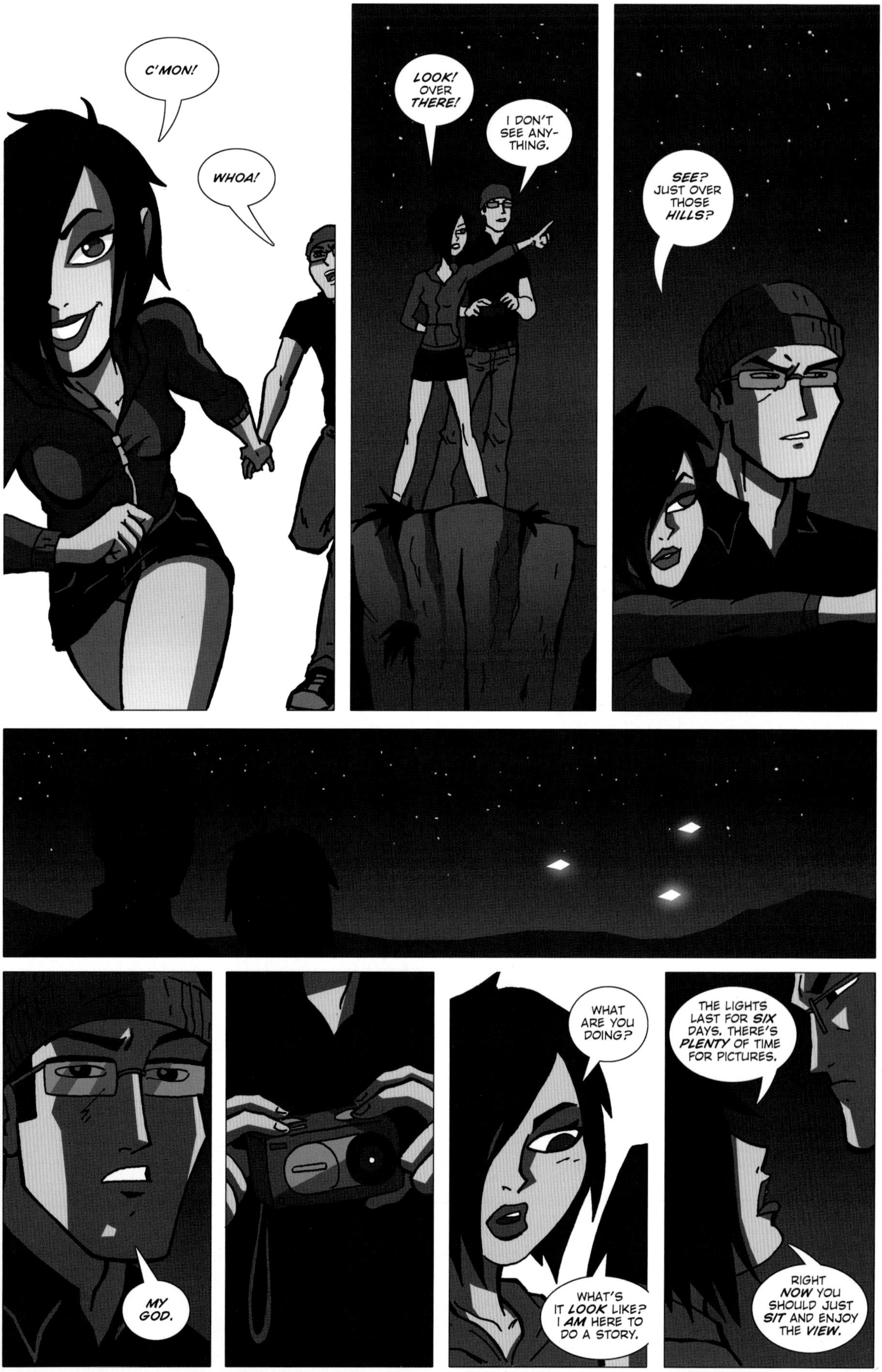
C'MON!
WHOA!
LOOK! OVER THERE!
I DON'T SEE ANY-THING.
SEE? JUST OVER THOSE HILLS?
MY GOD.
WHAT ARE YOU DOING?
WHAT'S IT LOOK LIKE? I AM HERE TO DO A STORY.
THE LIGHTS LAST FOR SIX DAYS. THERE'S PLENTY OF TIME FOR PICTURES.
RIGHT NOW YOU SHOULD JUST SIT AND ENJOY THE VIEW.

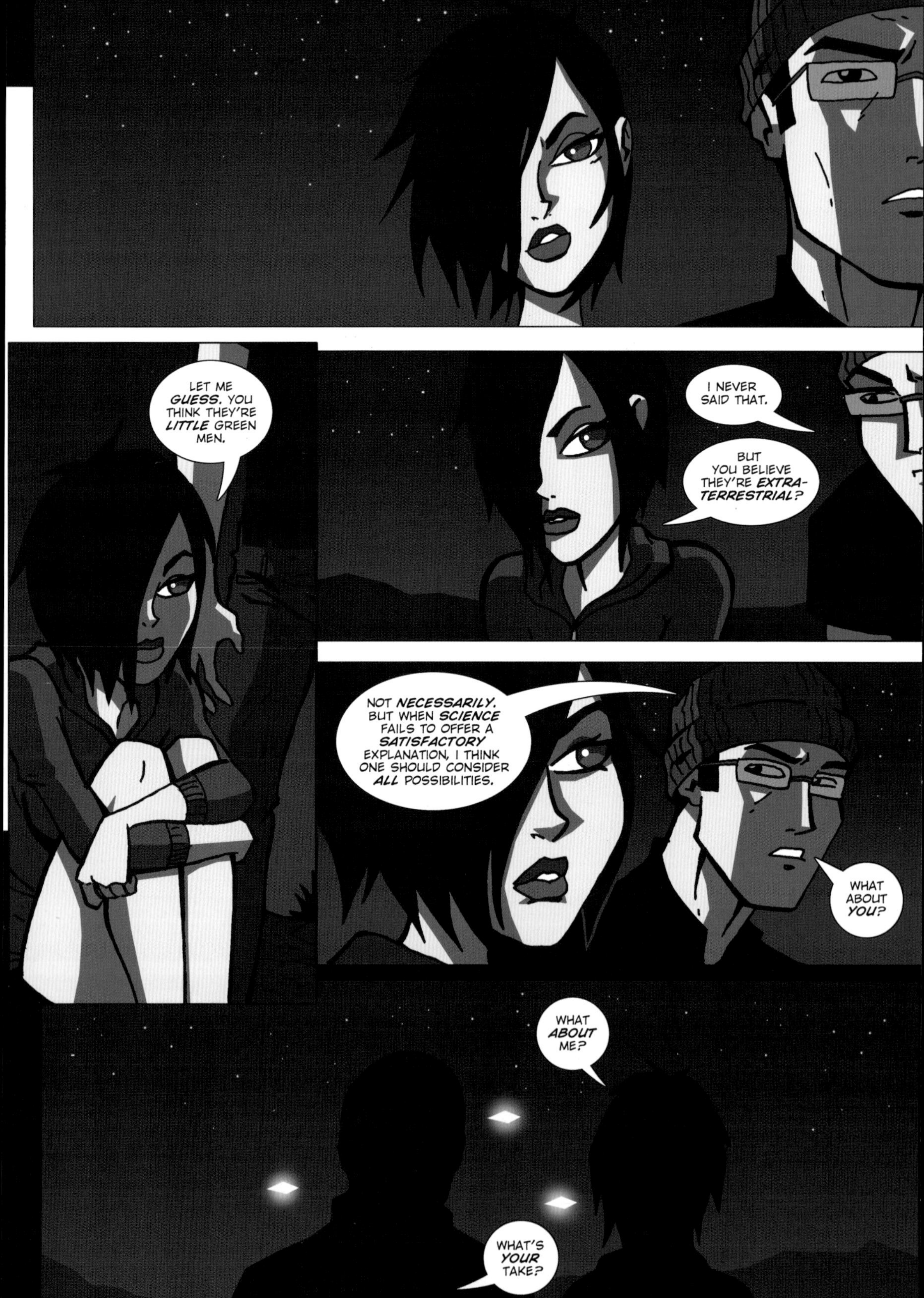
LET ME GUESS. YOU THINK THEY'RE LITTLE GREEN MEN.
I NEVER SAID THAT.
BUT YOU BELIEVE THEY'RE EXTRA-TERRESTRIAL?
NOT NECESSARILY. BUT WHEN SCIENCE FAILS TO OFFER A SATISFACTORY EXPLANATION, I THINK ONE SHOULD CONSIDER ALL POSSIBILITIES.
WHAT ABOUT YOU?
WHAT ABOUT ME?
WHAT'S YOUR TAKE?

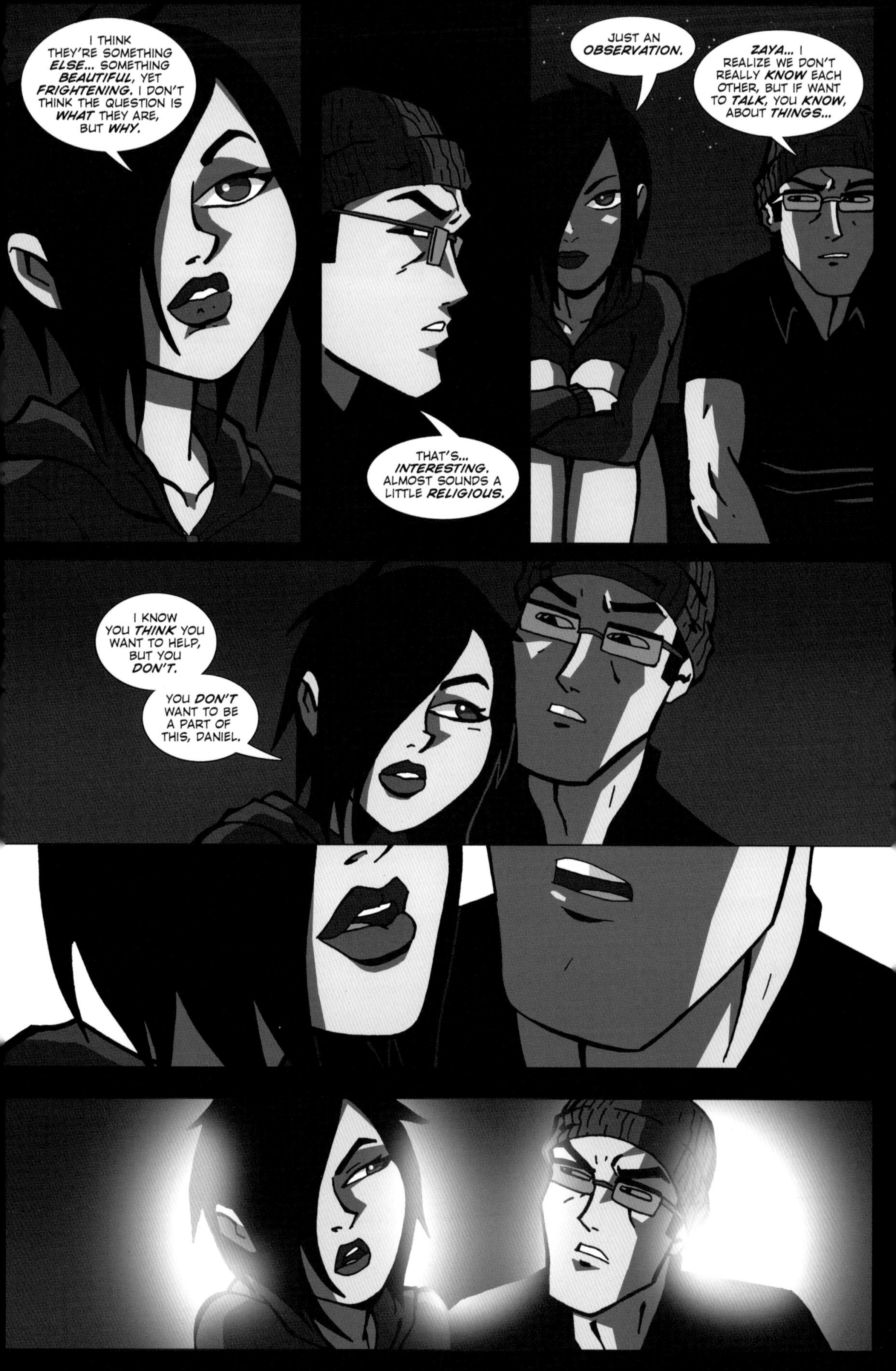
I THINK THEY'RE SOMETHING ELSE... SOMETHING BEAUTIFUL, YET FRIGHTENING. I DON'T THINK THE QUESTION IS WHAT THEY ARE, BUT WHY.
THAT'S... INTERESTING. ALMOST SOUNDS A LITTLE RELIGIOUS.
JUST AN OBSERVATION.
ZAYA... I REALIZE WE DON'T REALLY KNOW EACH OTHER, BUT IF WANT TO TALK, YOU KNOW, ABOUT THINGS...
I KNOW YOU THINK YOU WANT TO HELP, BUT YOU DON'T.
YOU DON'T WANT TO BE A PART OF THIS, DANIEL.

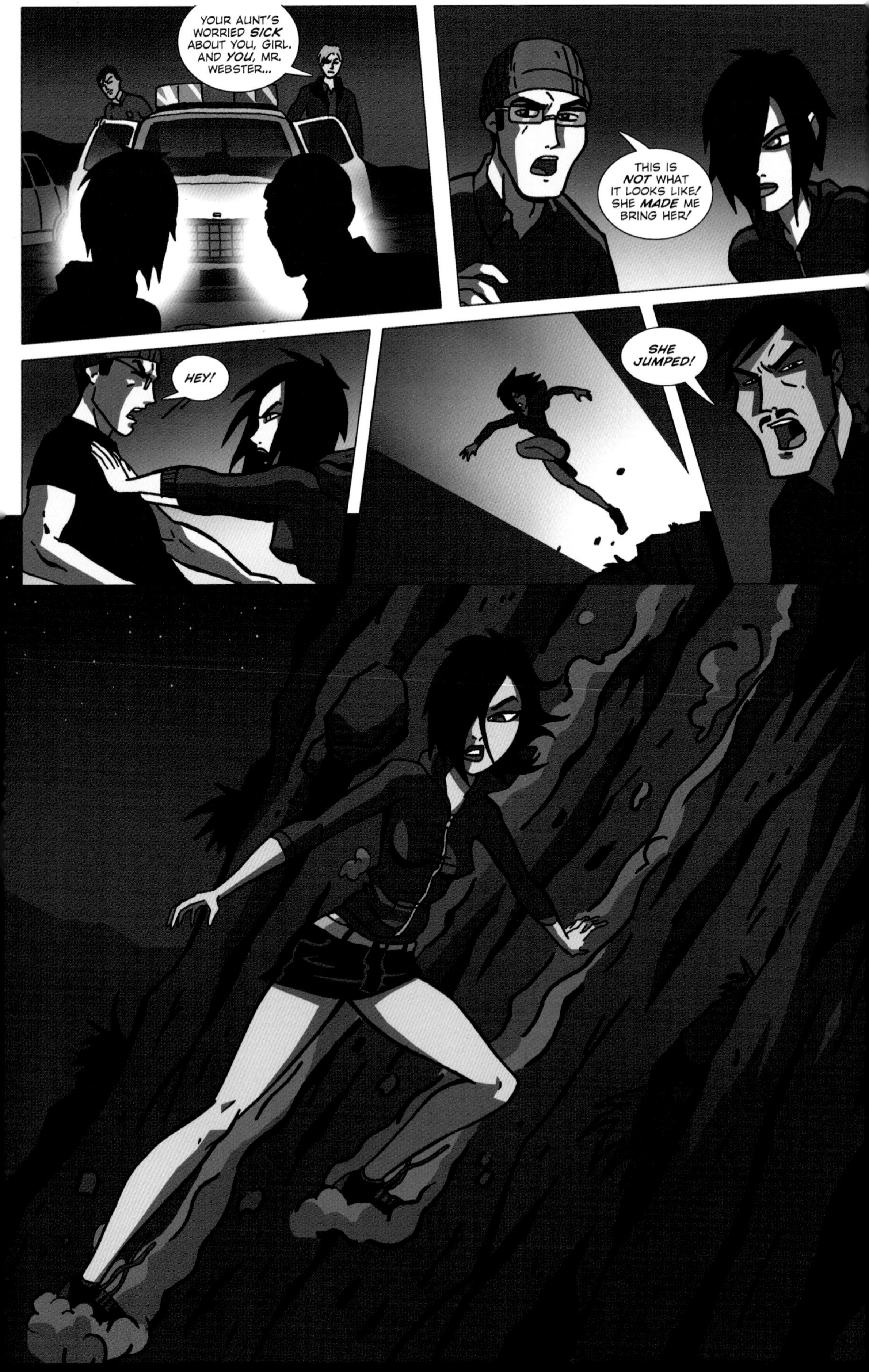
YOUR AUNT'S WORRIED SICK ABOUT YOU, GIRL. AND YOU, MR. WEBSTER...
THIS IS NOT WHAT IT LOOKS LIKE! SHE MADE ME BRING HER!
HEY!
SHE JUMPED!

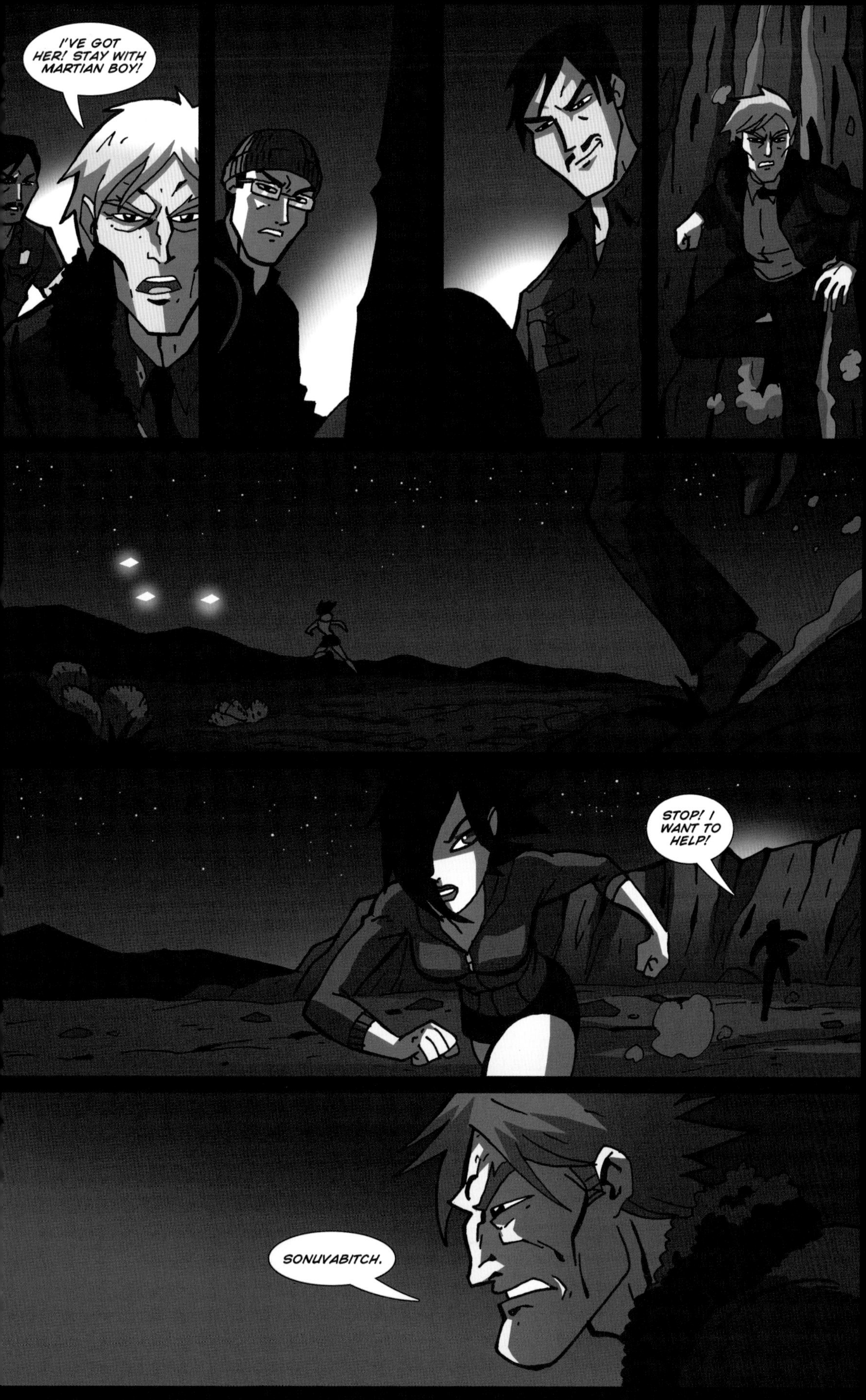
I'VE GOT HER! STAY WITH MARTIAN BOY!
STOP! I WANT TO HELP!
SONUVABITCH.

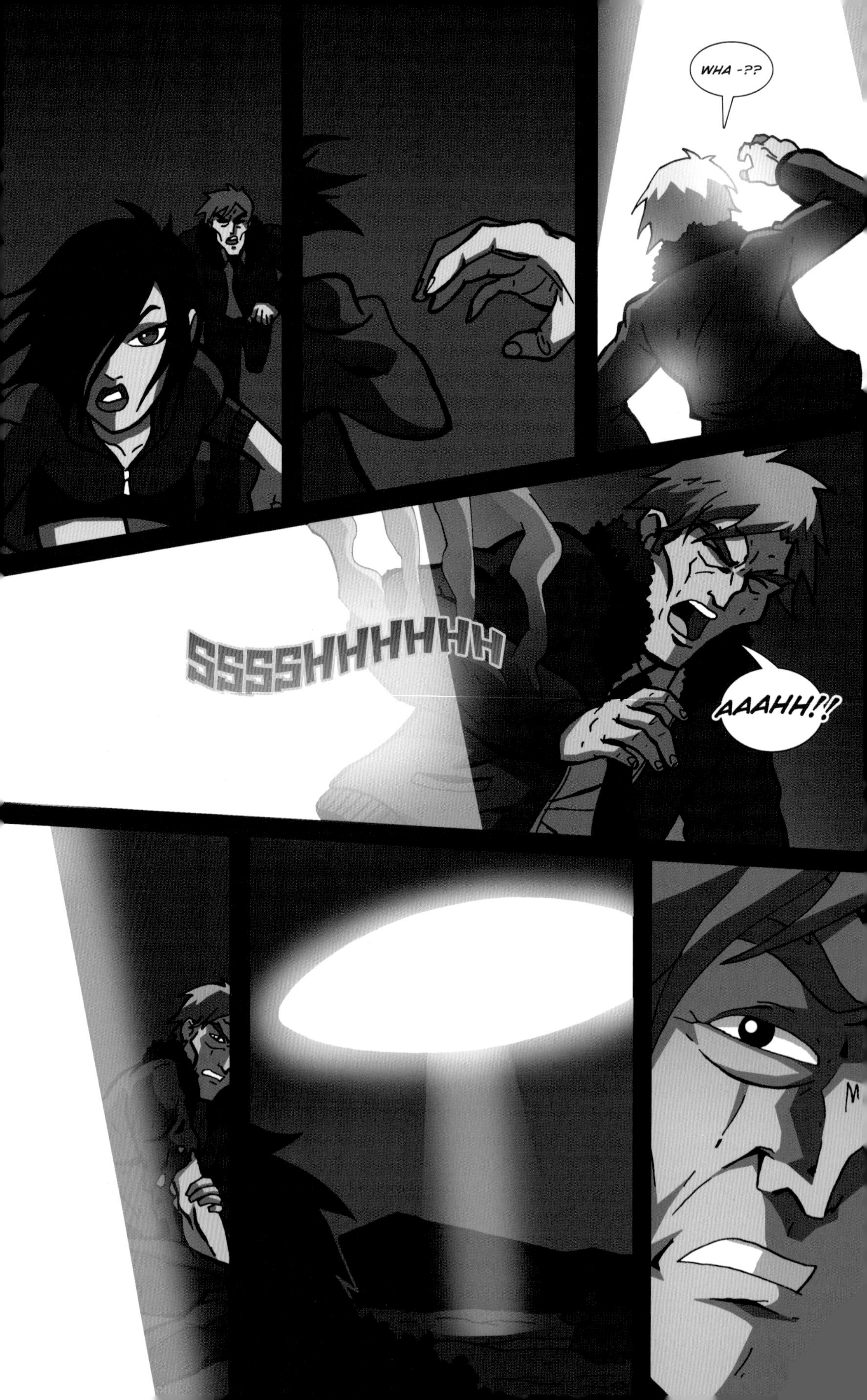
WHA -??
SSSSHHHHHH
AAAHH!!

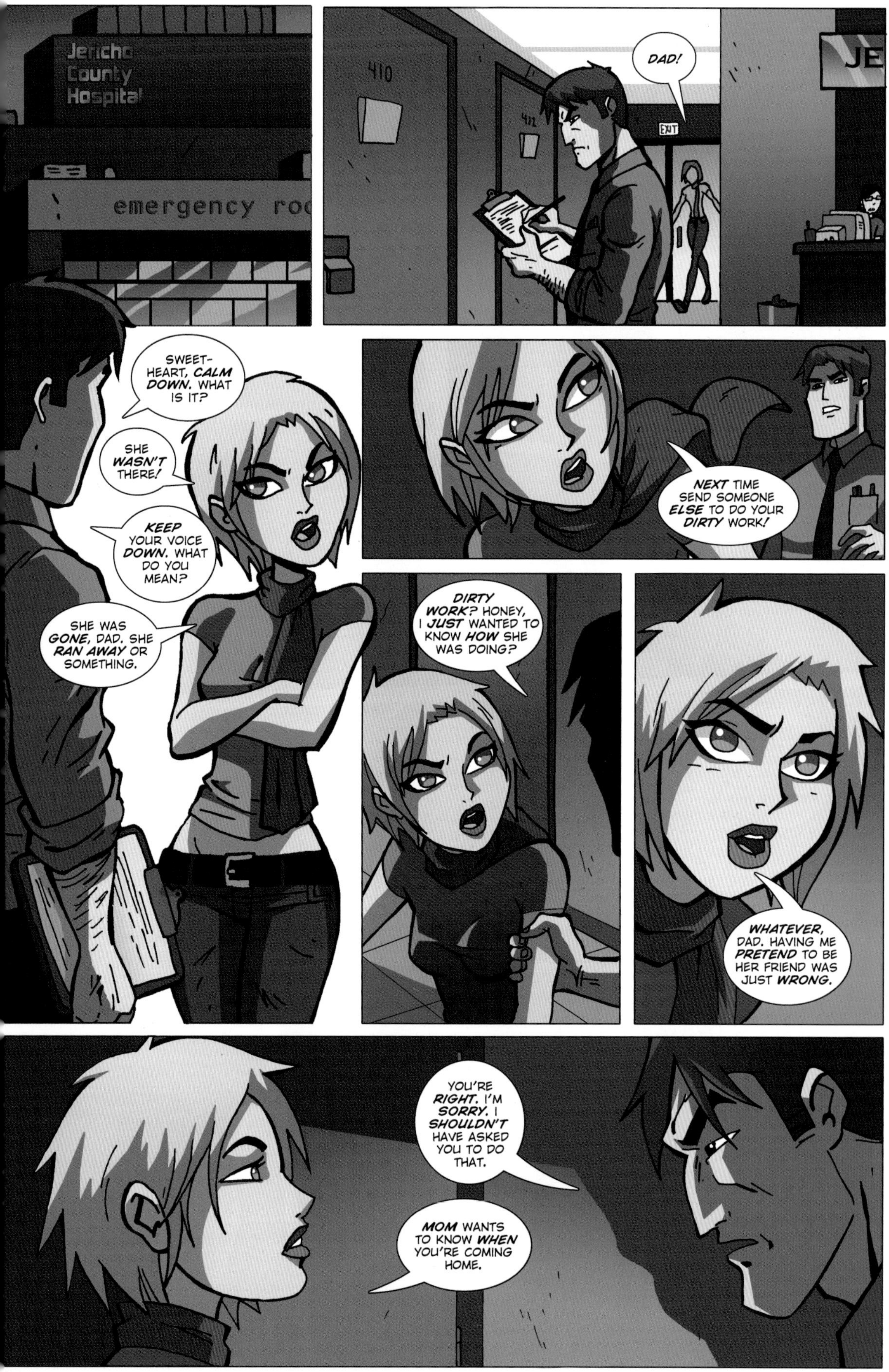
Jericho County Hospital
emergency roo
410
412
DAD!
EXIT
JE
SWEET-HEART, CALM DOWN. WHAT IS IT?
SHE WASN'T THERE!
KEEP YOUR VOICE DOWN. WHAT DO YOU MEAN?
SHE WAS GONE, DAD. SHE RAN AWAY OR SOMETHING.
NEXT TIME SEND SOMEONE ELSE TO DO YOUR DIRTY WORK!
DIRTY WORK? HONEY, I JUST WANTED TO KNOW HOW SHE WAS DOING?
WHATEVER, DAD. HAVING ME PRETEND TO BE HER FRIEND WAS JUST WRONG.
YOU'RE RIGHT. I'M SORRY. I SHOULDN'T HAVE ASKED YOU TO DO THAT.
MOM WANTS TO KNOW WHEN YOU'RE COMING HOME.

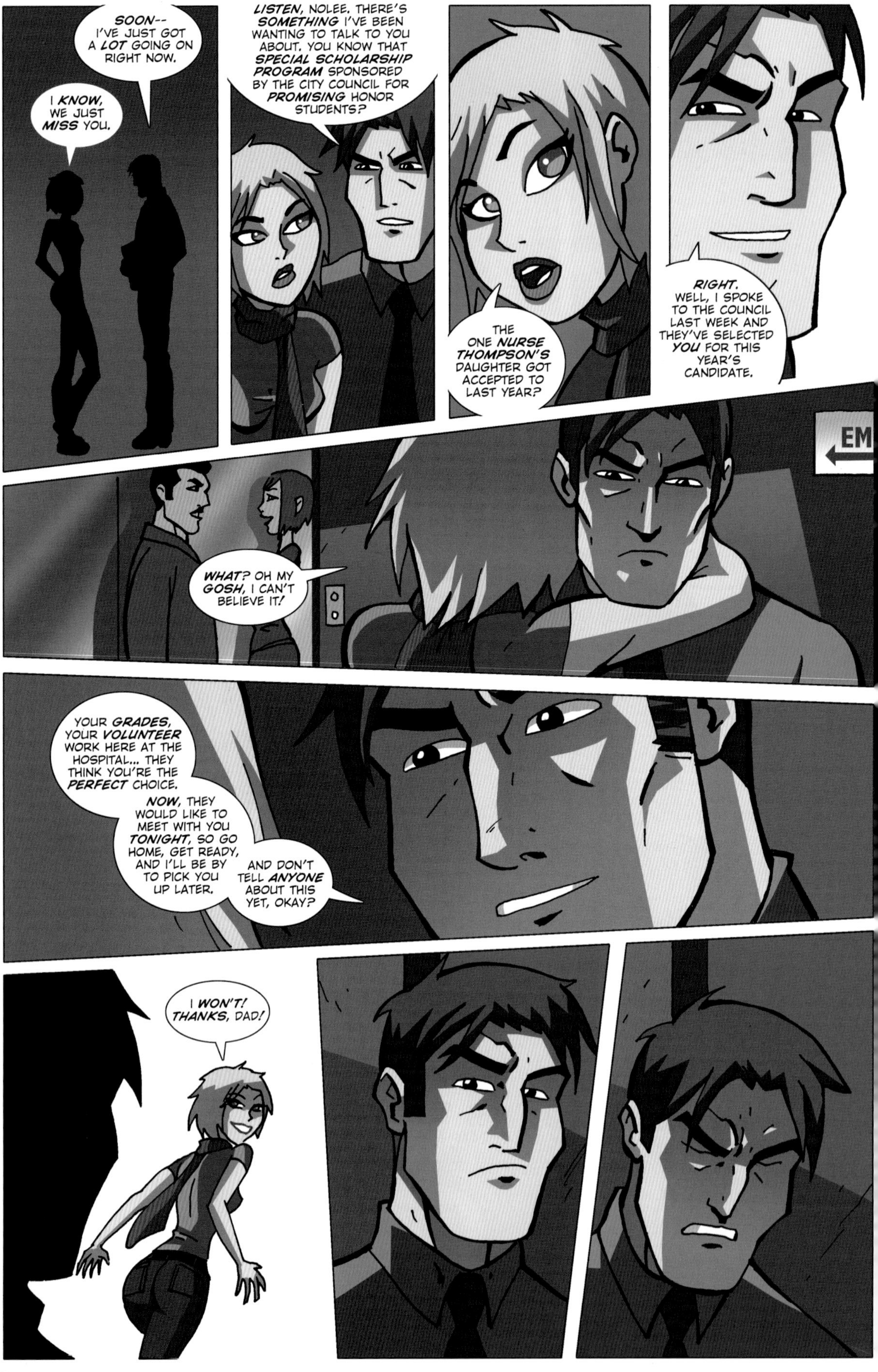
SOON-- I'VE JUST GOT A LOT GOING ON RIGHT NOW.
I KNOW, WE JUST MISS YOU.
LISTEN, NOLEE. THERE'S SOMETHING I'VE BEEN WANTING TO TALK TO YOU ABOUT. YOU KNOW THAT SPECIAL SCHOLARSHIP PROGRAM SPONSORED BY THE CITY COUNCIL FOR PROMISING HONOR STUDENTS?
THE ONE NURSE THOMPSON'S DAUGHTER GOT ACCEPTED TO LAST YEAR?
RIGHT. WELL, I SPOKE TO THE COUNCIL LAST WEEK AND THEY'VE SELECTED YOU FOR THIS YEAR'S CANDIDATE.
EM
WHAT? OH MY GOSH, I CAN'T BELIEVE IT!
YOUR GRADES, YOUR VOLUNTEER WORK HERE AT THE HOSPITAL... THEY THINK YOU'RE THE PERFECT CHOICE.
NOW, THEY WOULD LIKE TO MEET WITH YOU TONIGHT, SO GO HOME, GET READY, AND I'LL BE BY TO PICK YOU UP LATER.
AND DON'T TELL ANYONE ABOUT THIS YET, OKAY?
I WON'T! THANKS, DAD!

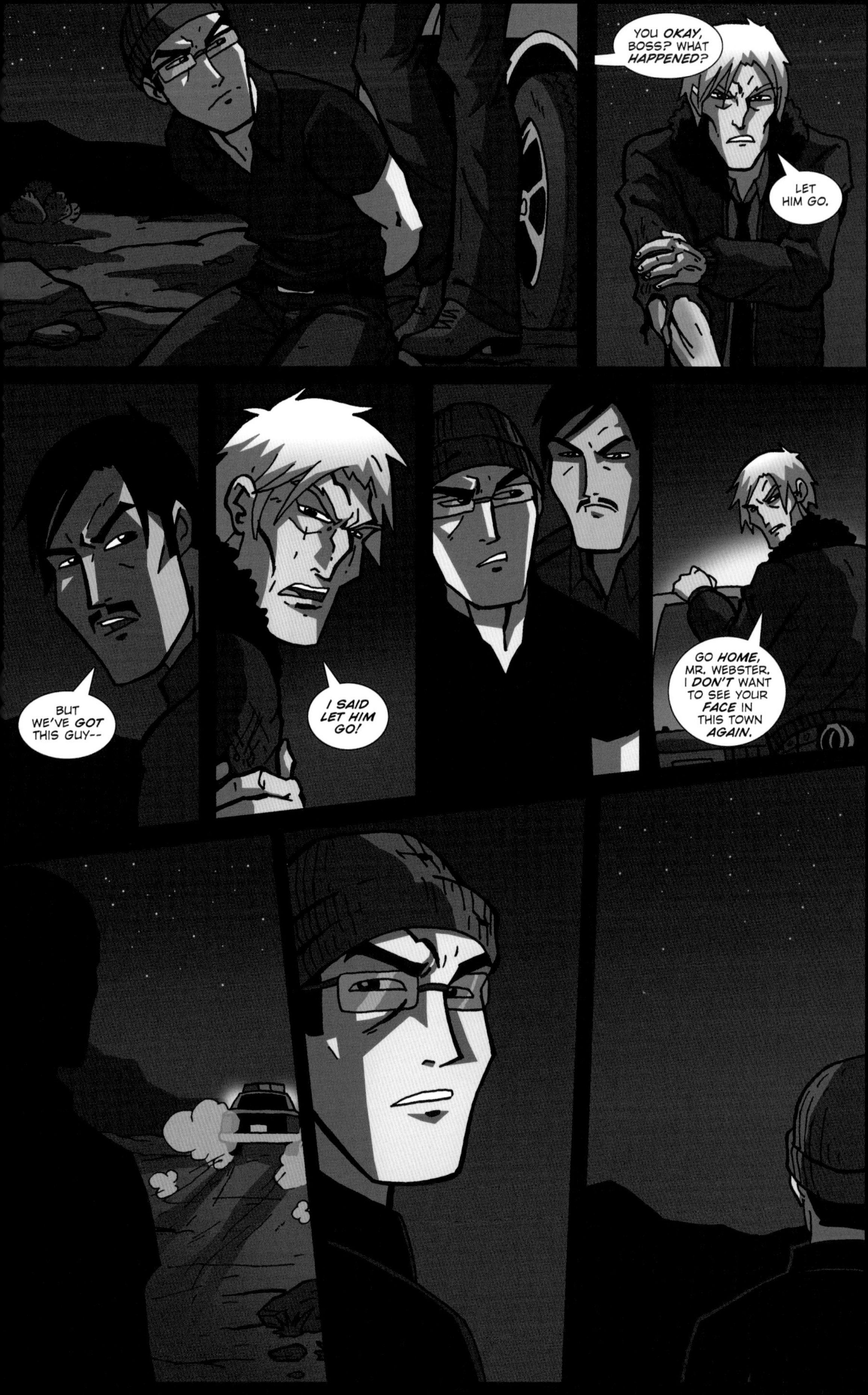
YOU OKAY, BOSS? WHAT HAPPENED?
LET HIM GO.
BUT WE'VE GOT THIS GUY--
I SAID LET HIM GO!
GO HOME, MR. WEBSTER. I DON'T WANT TO SEE YOUR FACE IN THIS TOWN AGAIN.

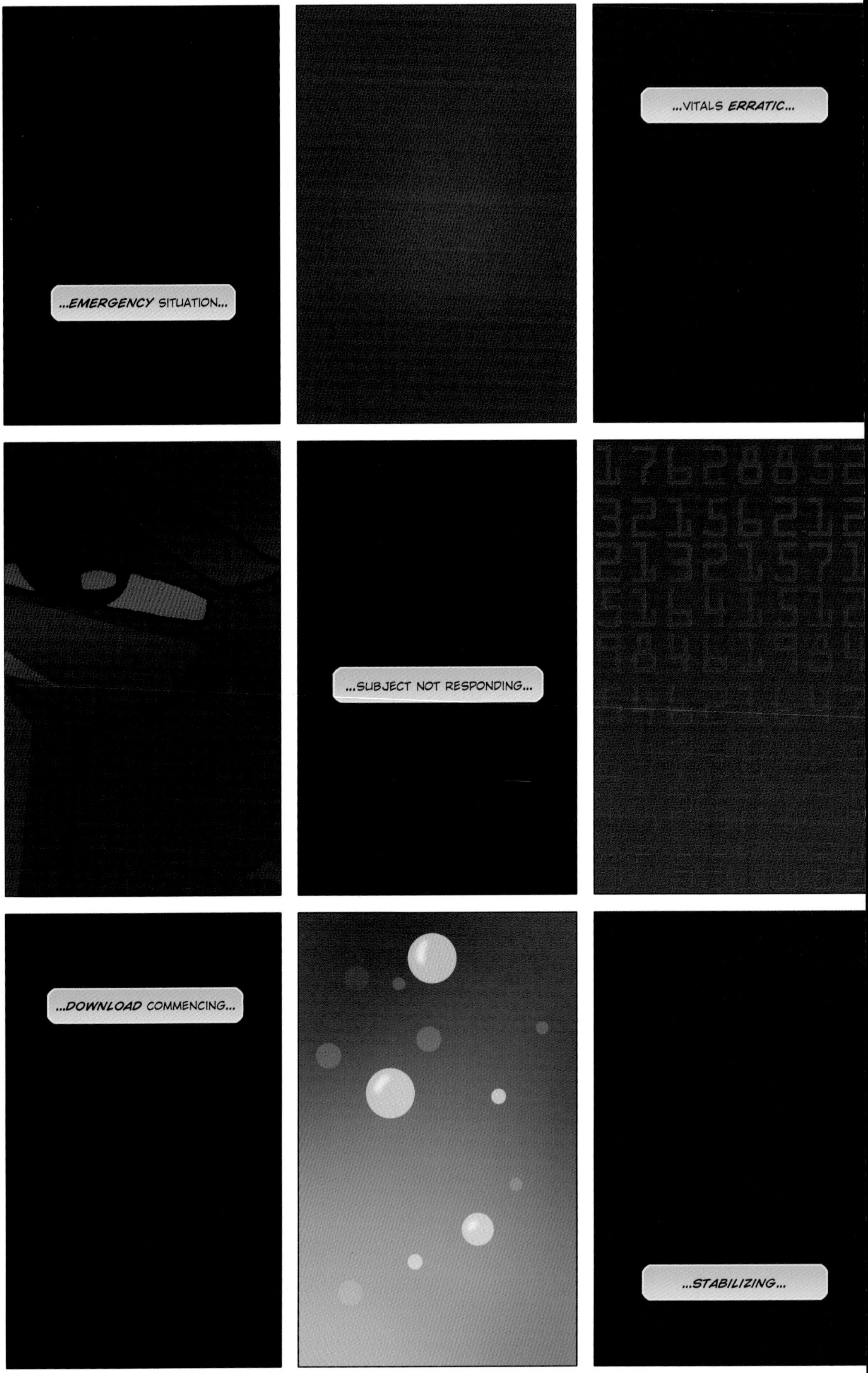
...EMERGENCY SITUATION...
...VITALS ERRATIC...
...SUBJECT NOT RESPONDING...
...DOWNLOAD COMMENCING...
...STABILIZING...

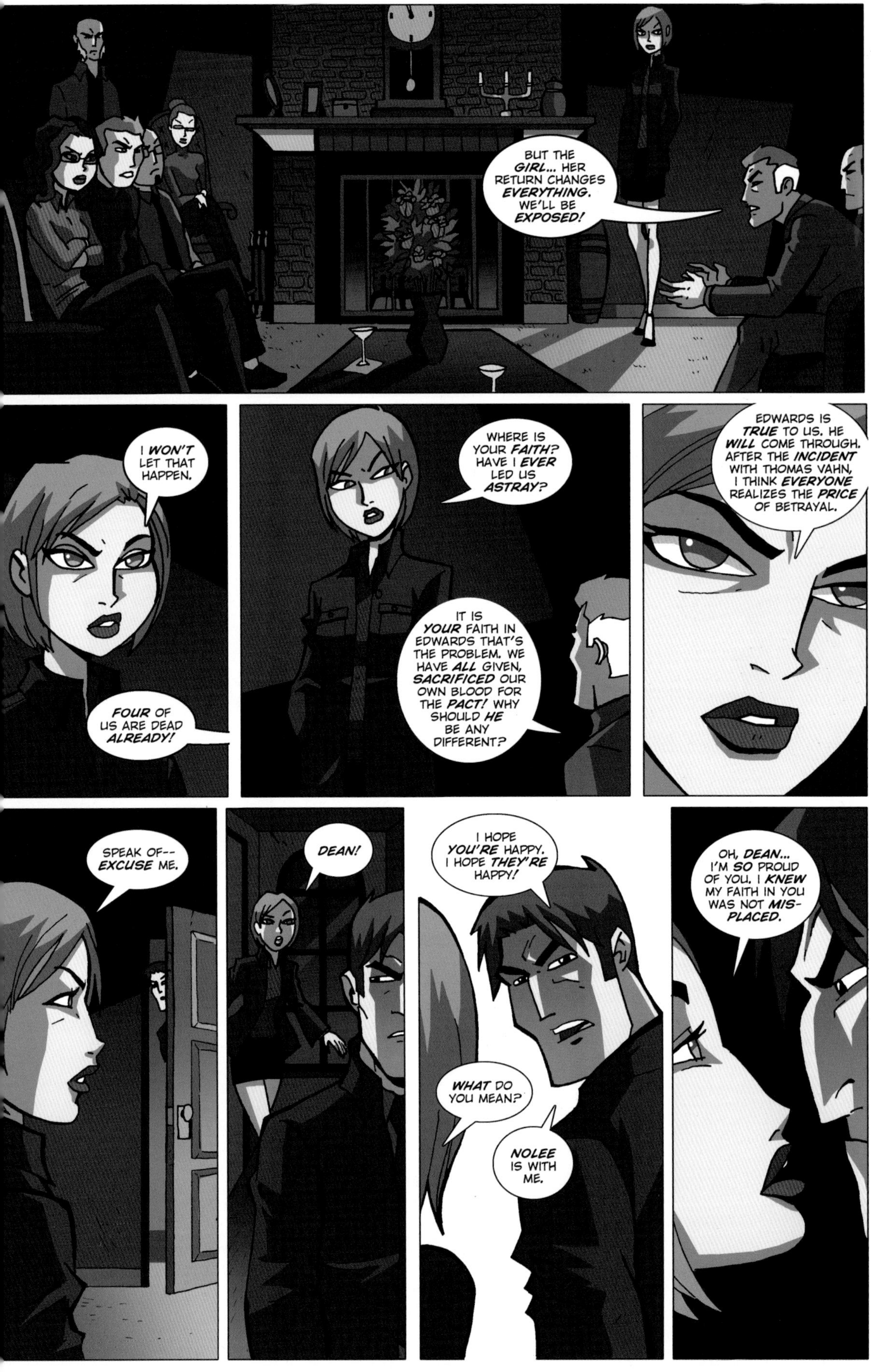
BUT THE GIRL... HER RETURN CHANGES EVERYTHING. WE'LL BE EXPOSED!
I WON'T LET THAT HAPPEN.
FOUR OF US ARE DEAD ALREADY!
WHERE IS YOUR FAITH? HAVE I EVER LED US ASTRAY?
IT IS YOUR FAITH IN EDWARDS THAT'S THE PROBLEM. WE HAVE ALL GIVEN, SACRIFICED OUR OWN BLOOD FOR THE PACT! WHY SHOULD HE BE ANY DIFFERENT?
EDWARDS IS TRUE TO US. HE WILL COME THROUGH. AFTER THE INCIDENT WITH THOMAS VAHN, I THINK EVERYONE REALIZES THE PRICE OF BETRAYAL.
SPEAK OF-- EXCUSE ME.
DEAN!
I HOPE YOU'RE HAPPY. I HOPE THEY'RE HAPPY!
WHAT DO YOU MEAN?
NOLEE IS WITH ME.
OH, DEAN... I'M SO PROUD OF YOU. I KNEW MY FAITH IN YOU WAS NOT MIS-PLACED.

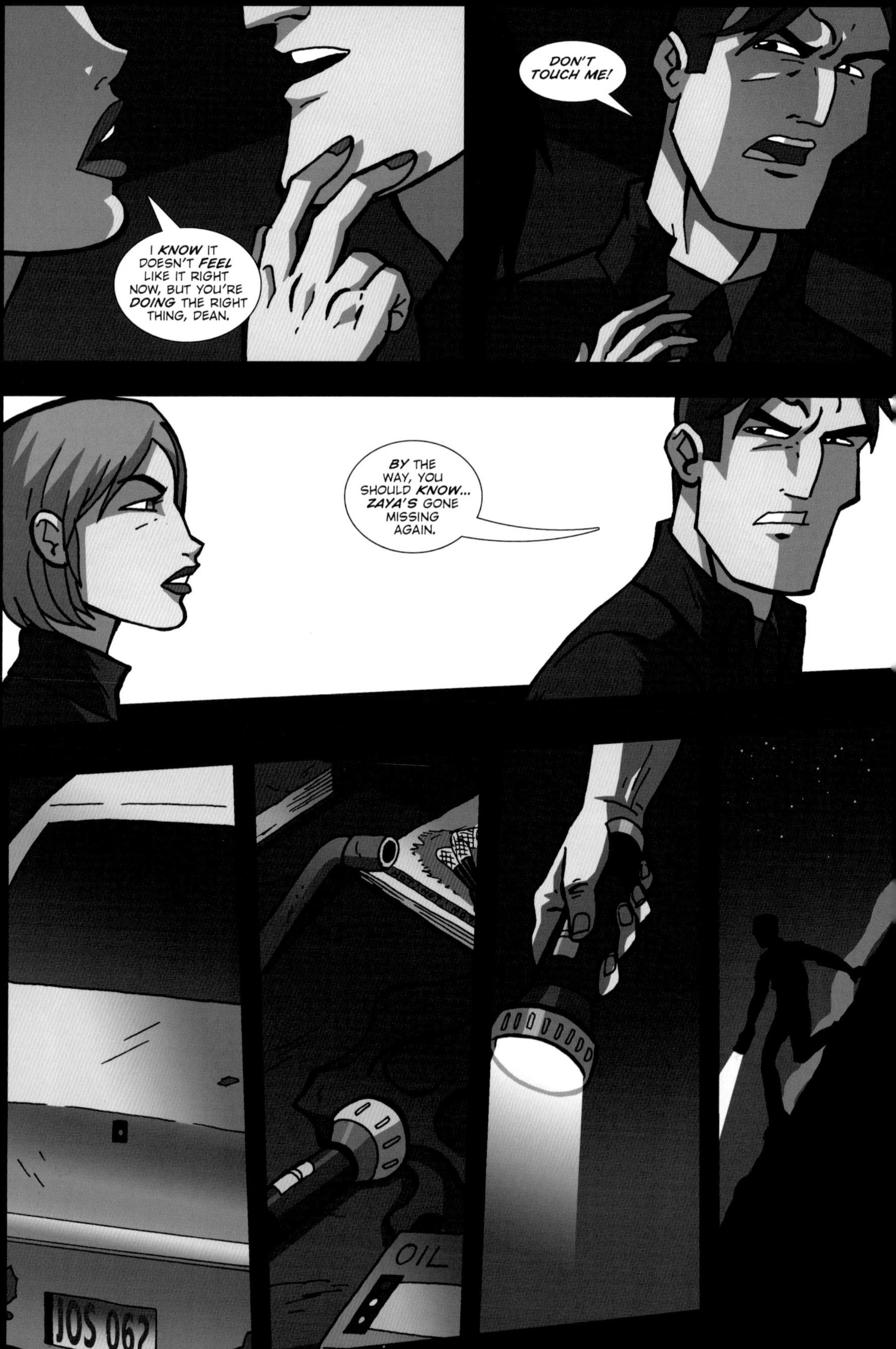
I KNOW IT DOESN'T FEEL LIKE IT RIGHT NOW, BUT YOU'RE DOING THE RIGHT THING, DEAN.
DON'T TOUCH ME!
BY THE WAY, YOU SHOULD KNOW... ZAYA'S GONE MISSING AGAIN.
OIL
JOS 062

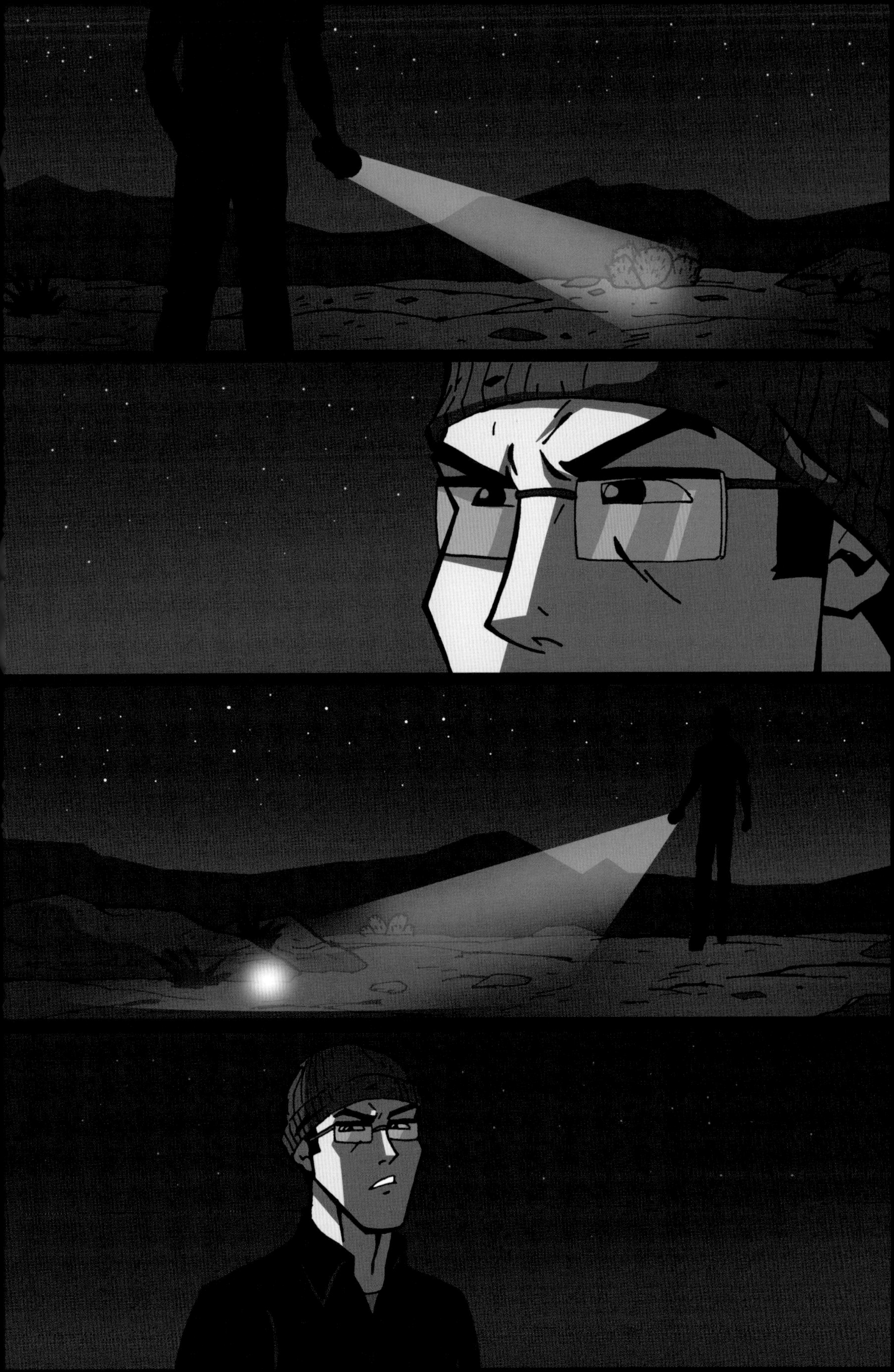

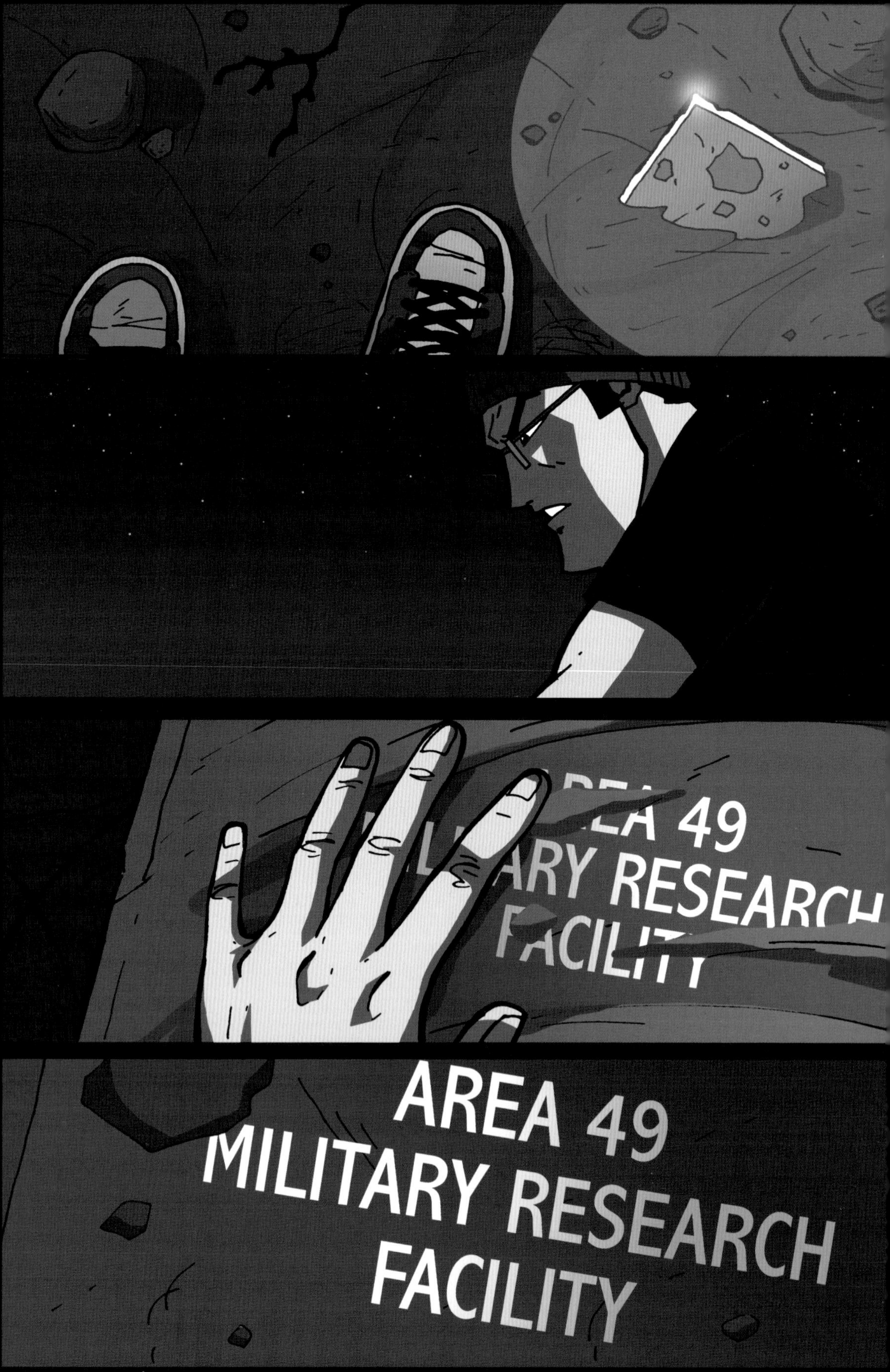
AREA 49
MILITARY RESEARCH
FACILITY

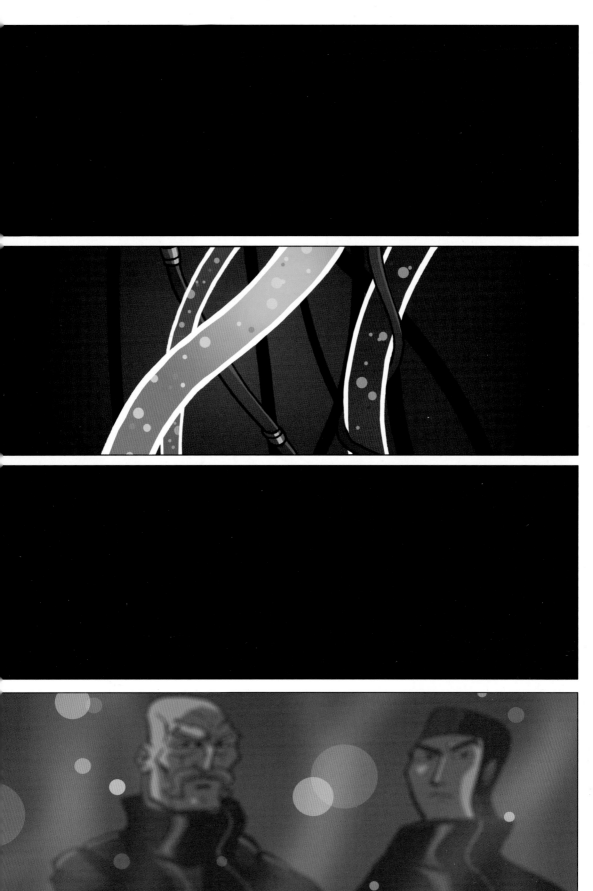

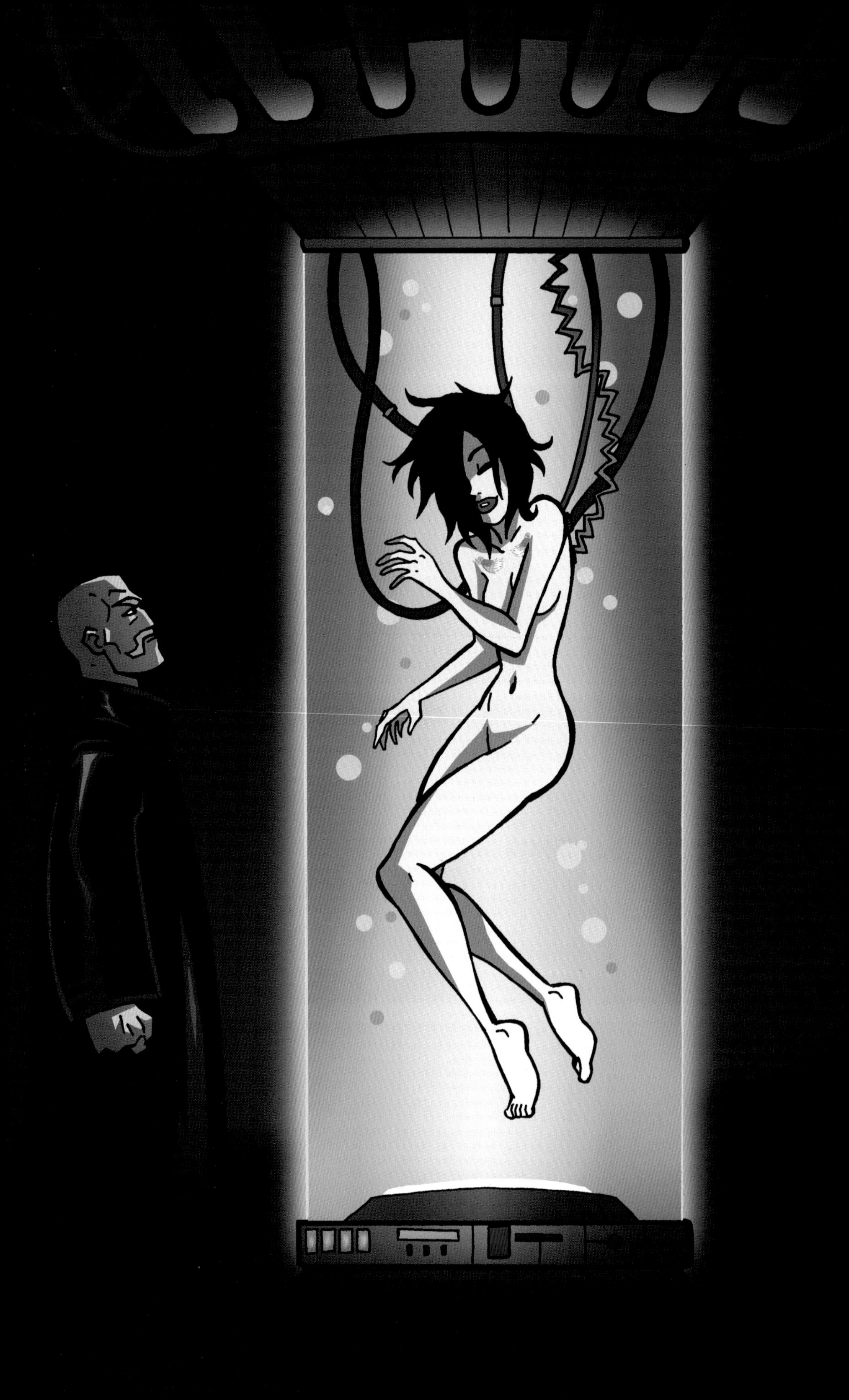

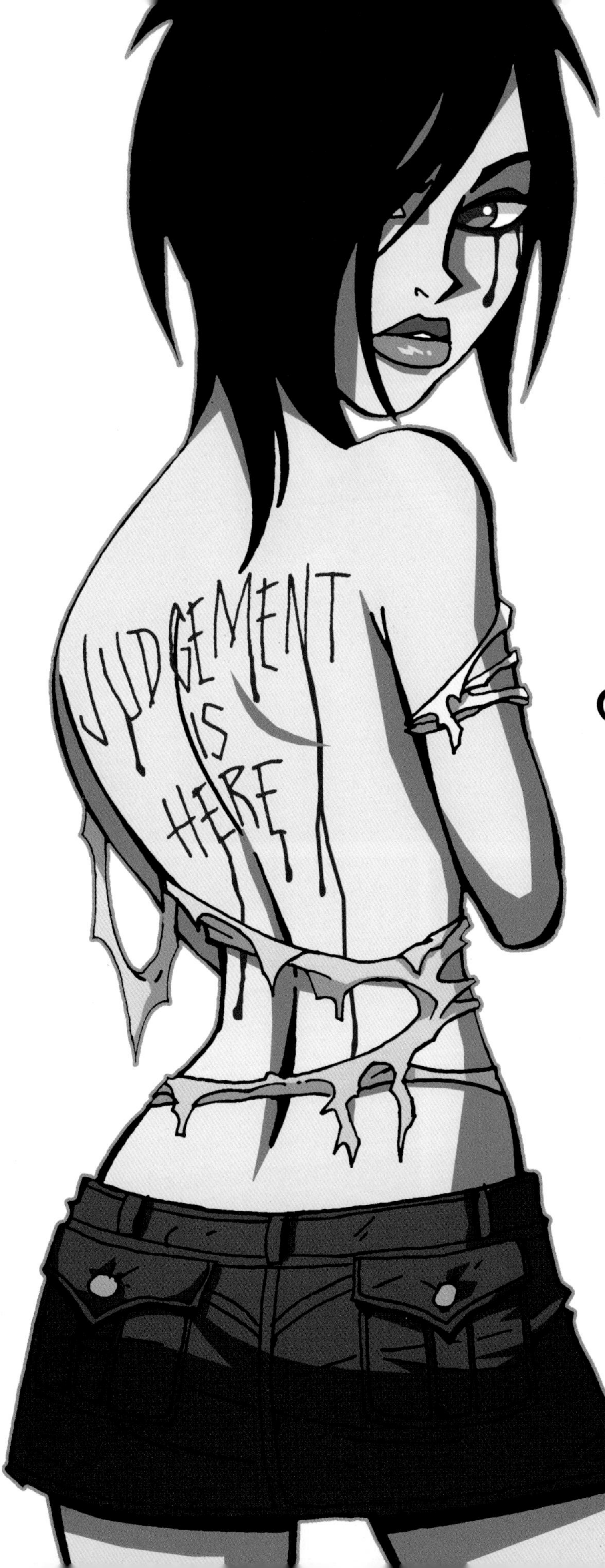
JUDGEMENT
IS
HERE

chapter 4

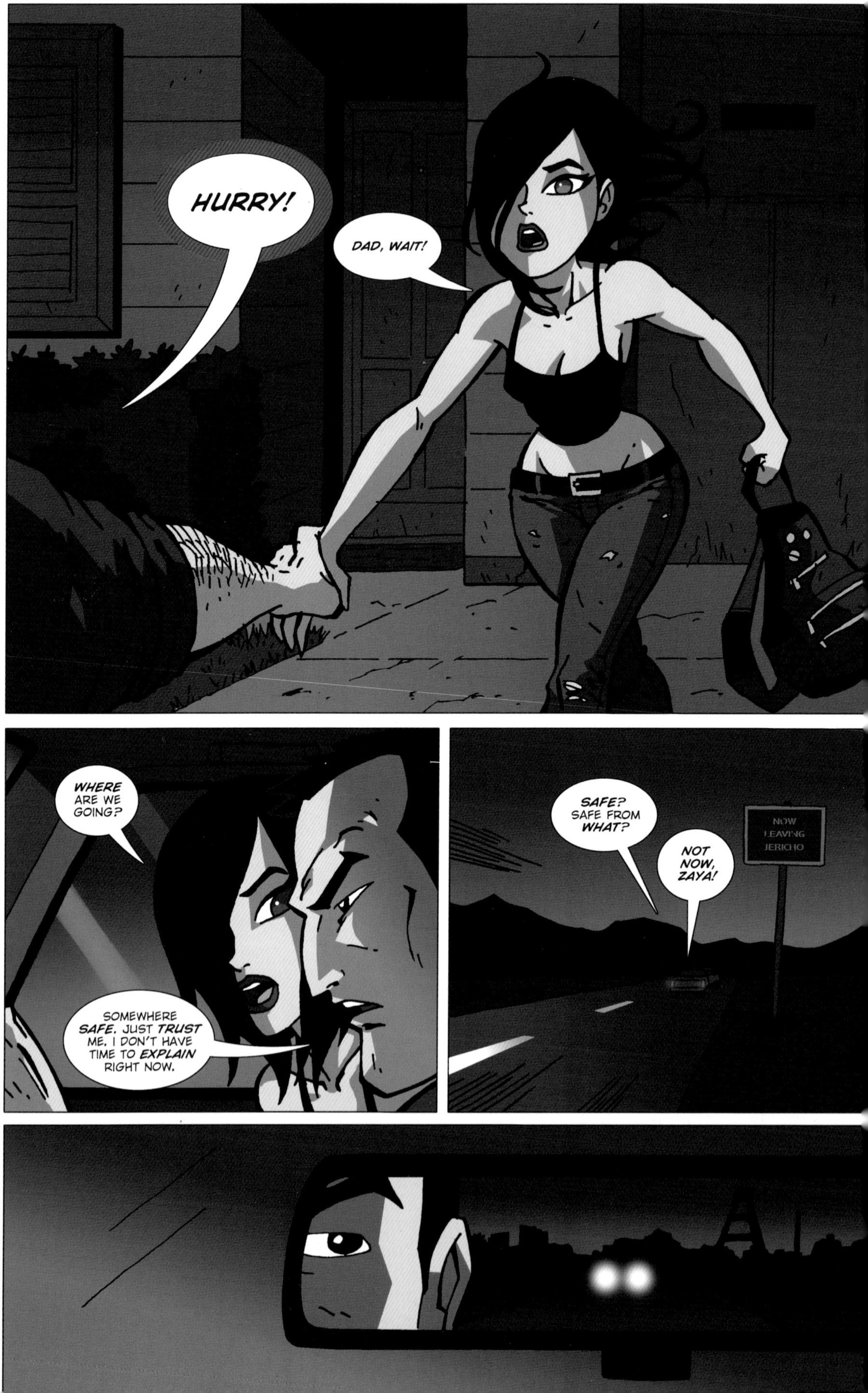
HURRY!
DAD, WAIT!
WHERE ARE WE GOING?
SOMEWHERE SAFE. JUST TRUST ME. I DON'T HAVE TIME TO EXPLAIN RIGHT NOW.
SAFE? SAFE FROM WHAT?
NOT NOW, ZAYA!
NOW LEAVING JERICHO

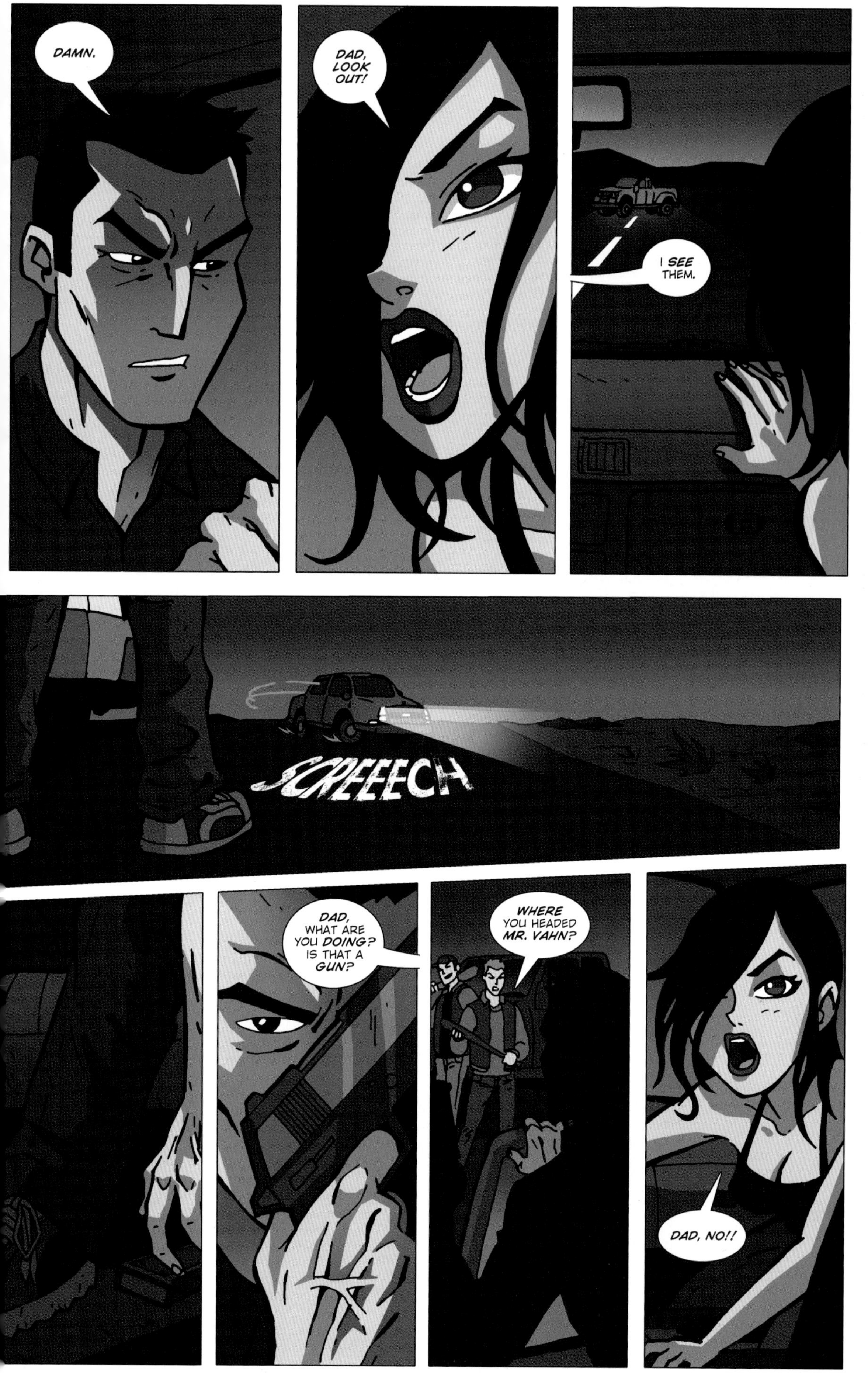
DAMN.
DAD, LOOK OUT!
I SEE THEM.
SCREEECH
DAD, WHAT ARE YOU DOING? IS THAT A GUN?
WHERE YOU HEADED MR. VAHN?
DAD, NO!!

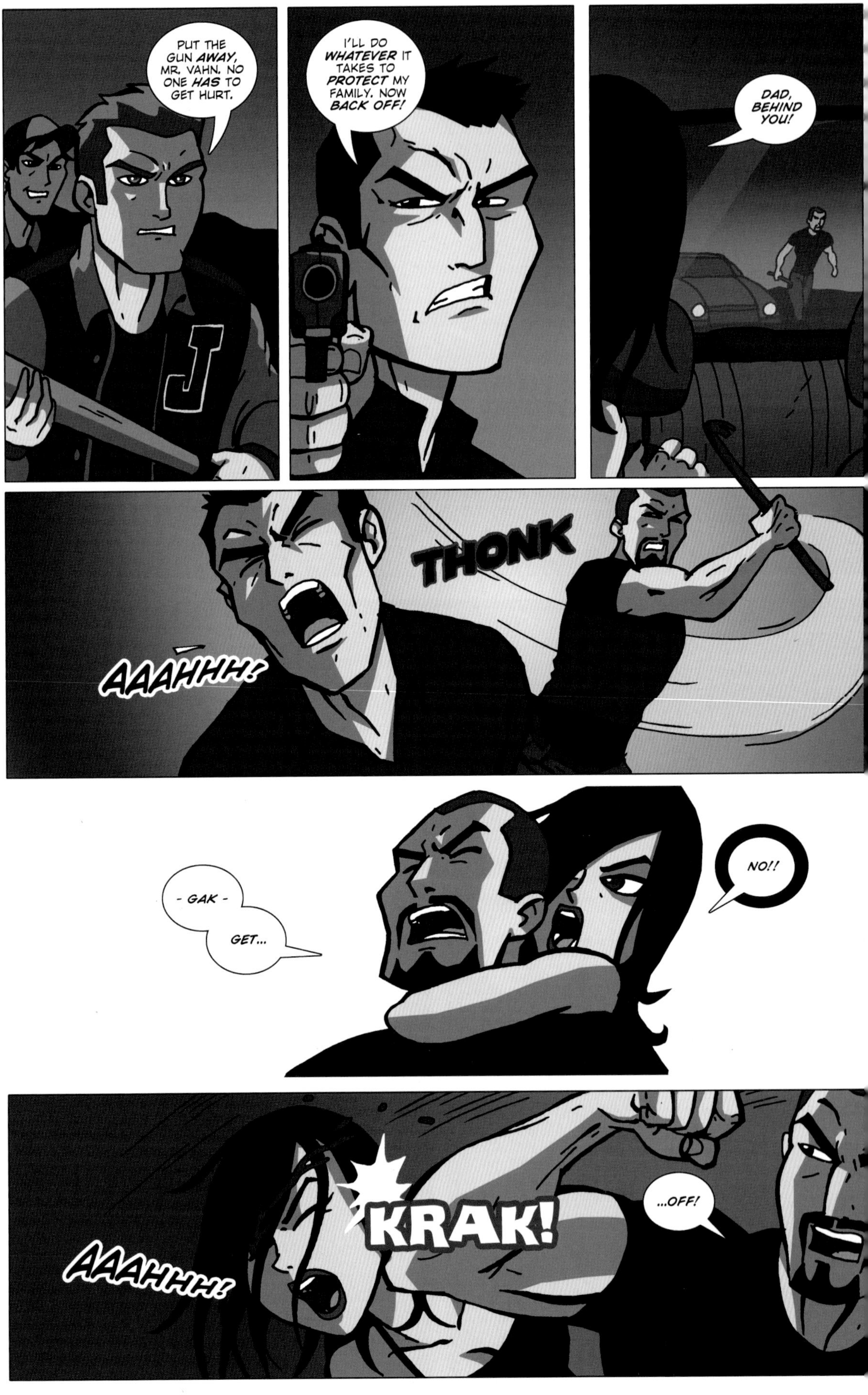
PUT THE GUN AWAY, MR. VAHN. NO ONE HAS TO GET HURT.
I'LL DO WHATEVER IT TAKES TO PROTECT MY FAMILY. NOW BACK OFF!
DAD, BEHIND YOU!
THONK
AAAHHH!
- GAK -
GET...
NO!!
KRAK!
...OFF!
AAAHHH!

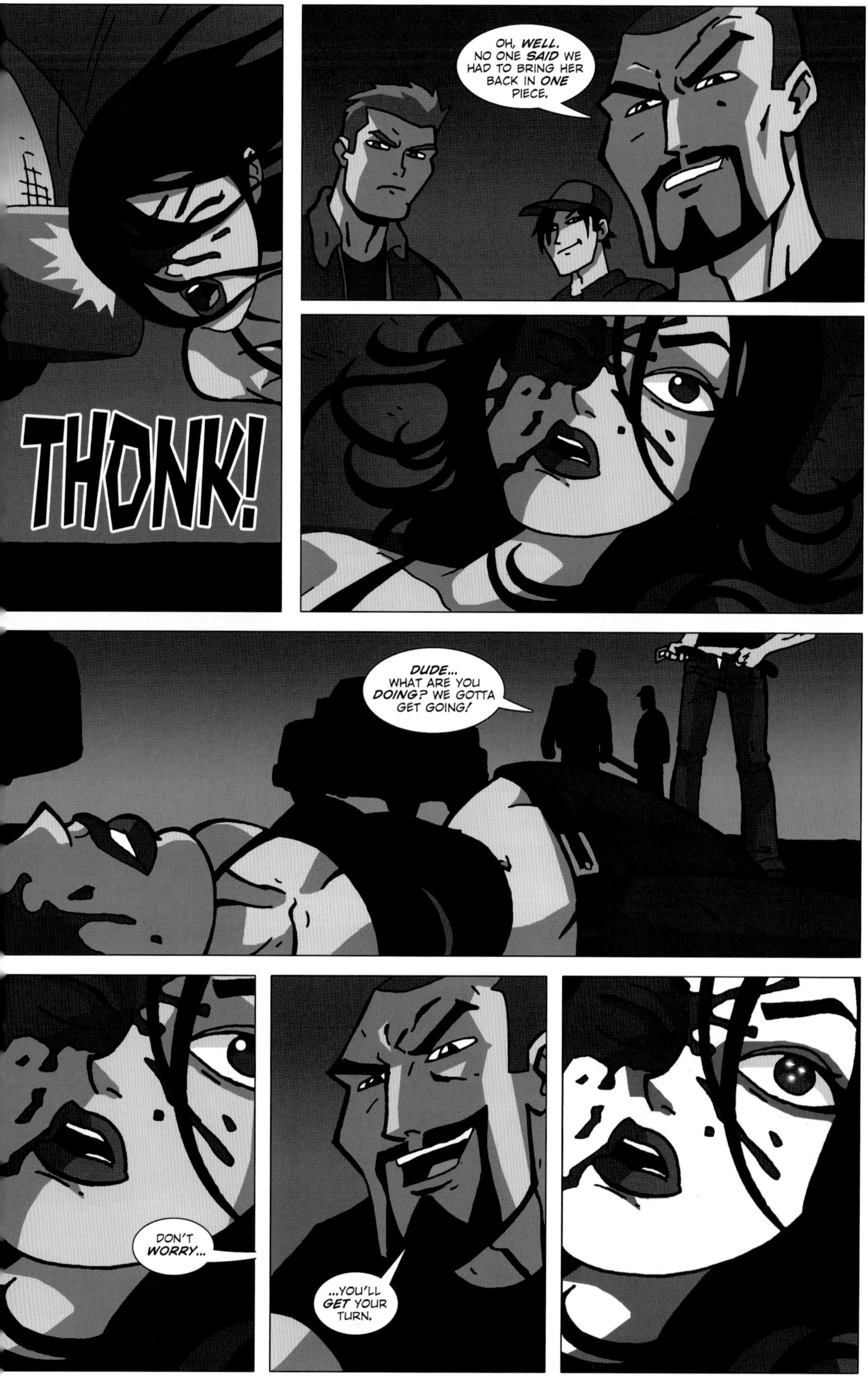
THONK!
OH, WELL. NO ONE SAID WE HAD TO BRING HER BACK IN ONE PIECE.
DUDE... WHAT ARE YOU DOING? WE GOTTA GET GOING!
DON'T WORRY...
...YOU'LL GET YOUR TURN.

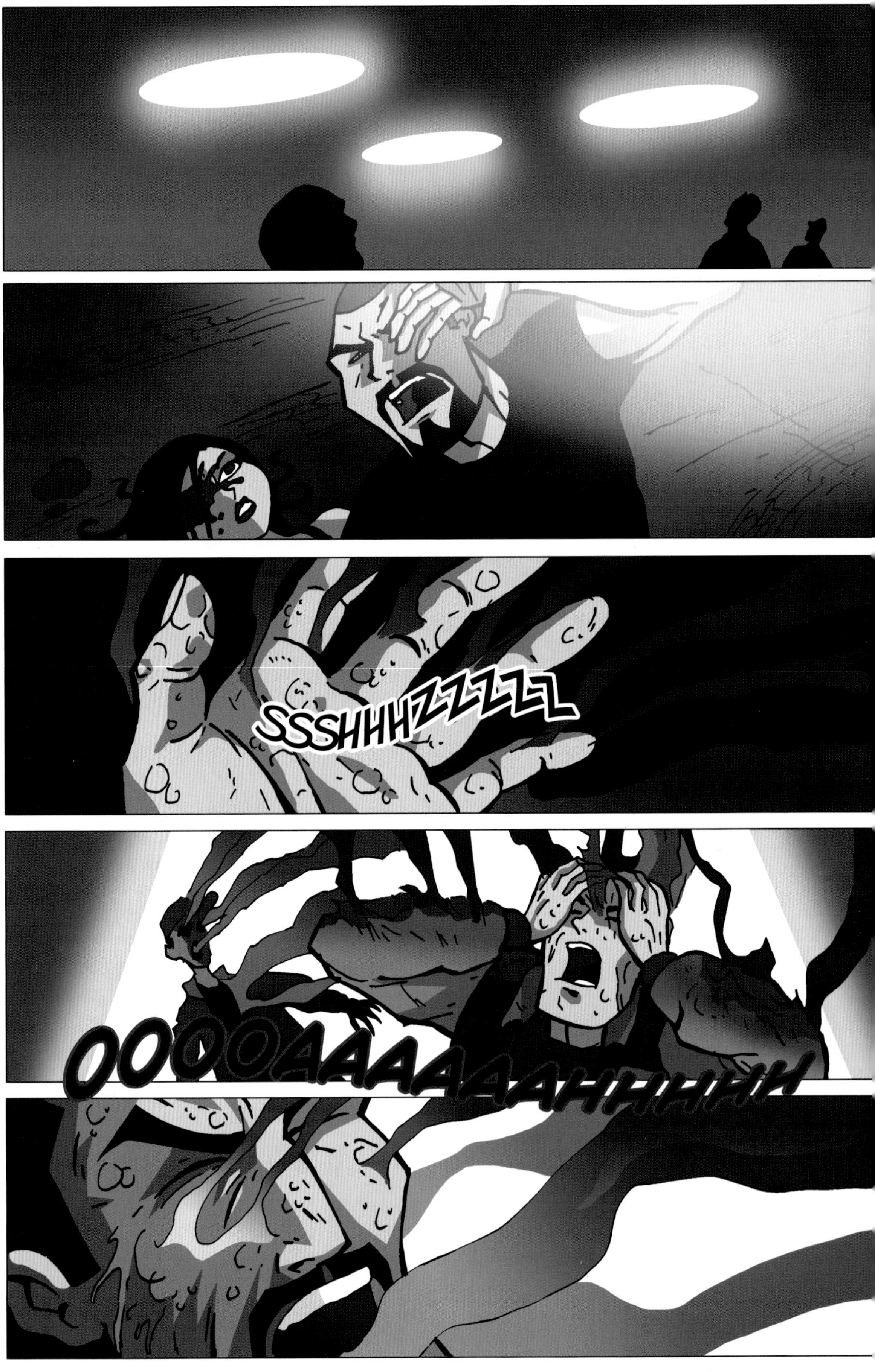
SSSHHHZZZZZ
OOOOAAAAAAAHHHHHH

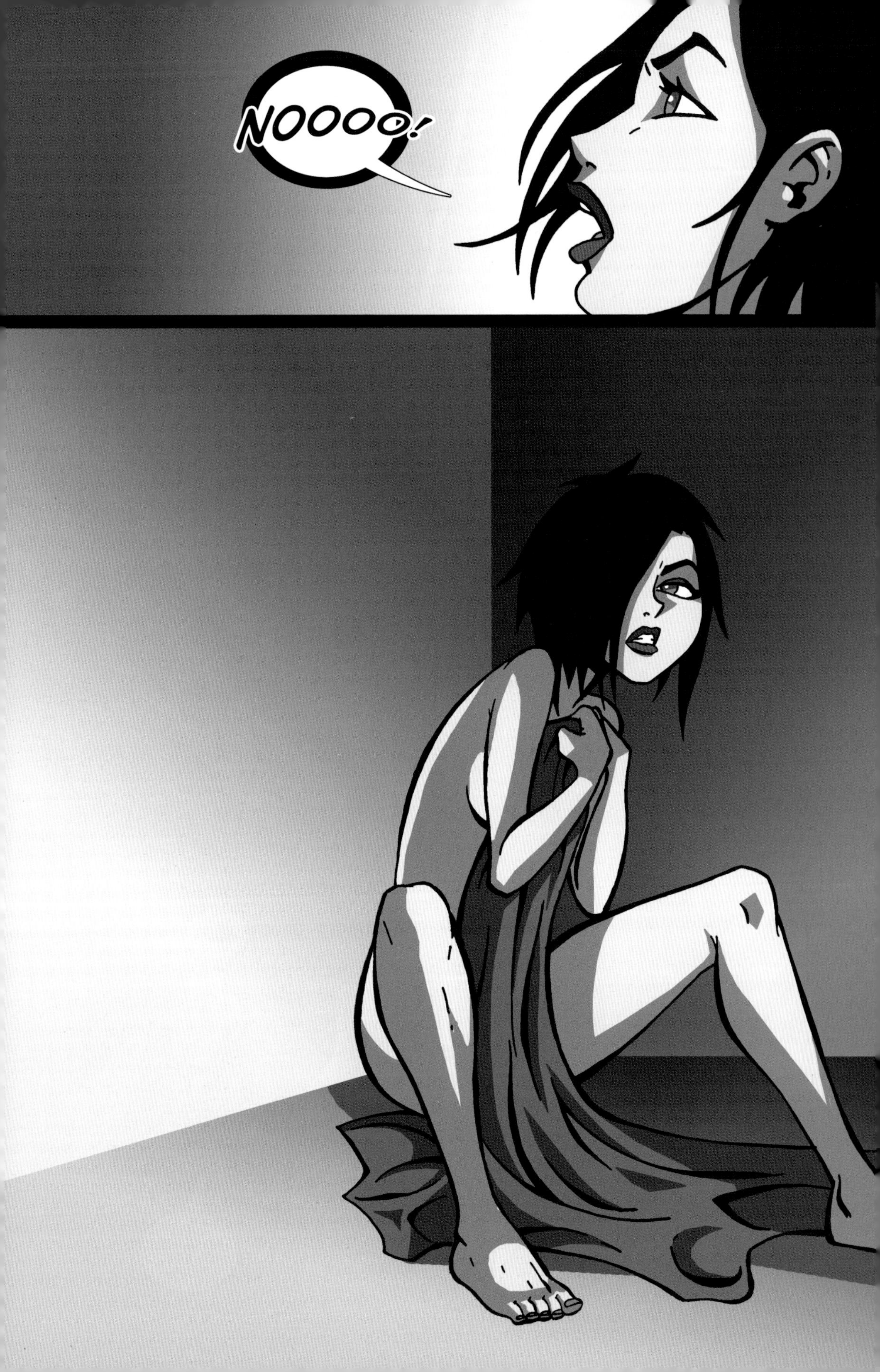
NOOOO!

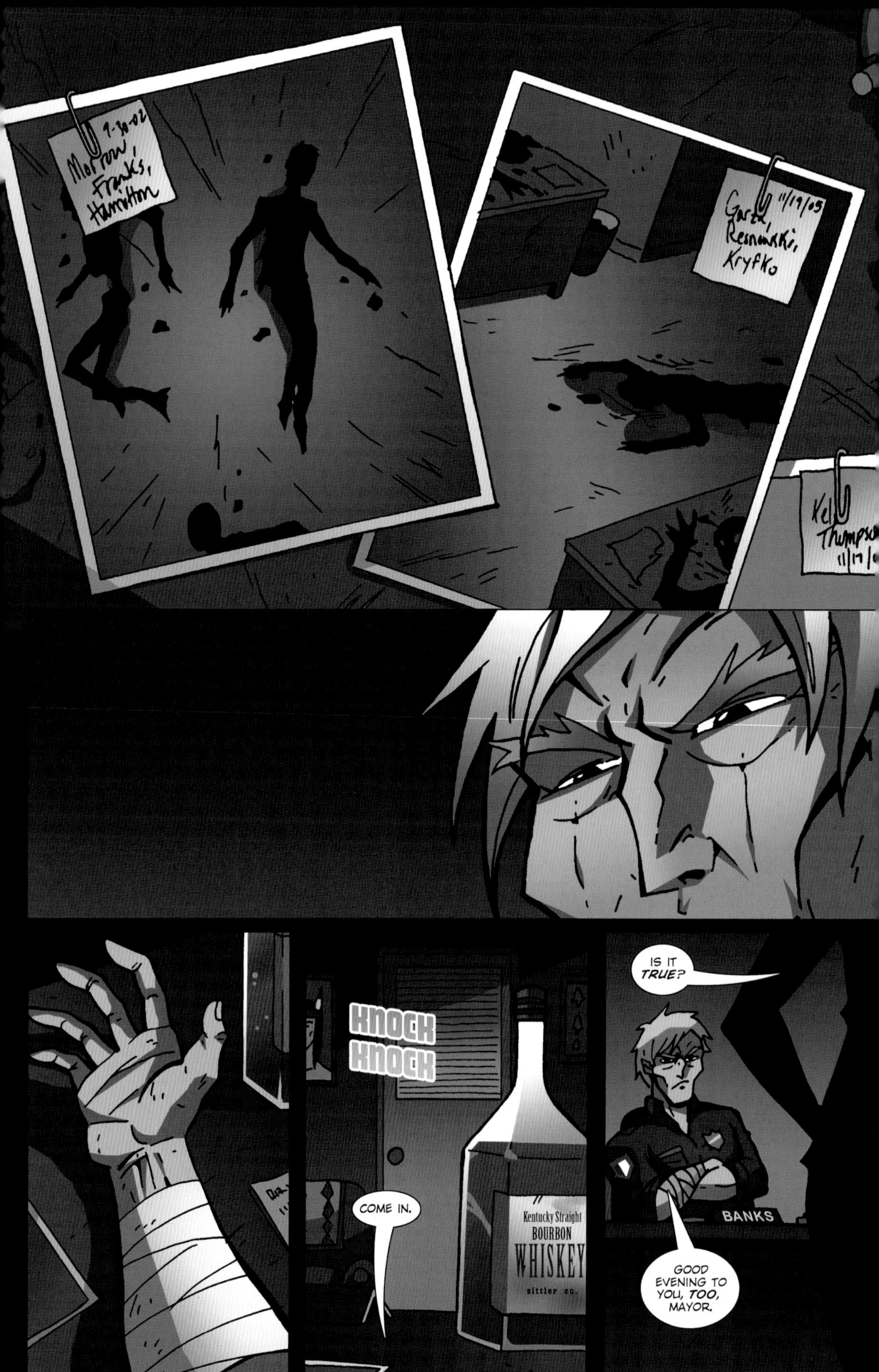
9-30-02
Morrow, Franks, Harrilton
11/19/05
Garza, Resnowski, Kryfko
KNOCK
KNOCK
COME IN.
Kentucky Straight
BOURBON
WHISKEY
sittler co.
IS IT *TRUE?*
BANKS
GOOD EVENING TO YOU, *TOO,* MAYOR.

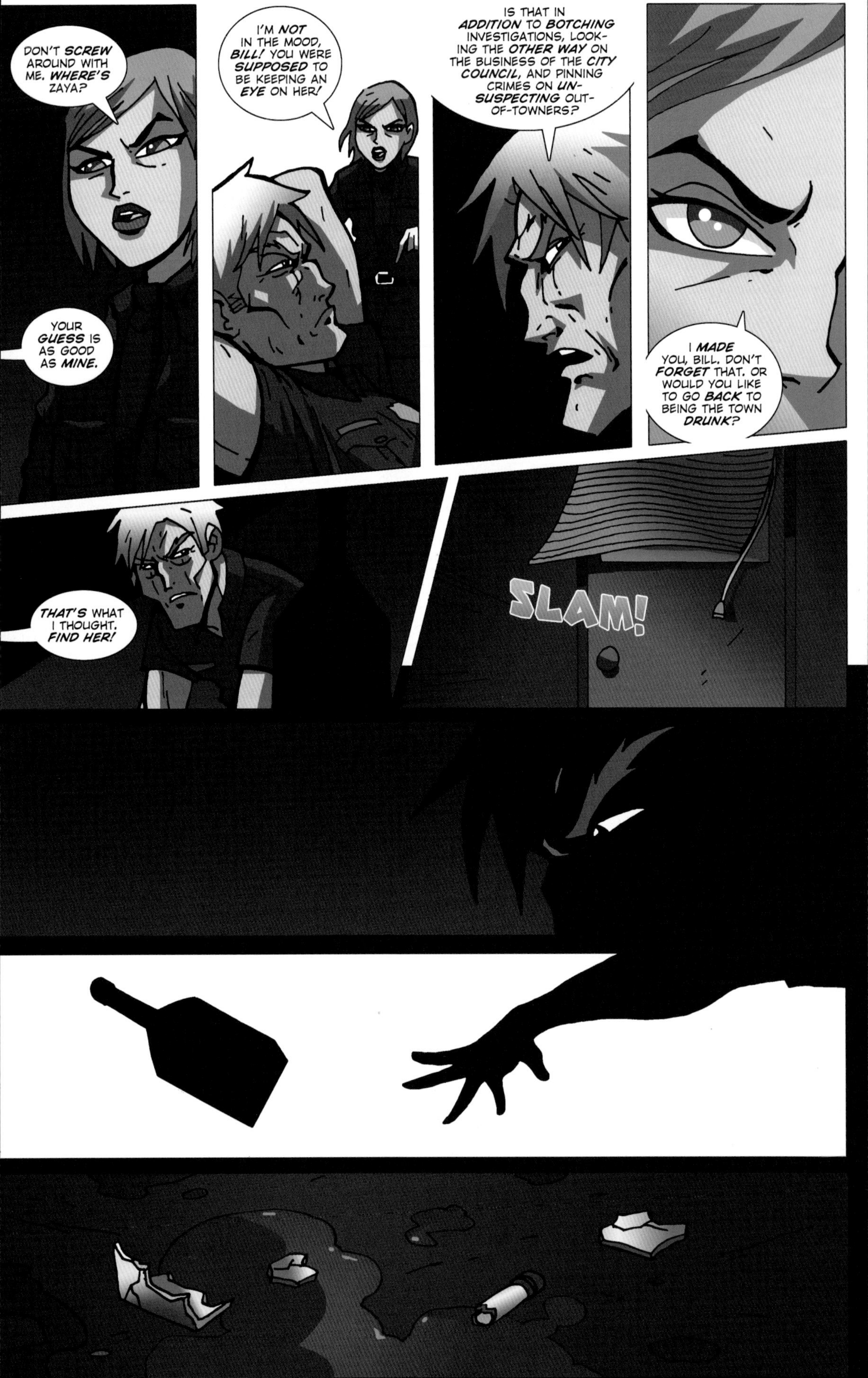
DON'T SCREW AROUND WITH ME. WHERE'S ZAYA?
YOUR GUESS IS AS GOOD AS MINE.
I'M NOT IN THE MOOD, BILL! YOU WERE SUPPOSED TO BE KEEPING AN EYE ON HER!
IS THAT IN ADDITION TO BOTCHING INVESTIGATIONS, LOOKING THE OTHER WAY ON THE BUSINESS OF THE CITY COUNCIL, AND PINNING CRIMES ON UNSUSPECTING OUT-OF-TOWNERS?
I MADE YOU, BILL. DON'T FORGET THAT. OR WOULD YOU LIKE TO GO BACK TO BEING THE TOWN DRUNK?
THAT'S WHAT I THOUGHT. FIND HER!
SLAM!

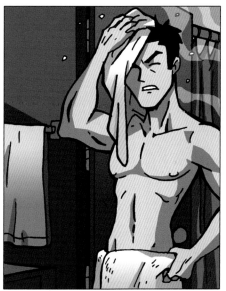

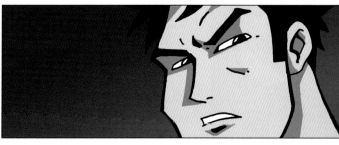

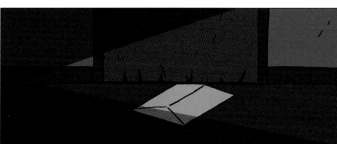

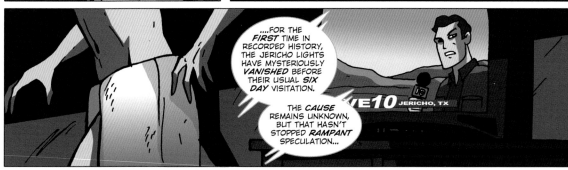

....FOR THE FIRST TIME IN RECORDED HISTORY, THE JERICHO LIGHTS HAVE MYSTERIOUSLY VANISHED BEFORE THEIR USUAL SIX DAY VISITATION.
THE CAUSE REMAINS UNKNOWN, BUT THAT HASN'T STOPPED RAMPANT SPECULATION...
VE10 JERICHO, TX
44106-1
4th & Main
- basement
- AA-001X
- a friend

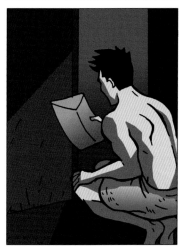

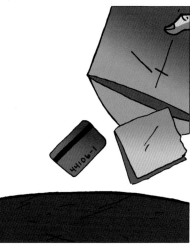

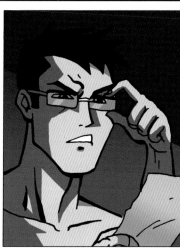

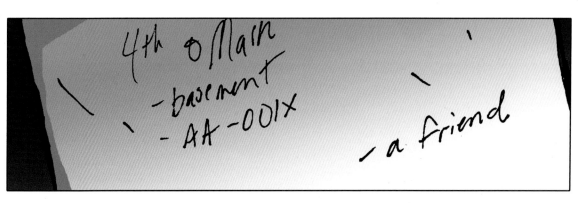

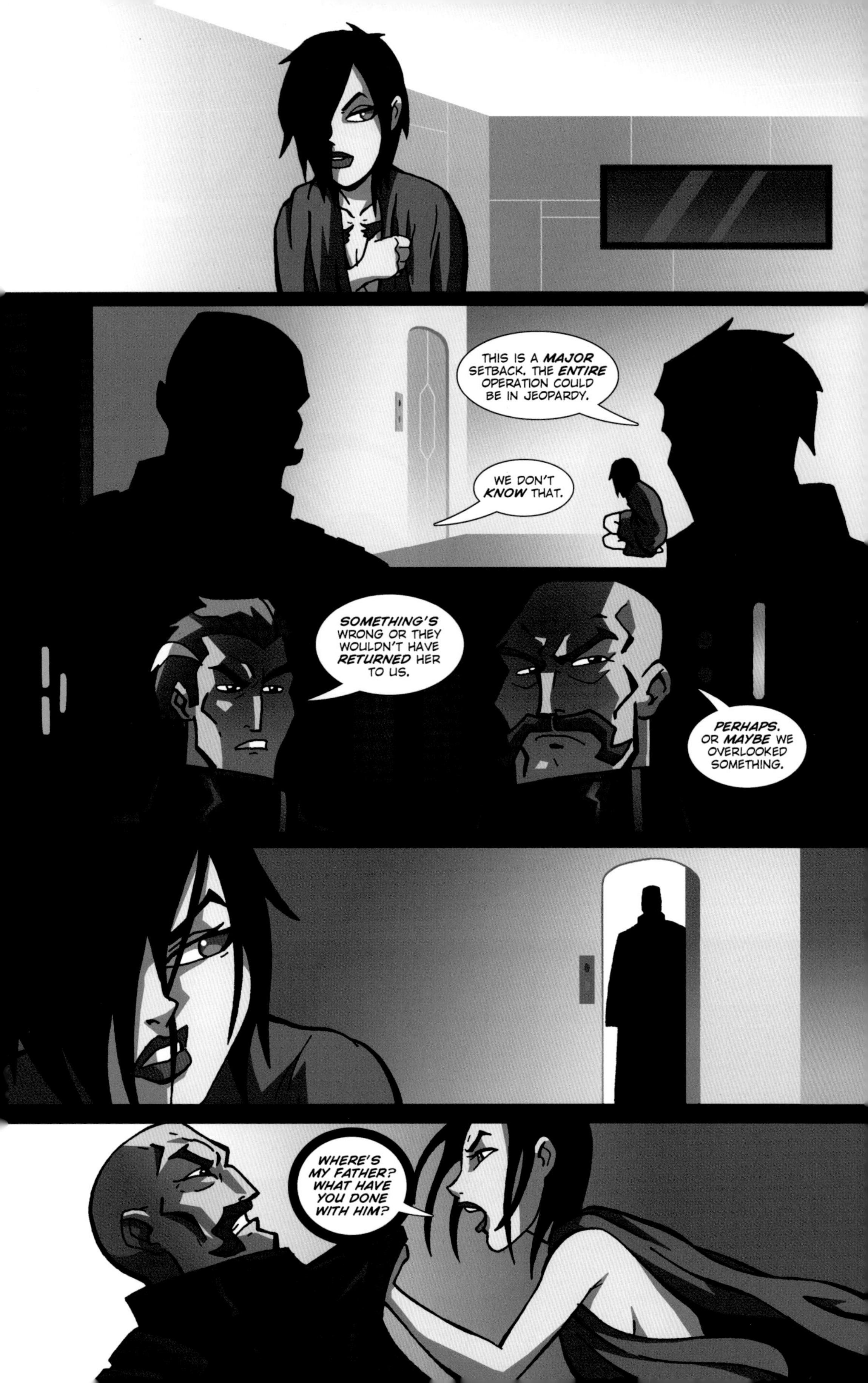
THIS IS A MAJOR SETBACK. THE ENTIRE OPERATION COULD BE IN JEOPARDY.
WE DON'T KNOW THAT.
SOMETHING'S WRONG OR THEY WOULDN'T HAVE RETURNED HER TO US.
PERHAPS. OR MAYBE WE OVERLOOKED SOMETHING.
WHERE'S MY FATHER? WHAT HAVE YOU DONE WITH HIM?

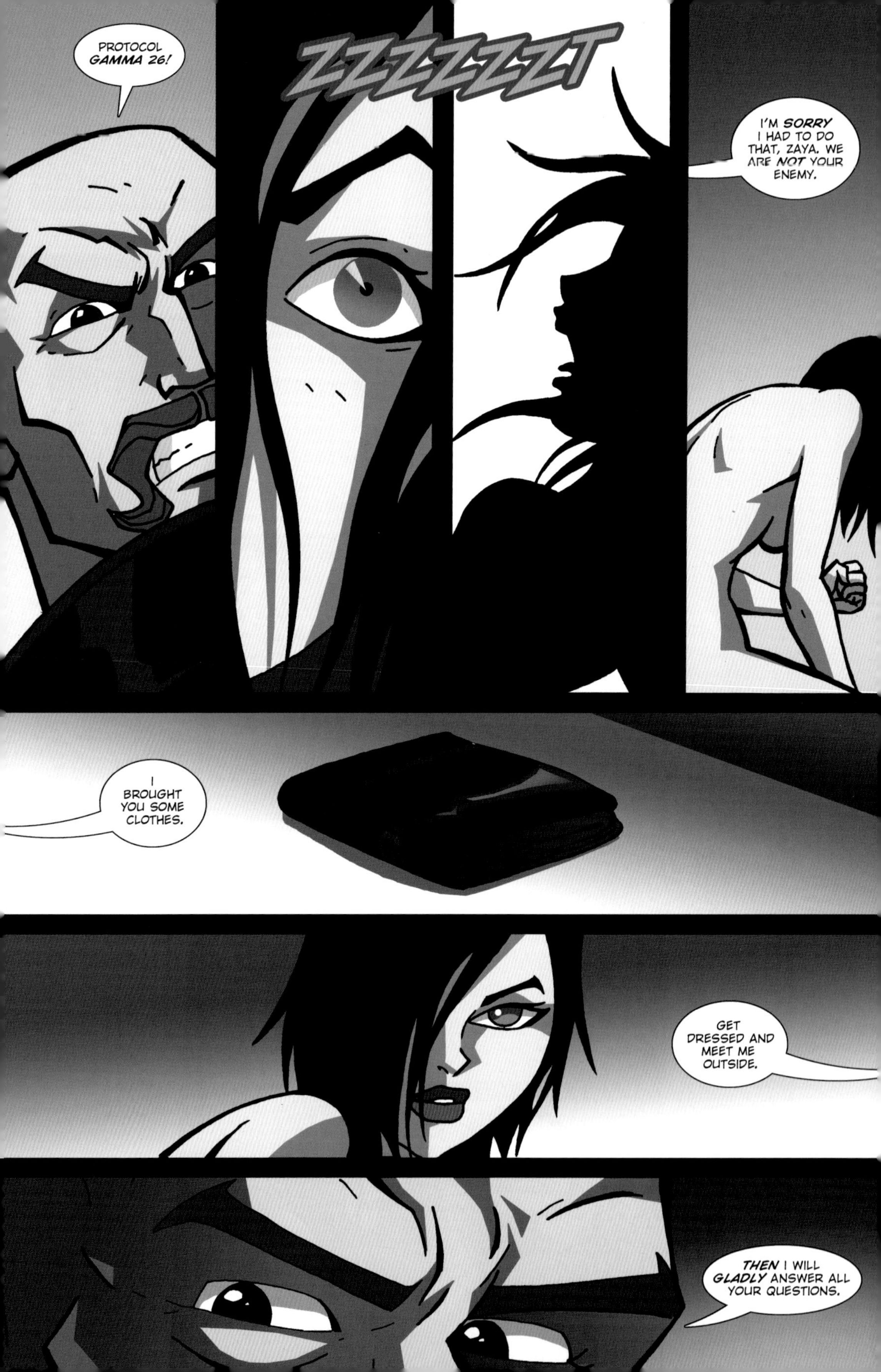
PROTOCOL GAMMA 26!
ZZZZZZZT
I'M SORRY I HAD TO DO THAT, ZAYA. WE ARE NOT YOUR ENEMY.
I BROUGHT YOU SOME CLOTHES.
GET DRESSED AND MEET ME OUTSIDE.
THEN I WILL GLADLY ANSWER ALL YOUR QUESTIONS.

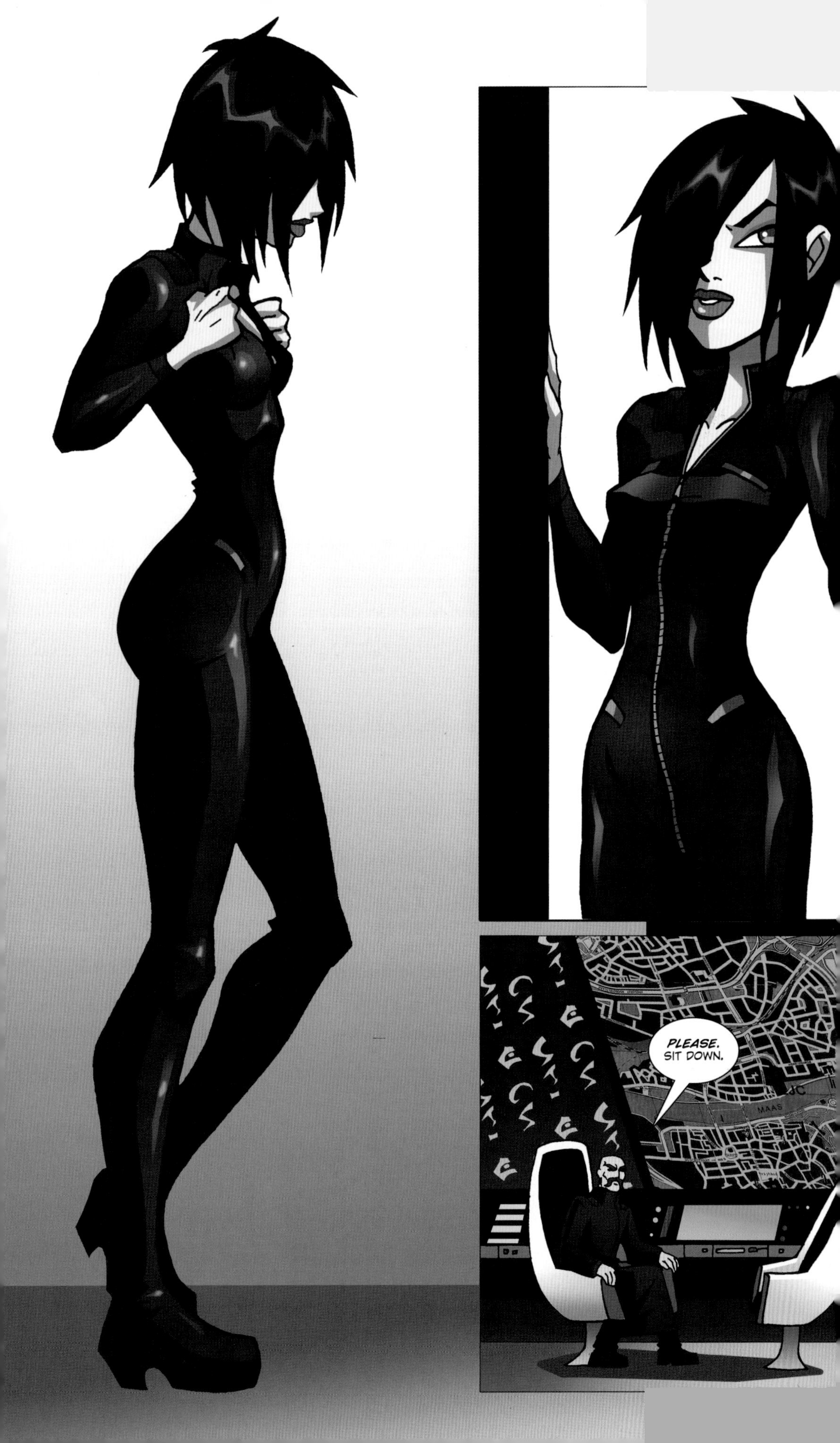
PLEASE. SIT DOWN.
MAAS

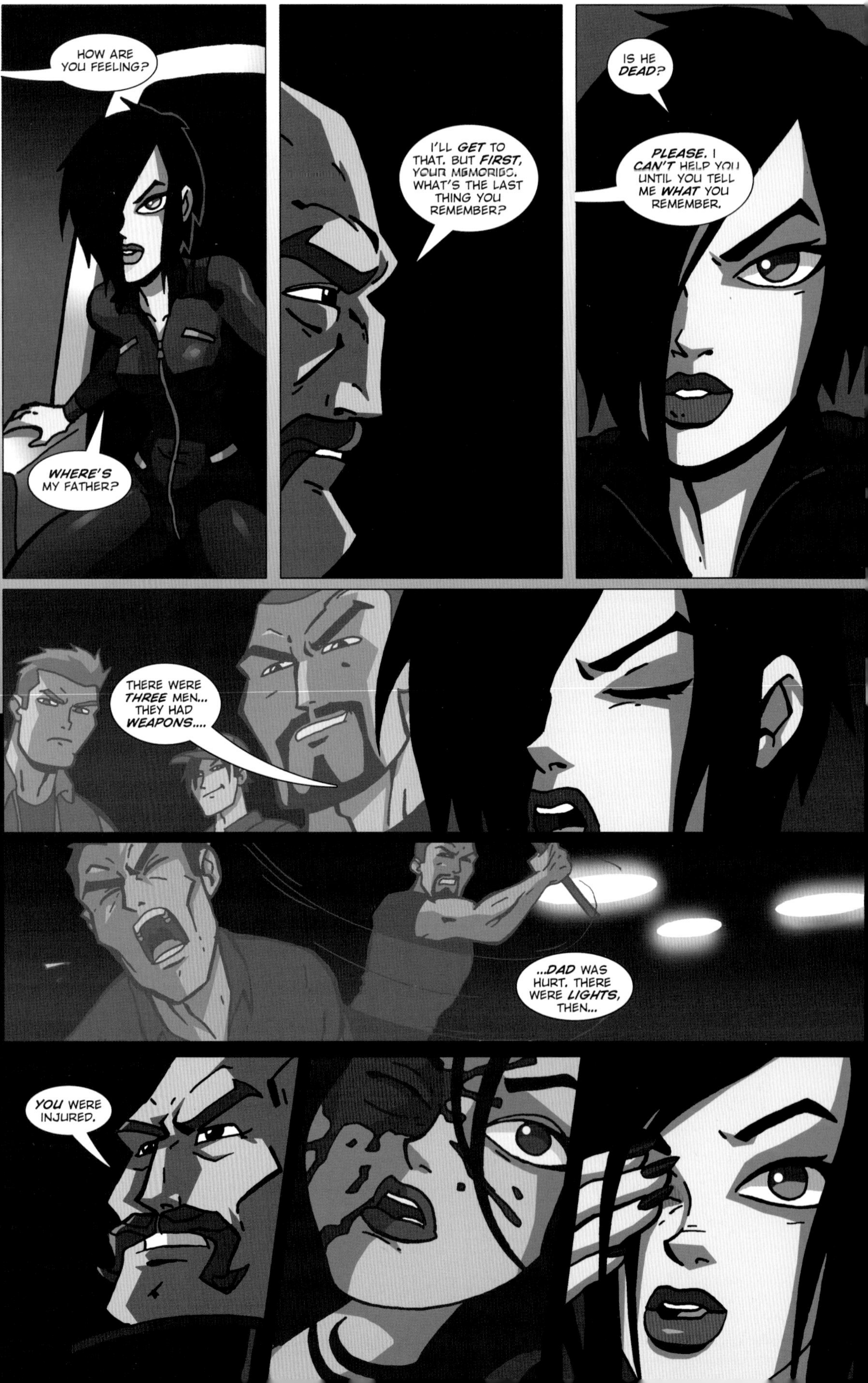
HOW ARE YOU FEELING?
WHERE'S MY FATHER?
I'LL GET TO THAT. BUT FIRST, YOUR MEMORIES. WHAT'S THE LAST THING YOU REMEMBER?
IS HE DEAD?
PLEASE. I CAN'T HELP YOU UNTIL YOU TELL ME WHAT YOU REMEMBER.
THERE WERE THREE MEN... THEY HAD WEAPONS....
...DAD WAS HURT. THERE WERE LIGHTS, THEN...
YOU WERE INJURED.

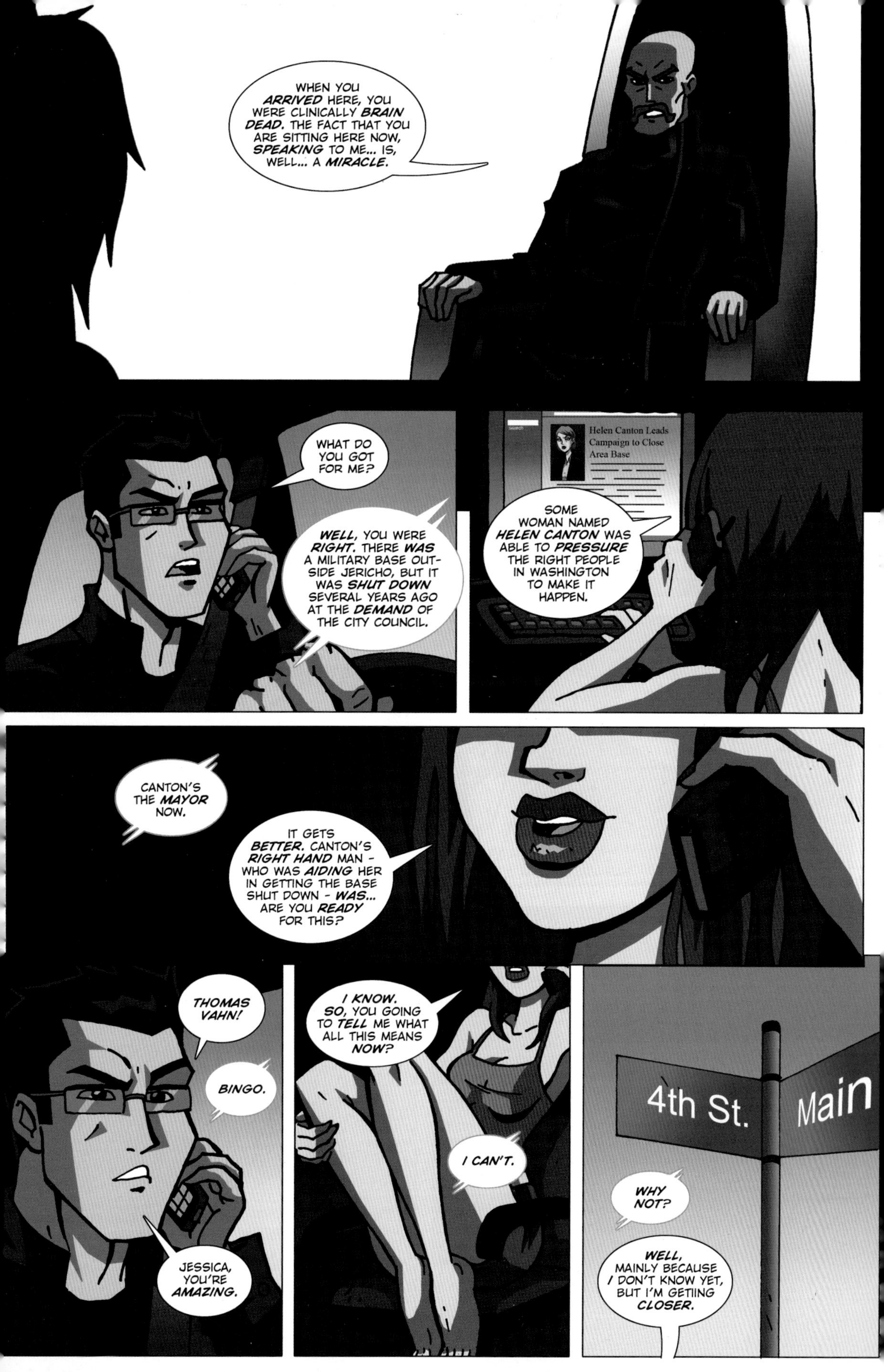
WHEN YOU ARRIVED HERE, YOU WERE CLINICALLY BRAIN DEAD. THE FACT THAT YOU ARE SITTING HERE NOW, SPEAKING TO ME... IS, WELL... A MIRACLE.
WHAT DO YOU GOT FOR ME?
WELL, YOU WERE RIGHT. THERE WAS A MILITARY BASE OUTSIDE JERICHO, BUT IT WAS SHUT DOWN SEVERAL YEARS AGO AT THE DEMAND OF THE CITY COUNCIL.
Helen Canton Leads Campaign to Close Area Base
SOME WOMAN NAMED HELEN CANTON WAS ABLE TO PRESSURE THE RIGHT PEOPLE IN WASHINGTON TO MAKE IT HAPPEN.
CANTON'S THE MAYOR NOW.
IT GETS BETTER. CANTON'S RIGHT HAND MAN - WHO WAS AIDING HER IN GETTING THE BASE SHUT DOWN - WAS... ARE YOU READY FOR THIS?
THOMAS VAHN!
BINGO.
JESSICA, YOU'RE AMAZING.
I KNOW. SO, YOU GOING TO TELL ME WHAT ALL THIS MEANS NOW?
I CAN'T.
4th St.
Main
WHY NOT?
WELL, MAINLY BECAUSE I DON'T KNOW YET, BUT I'M GETIING CLOSER.

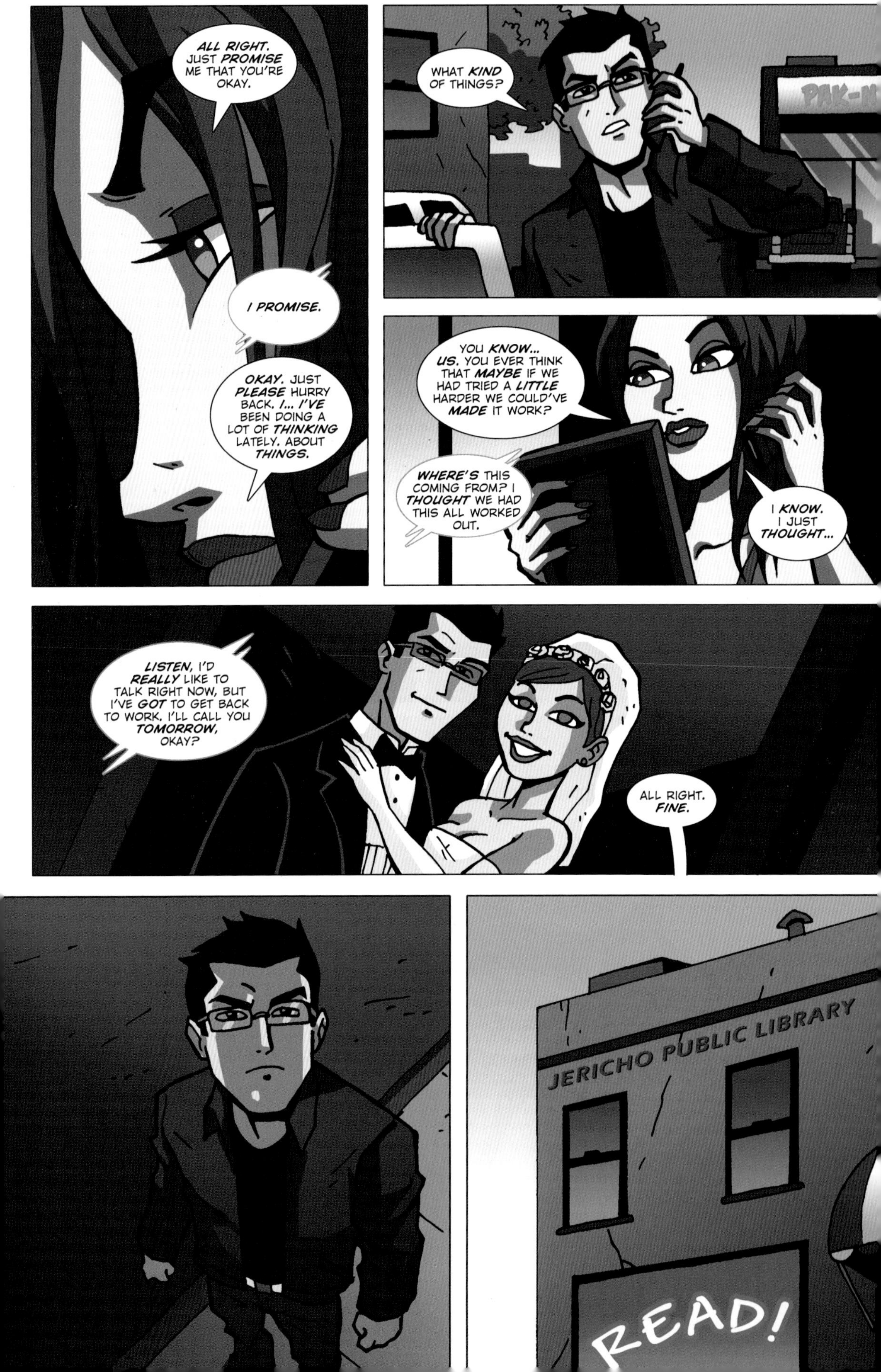
ALL RIGHT. JUST PROMISE ME THAT YOU'RE OKAY.
I PROMISE.
OKAY. JUST PLEASE HURRY BACK. I... I'VE BEEN DOING A LOT OF THINKING LATELY. ABOUT THINGS.
WHAT KIND OF THINGS?
PAK-N
YOU KNOW... US. YOU EVER THINK THAT MAYBE IF WE HAD TRIED A LITTLE HARDER WE COULD'VE MADE IT WORK?
WHERE'S THIS COMING FROM? I THOUGHT WE HAD THIS ALL WORKED OUT.
I KNOW. I JUST THOUGHT...
LISTEN, I'D REALLY LIKE TO TALK RIGHT NOW, BUT I'VE GOT TO GET BACK TO WORK. I'LL CALL YOU TOMORROW, OKAY?
ALL RIGHT. FINE.
JERICHO PUBLIC LIBRARY
READ!

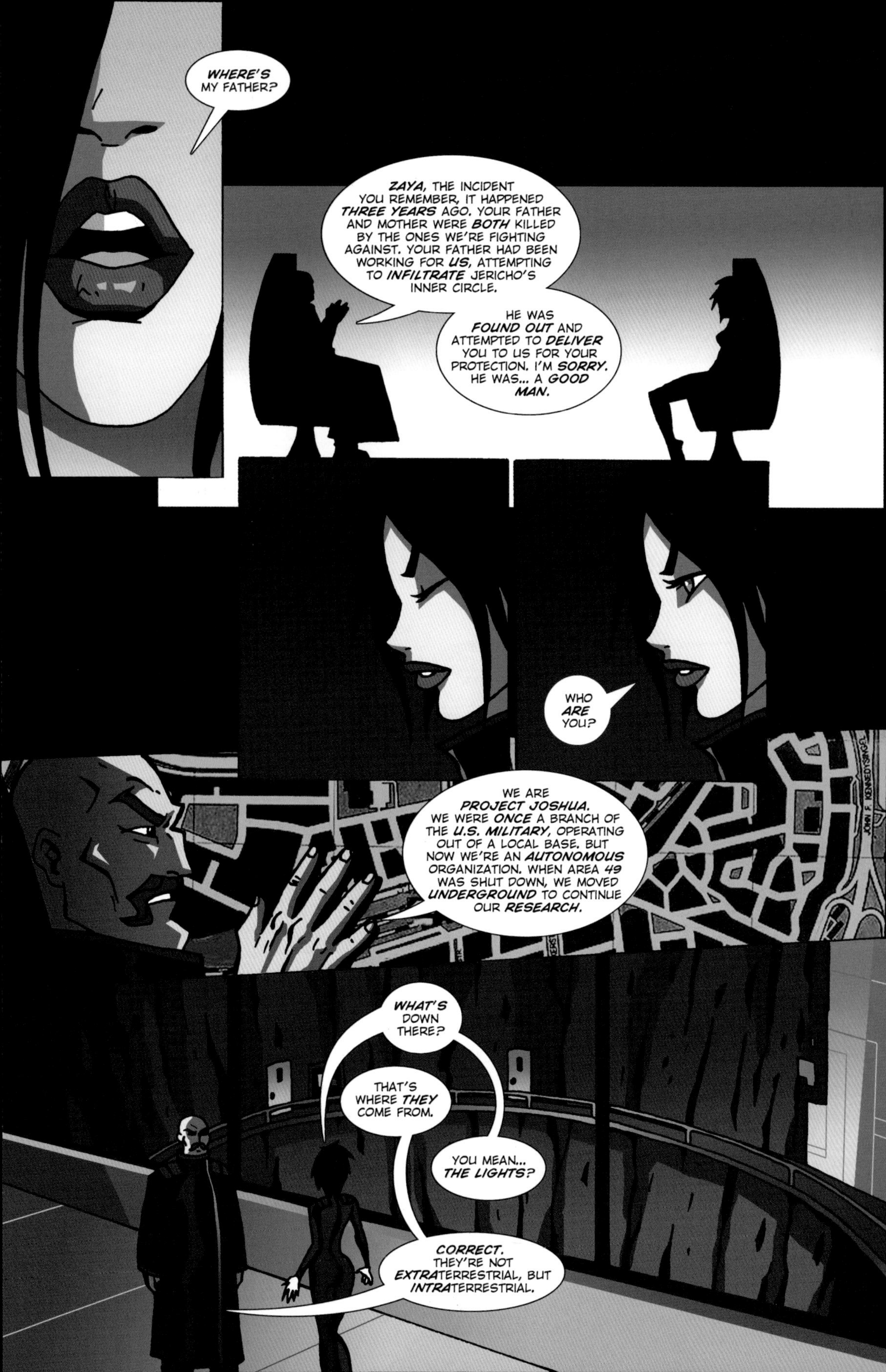
WHERE'S MY FATHER?
ZAYA, THE INCIDENT YOU REMEMBER, IT HAPPENED THREE YEARS AGO. YOUR FATHER AND MOTHER WERE BOTH KILLED BY THE ONES WE'RE FIGHTING AGAINST. YOUR FATHER HAD BEEN WORKING FOR US, ATTEMPTING TO INFILTRATE JERICHO'S INNER CIRCLE.
HE WAS FOUND OUT AND ATTEMPTED TO DELIVER YOU TO US FOR YOUR PROTECTION. I'M SORRY. HE WAS... A GOOD MAN.
WHO ARE YOU?
WE ARE PROJECT JOSHUA. WE WERE ONCE A BRANCH OF THE U.S. MILITARY, OPERATING OUT OF A LOCAL BASE. BUT NOW WE'RE AN AUTONOMOUS ORGANIZATION. WHEN AREA 49 WAS SHUT DOWN, WE MOVED UNDERGROUND TO CONTINUE OUR RESEARCH.
WHAT'S DOWN THERE?
THAT'S WHERE THEY COME FROM.
YOU MEAN... THE LIGHTS?
CORRECT. THEY'RE NOT EXTRATERRESTRIAL, BUT INTRATERRESTRIAL.

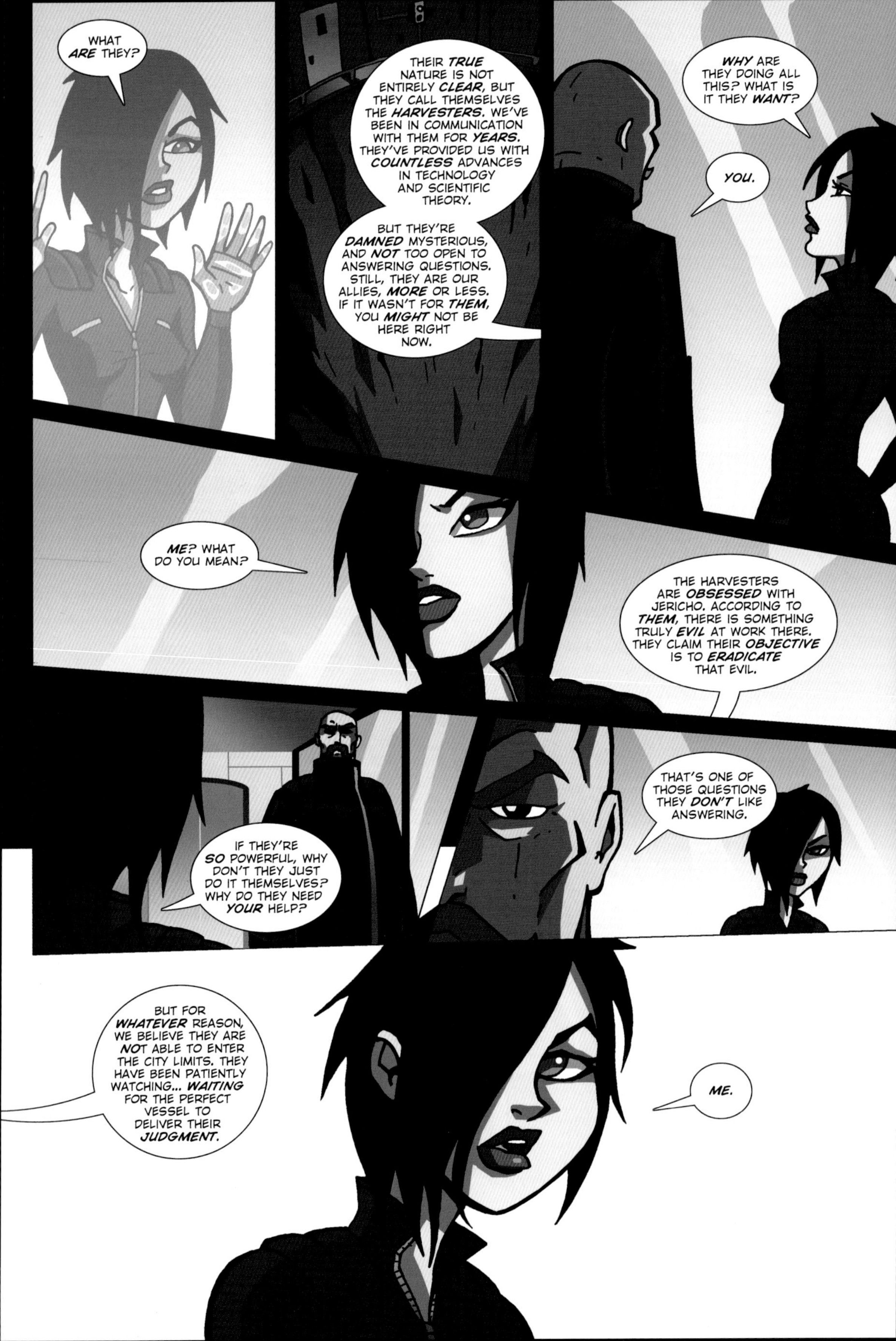
WHAT ARE THEY?
THEIR TRUE NATURE IS NOT ENTIRELY CLEAR, BUT THEY CALL THEMSELVES THE HARVESTERS. WE'VE BEEN IN COMMUNICATION WITH THEM FOR YEARS. THEY'VE PROVIDED US WITH COUNTLESS ADVANCES IN TECHNOLOGY AND SCIENTIFIC THEORY.
BUT THEY'RE DAMNED MYSTERIOUS, AND NOT TOO OPEN TO ANSWERING QUESTIONS. STILL, THEY ARE OUR ALLIES, MORE OR LESS. IF IT WASN'T FOR THEM, YOU MIGHT NOT BE HERE RIGHT NOW.
WHY ARE THEY DOING ALL THIS? WHAT IS IT THEY WANT?
YOU.
ME? WHAT DO YOU MEAN?
THE HARVESTERS ARE OBSESSED WITH JERICHO. ACCORDING TO THEM, THERE IS SOMETHING TRULY EVIL AT WORK THERE. THEY CLAIM THEIR OBJECTIVE IS TO ERADICATE THAT EVIL.
IF THEY'RE SO POWERFUL, WHY DON'T THEY JUST DO IT THEMSELVES? WHY DO THEY NEED YOUR HELP?
THAT'S ONE OF THOSE QUESTIONS THEY DON'T LIKE ANSWERING.
BUT FOR WHATEVER REASON, WE BELIEVE THEY ARE NOT ABLE TO ENTER THE CITY LIMITS. THEY HAVE BEEN PATIENTLY WATCHING... WAITING FOR THE PERFECT VESSEL TO DELIVER THEIR JUDGMENT.
ME.

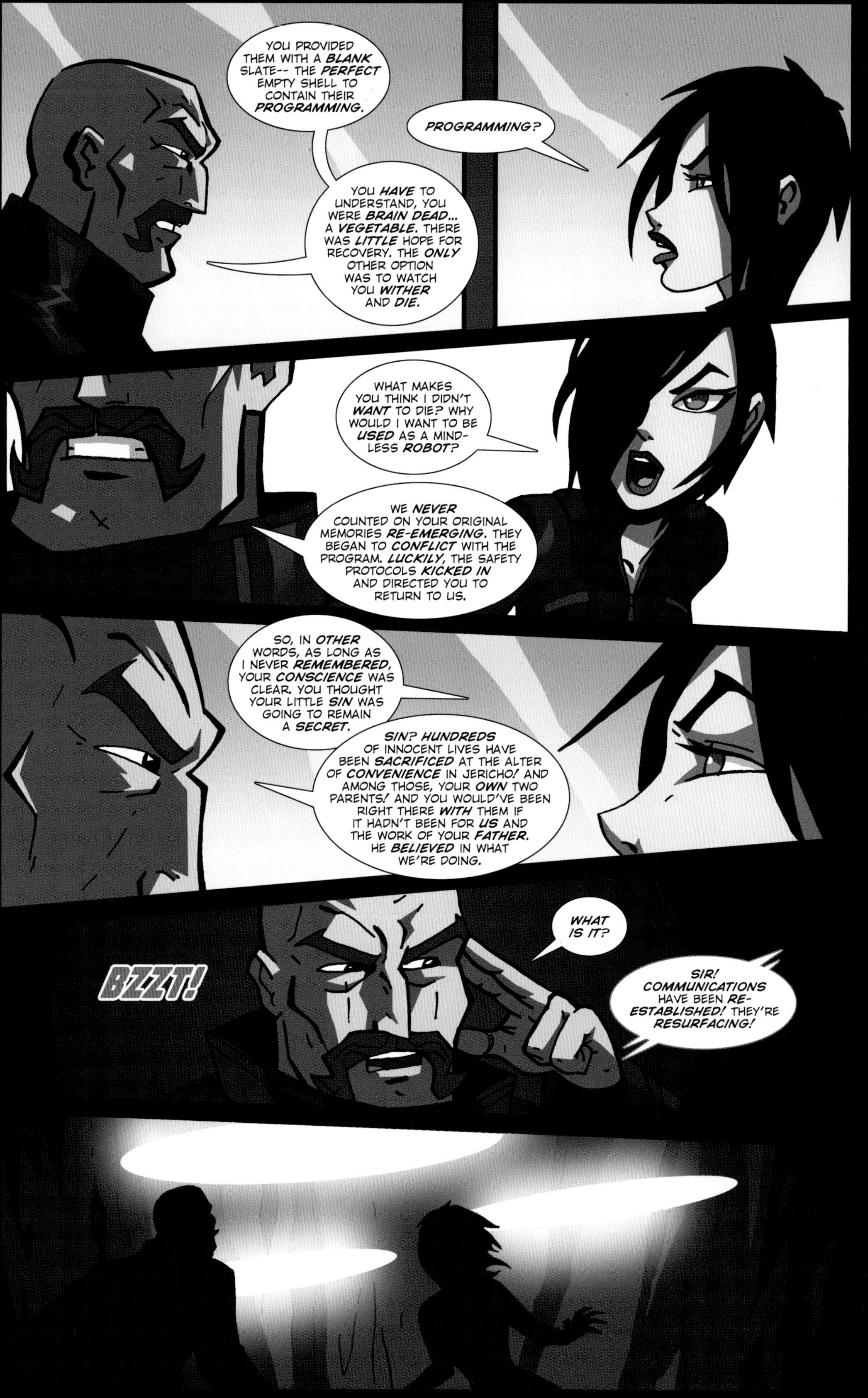
YOU PROVIDED THEM WITH A BLANK SLATE-- THE PERFECT EMPTY SHELL TO CONTAIN THEIR PROGRAMMING.
PROGRAMMING?
YOU HAVE TO UNDERSTAND, YOU WERE BRAIN DEAD... A VEGETABLE. THERE WAS LITTLE HOPE FOR RECOVERY. THE ONLY OTHER OPTION WAS TO WATCH YOU WITHER AND DIE.
WHAT MAKES YOU THINK I DIDN'T WANT TO DIE? WHY WOULD I WANT TO BE USED AS A MIND-LESS ROBOT?
WE NEVER COUNTED ON YOUR ORIGINAL MEMORIES RE-EMERGING. THEY BEGAN TO CONFLICT WITH THE PROGRAM. LUCKILY, THE SAFETY PROTOCOLS KICKED IN AND DIRECTED YOU TO RETURN TO US.
SO, IN OTHER WORDS, AS LONG AS I NEVER REMEMBERED, YOUR CONSCIENCE WAS CLEAR. YOU THOUGHT YOUR LITTLE SIN WAS GOING TO REMAIN A SECRET.
SIN? HUNDREDS OF INNOCENT LIVES HAVE BEEN SACRIFICED AT THE ALTER OF CONVENIENCE IN JERICHO! AND AMONG THOSE, YOUR OWN TWO PARENTS! AND YOU WOULD'VE BEEN RIGHT THERE WITH THEM IF IT HADN'T BEEN FOR US AND THE WORK OF YOUR FATHER. HE BELIEVED IN WHAT WE'RE DOING.
BZZT!
WHAT IS IT?
SIR! COMMUNICATIONS HAVE BEEN RE-ESTABLISHED! THEY'RE RESURFACING!

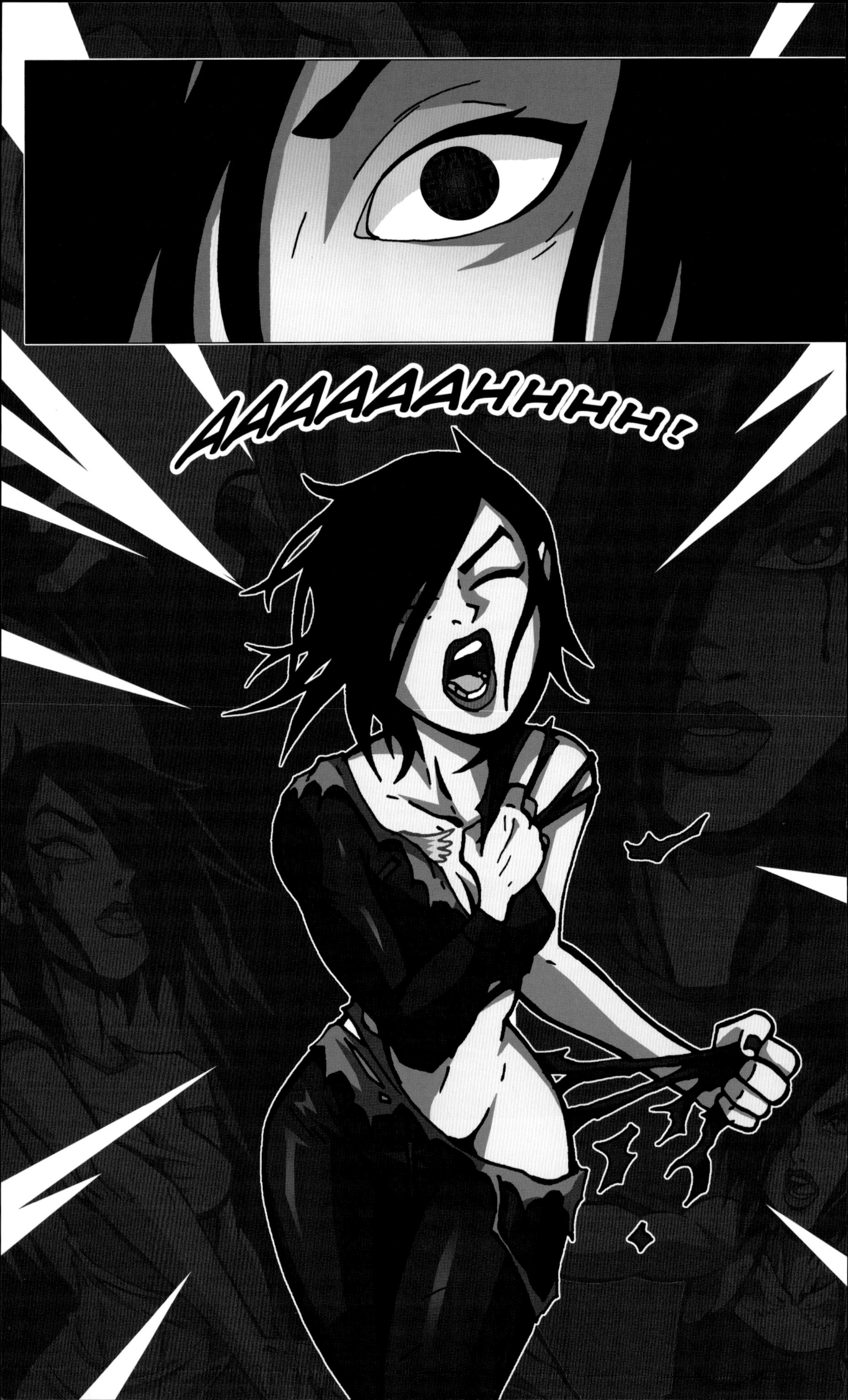
AAAAAAHHHHH!

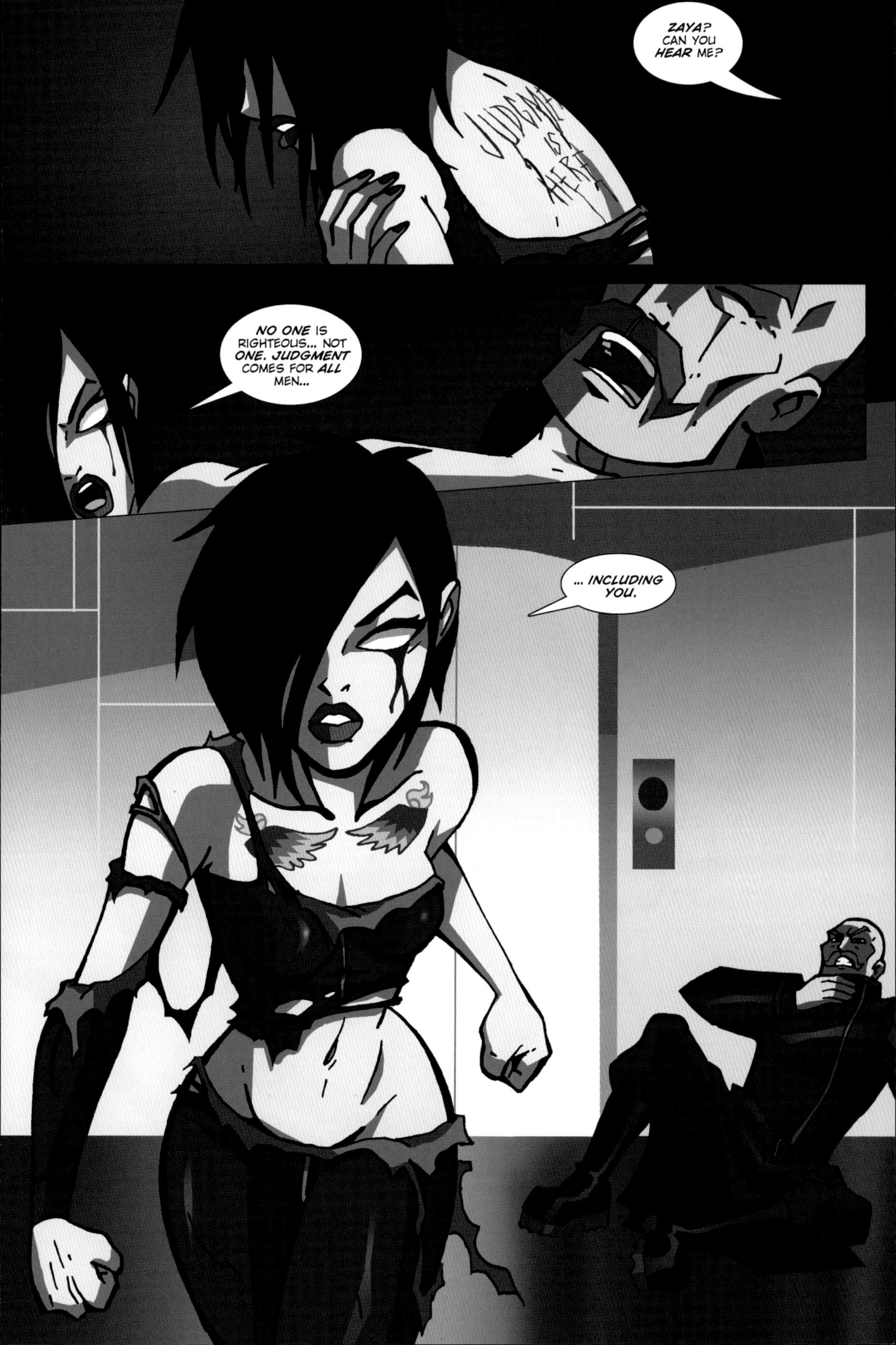
ZAYA? CAN YOU HEAR ME?
NO ONE IS RIGHTEOUS... NOT ONE. JUDGMENT COMES FOR ALL MEN...
... INCLUDING YOU.

chapter 5

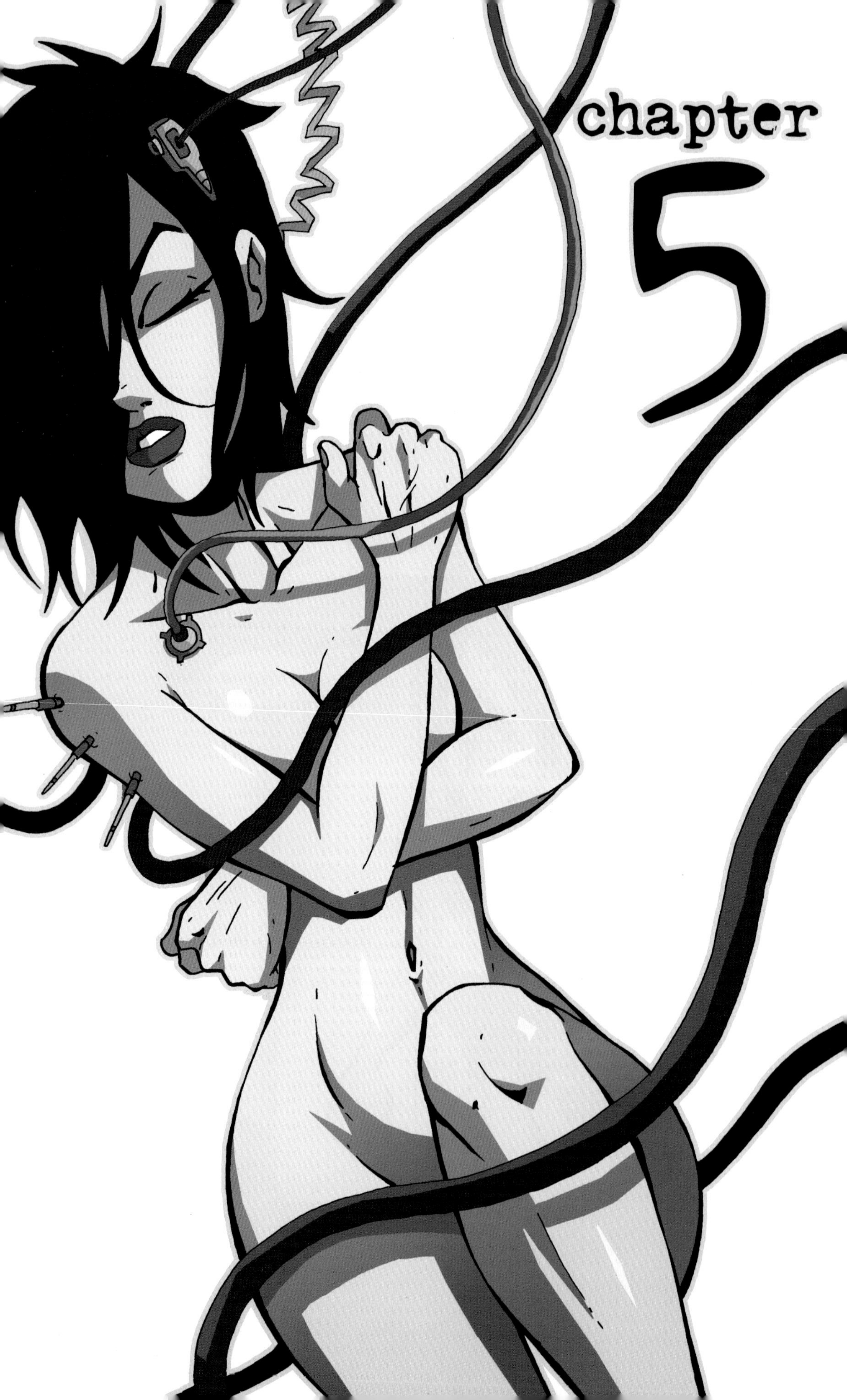

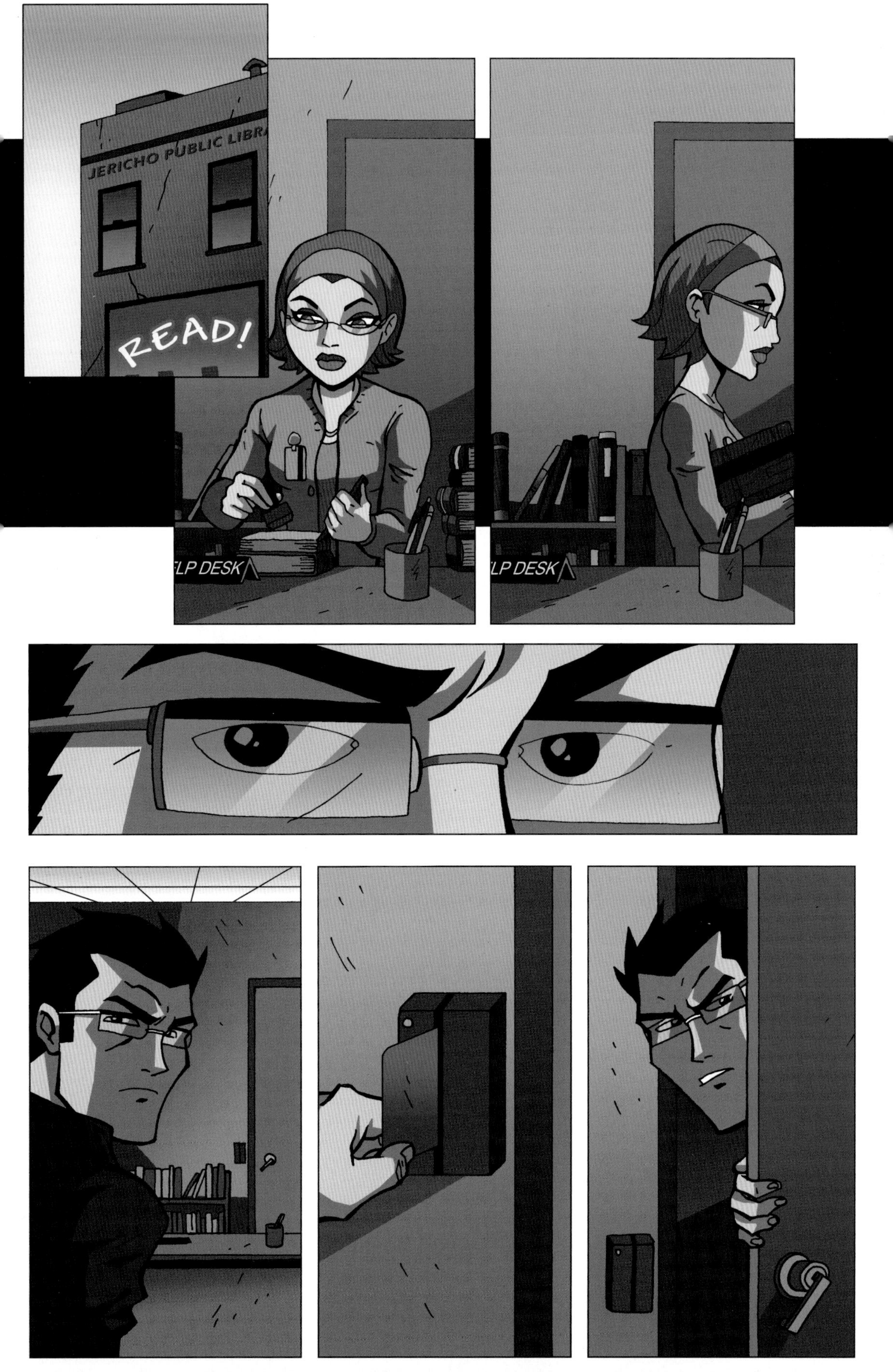
JERICHO PUBLIC LIBRA
READ!
ELP DESK
ELP DESK

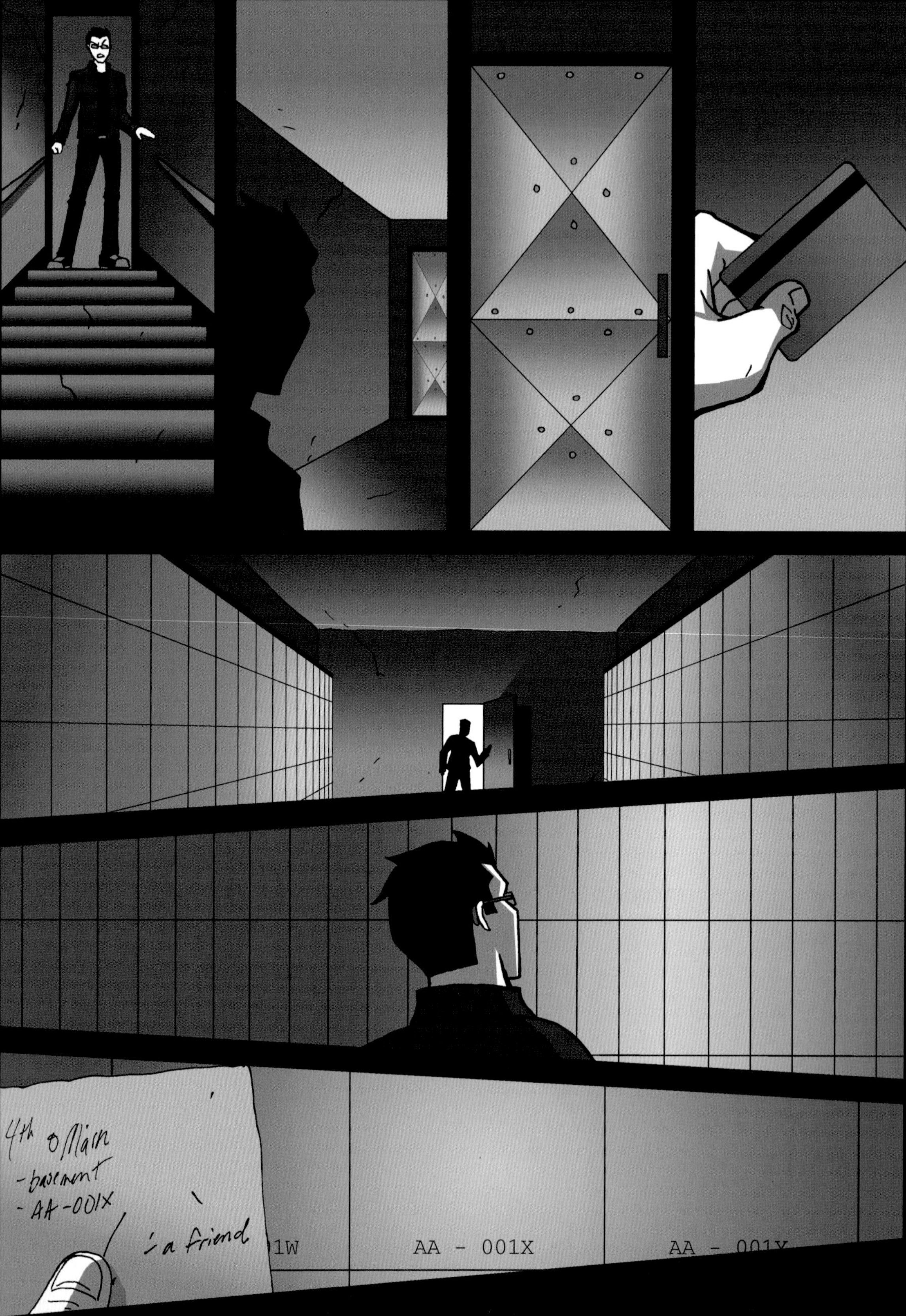
4th & Main
- basement
- AA-001X
: a friend
1W
AA - 001X

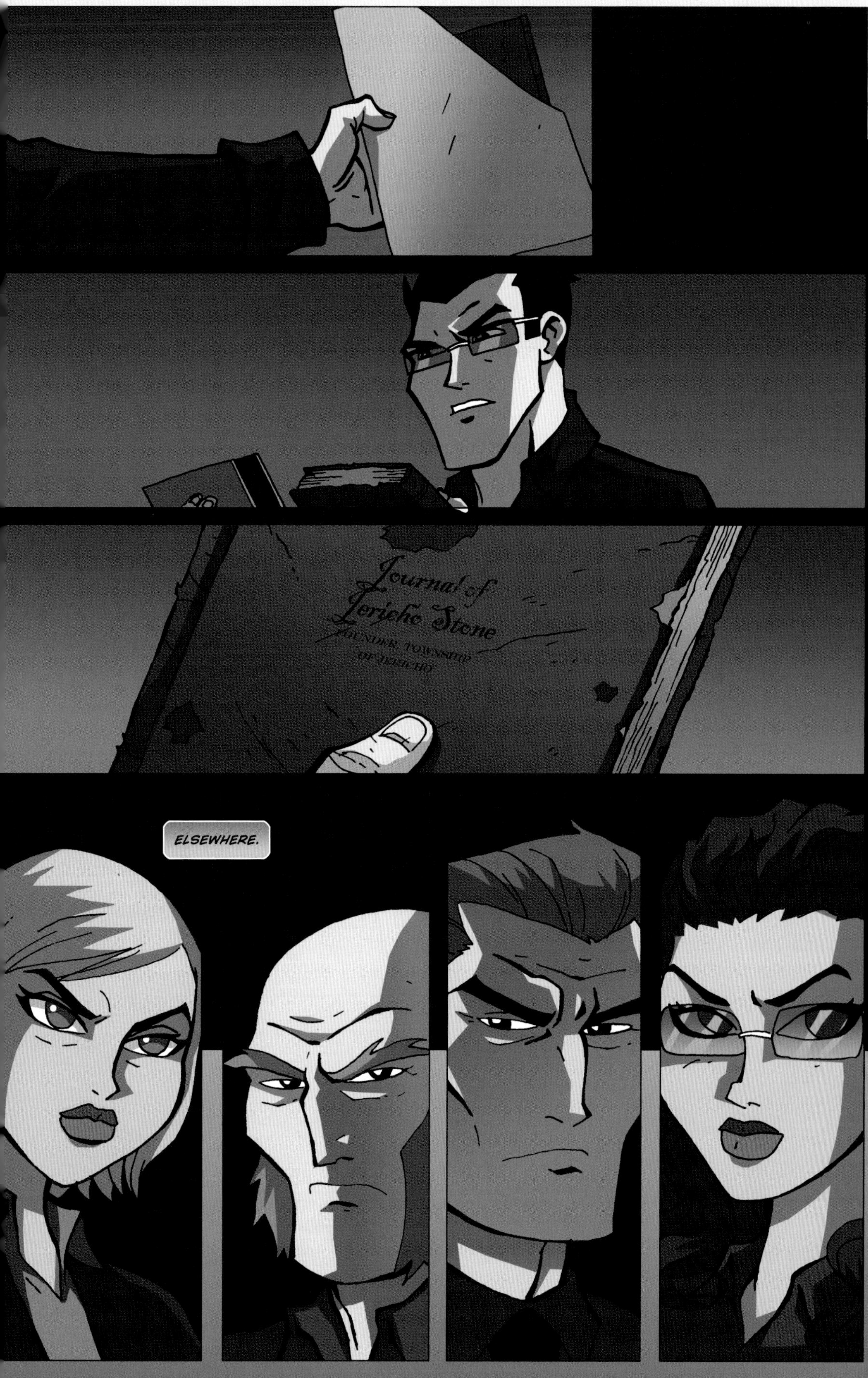
Journal of Jericho Stone
FOUNDER, TOWNSHIP OF JERICHO
ELSEWHERE.

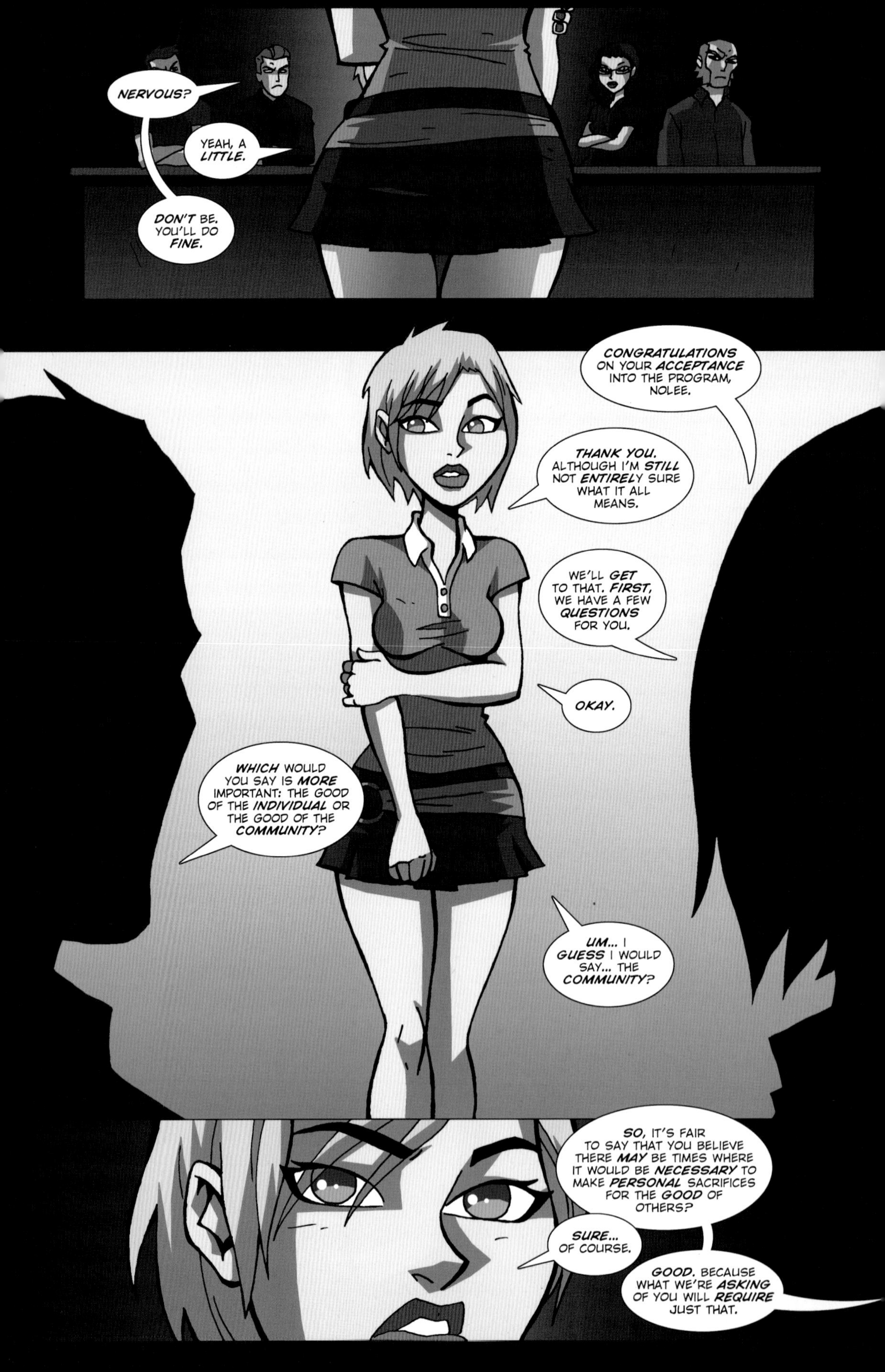
NERVOUS?
YEAH, A LITTLE.
DON'T BE. YOU'LL DO FINE.
CONGRATULATIONS ON YOUR ACCEPTANCE INTO THE PROGRAM, NOLEE.
THANK YOU. ALTHOUGH I'M STILL NOT ENTIRELY SURE WHAT IT ALL MEANS.
WE'LL GET TO THAT. FIRST, WE HAVE A FEW QUESTIONS FOR YOU.
OKAY.
WHICH WOULD YOU SAY IS MORE IMPORTANT: THE GOOD OF THE INDIVIDUAL OR THE GOOD OF THE COMMUNITY?
UM... I GUESS I WOULD SAY... THE COMMUNITY?
SO, IT'S FAIR TO SAY THAT YOU BELIEVE THERE MAY BE TIMES WHERE IT WOULD BE NECESSARY TO MAKE PERSONAL SACRIFICES FOR THE GOOD OF OTHERS?
SURE... OF COURSE.
GOOD. BECAUSE WHAT WE'RE ASKING OF YOU WILL REQUIRE JUST THAT.

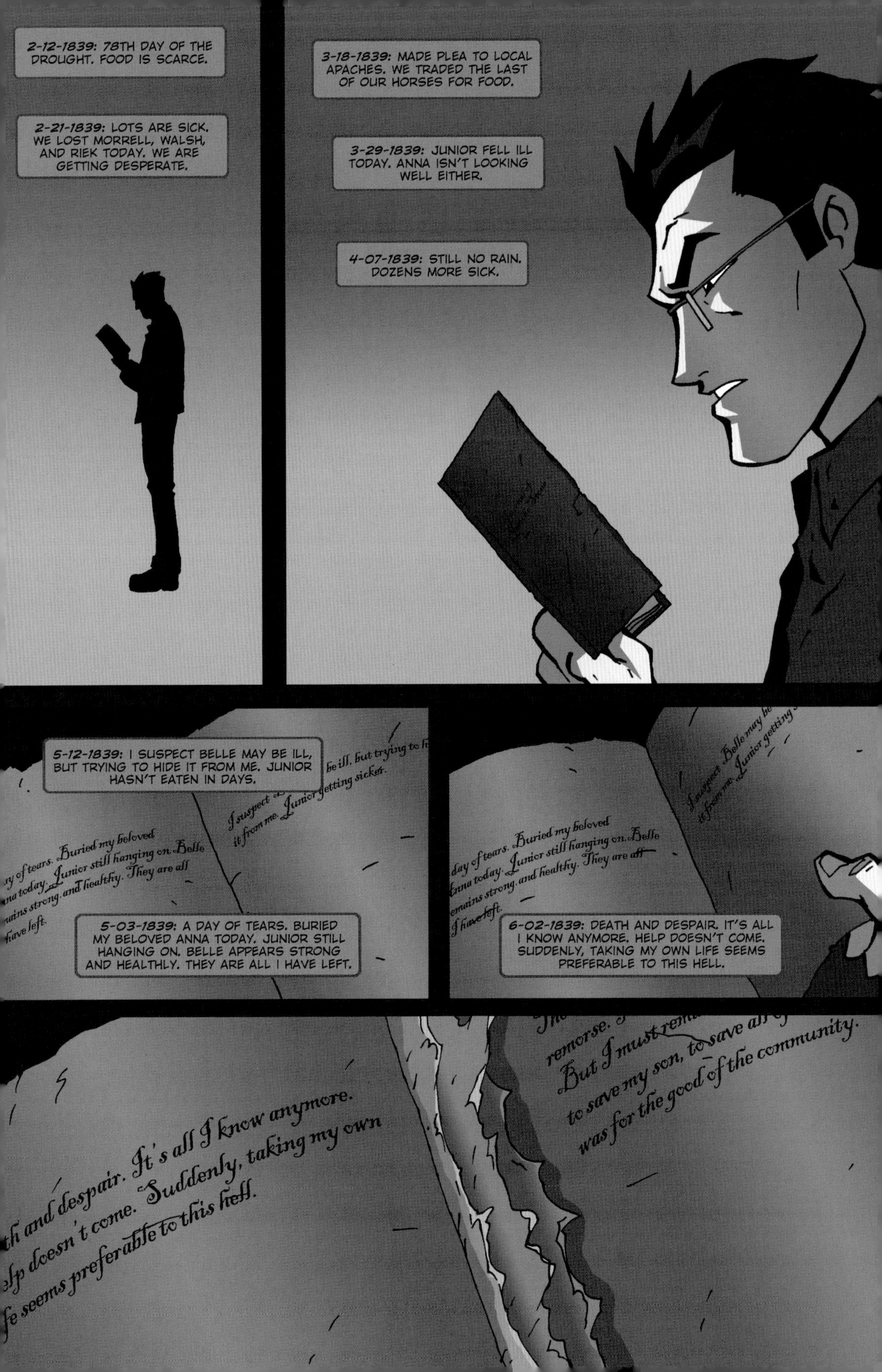

2-12-1839: 78TH DAY OF THE DROUGHT. FOOD IS SCARCE.
2-21-1839: LOTS ARE SICK. WE LOST MORRELL, WALSH, AND RIEK TODAY. WE ARE GETTING DESPERATE.
3-18-1839: MADE PLEA TO LOCAL APACHES. WE TRADED THE LAST OF OUR HORSES FOR FOOD.
3-29-1839: JUNIOR FELL ILL TODAY. ANNA ISN'T LOOKING WELL EITHER.
4-07-1839: STILL NO RAIN. DOZENS MORE SICK.
5-12-1839: I SUSPECT BELLE MAY BE ILL, BUT TRYING TO HIDE IT FROM ME. JUNIOR HASN'T EATEN IN DAYS.
5-03-1839: A DAY OF TEARS. BURIED MY BELOVED ANNA TODAY. JUNIOR STILL HANGING ON. BELLE APPEARS STRONG AND HEALTHLY. THEY ARE ALL I HAVE LEFT.
6-02-1839: DEATH AND DESPAIR. IT'S ALL I KNOW ANYMORE. HELP DOESN'T COME. SUDDENLY, TAKING MY OWN LIFE SEEMS PREFERABLE TO THIS HELL.

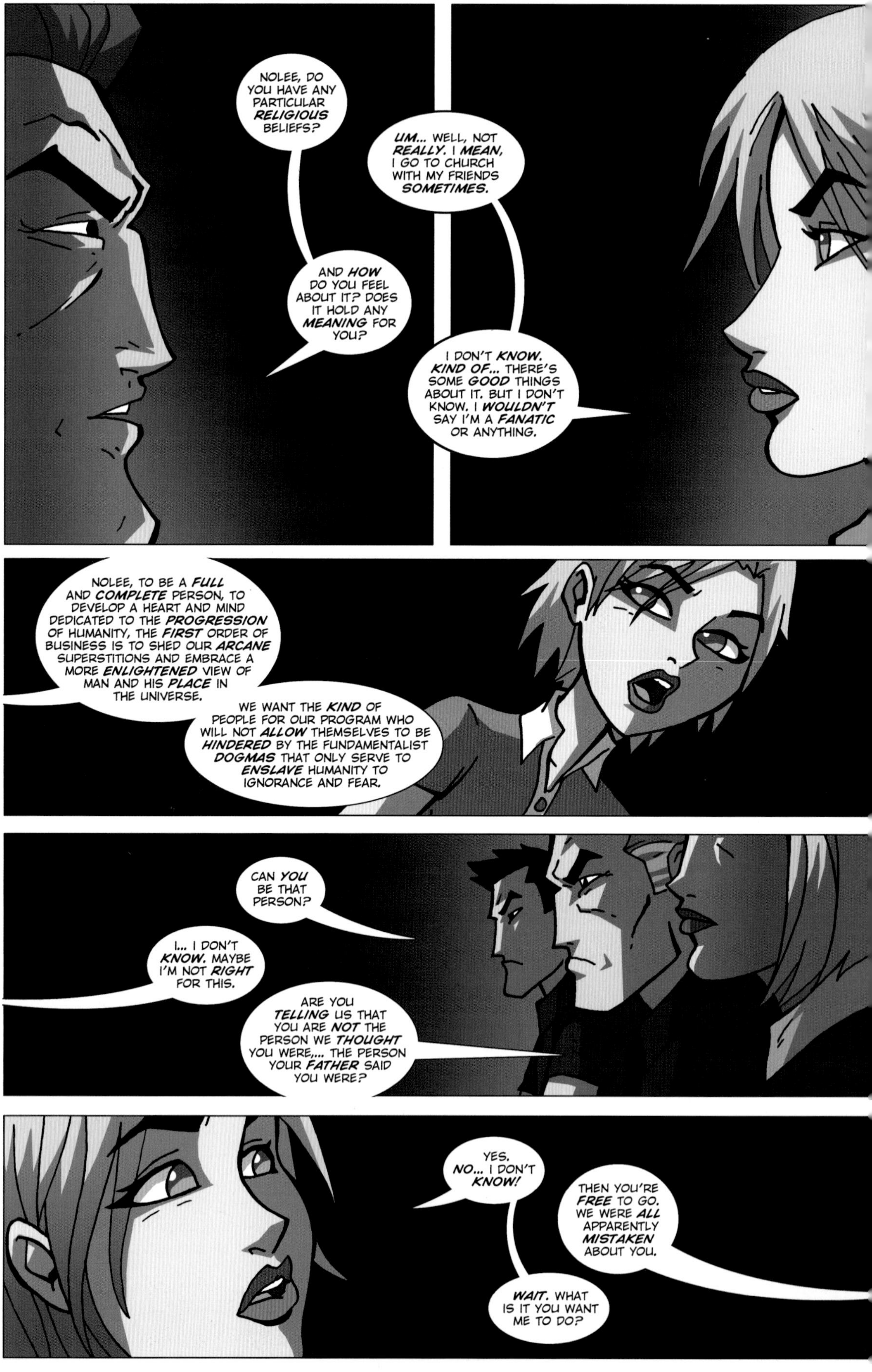
NOLEE, DO YOU HAVE ANY PARTICULAR RELIGIOUS BELIEFS?
UM... WELL, NOT REALLY. I MEAN, I GO TO CHURCH WITH MY FRIENDS SOMETIMES.
AND HOW DO YOU FEEL ABOUT IT? DOES IT HOLD ANY MEANING FOR YOU?
I DON'T KNOW. KIND OF... THERE'S SOME GOOD THINGS ABOUT IT. BUT I DON'T KNOW. I WOULDN'T SAY I'M A FANATIC OR ANYTHING.
NOLEE, TO BE A FULL AND COMPLETE PERSON, TO DEVELOP A HEART AND MIND DEDICATED TO THE PROGRESSION OF HUMANITY, THE FIRST ORDER OF BUSINESS IS TO SHED OUR ARCANE SUPERSTITIONS AND EMBRACE A MORE ENLIGHTENED VIEW OF MAN AND HIS PLACE IN THE UNIVERSE.
WE WANT THE KIND OF PEOPLE FOR OUR PROGRAM WHO WILL NOT ALLOW THEMSELVES TO BE HINDERED BY THE FUNDAMENTALIST DOGMAS THAT ONLY SERVE TO ENSLAVE HUMANITY TO IGNORANCE AND FEAR.
CAN YOU BE THAT PERSON?
I... I DON'T KNOW. MAYBE I'M NOT RIGHT FOR THIS.
ARE YOU TELLING US THAT YOU ARE NOT THE PERSON WE THOUGHT YOU WERE,... THE PERSON YOUR FATHER SAID YOU WERE?
YES. NO... I DON'T KNOW!
THEN YOU'RE FREE TO GO. WE WERE ALL APPARENTLY MISTAKEN ABOUT YOU.
WAIT. WHAT IS IT YOU WANT ME TO DO?

AUNT ELYSE.

OH, *HEAVENS! ZAYA...* YOU *SCARED* ME! WHERE HAVE YOU *BEEN?* I'VE BEEN WORRIED TO *DEATH!*

LISTEN TO ME. YOU *HAVE* TO LEAVE JERICHO.

WHAT? WHY?

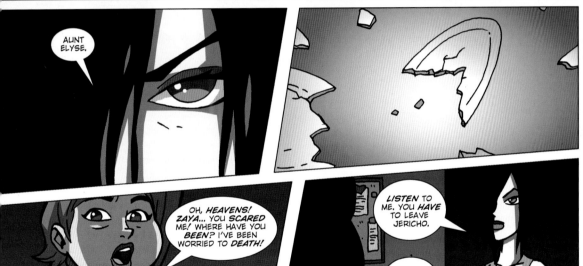

I *CAN'T* EXPLAIN. JUST *PLEASE* DO AS I ASK. THERE ARE *THINGS...* THINGS ABOUT TO *HAPPEN.* I JUST WANT YOU TO BE *SAFE.*

ZAYA, *WHAT* IS THIS ALL ABOUT?

SETTING THINGS *RIGHT.*

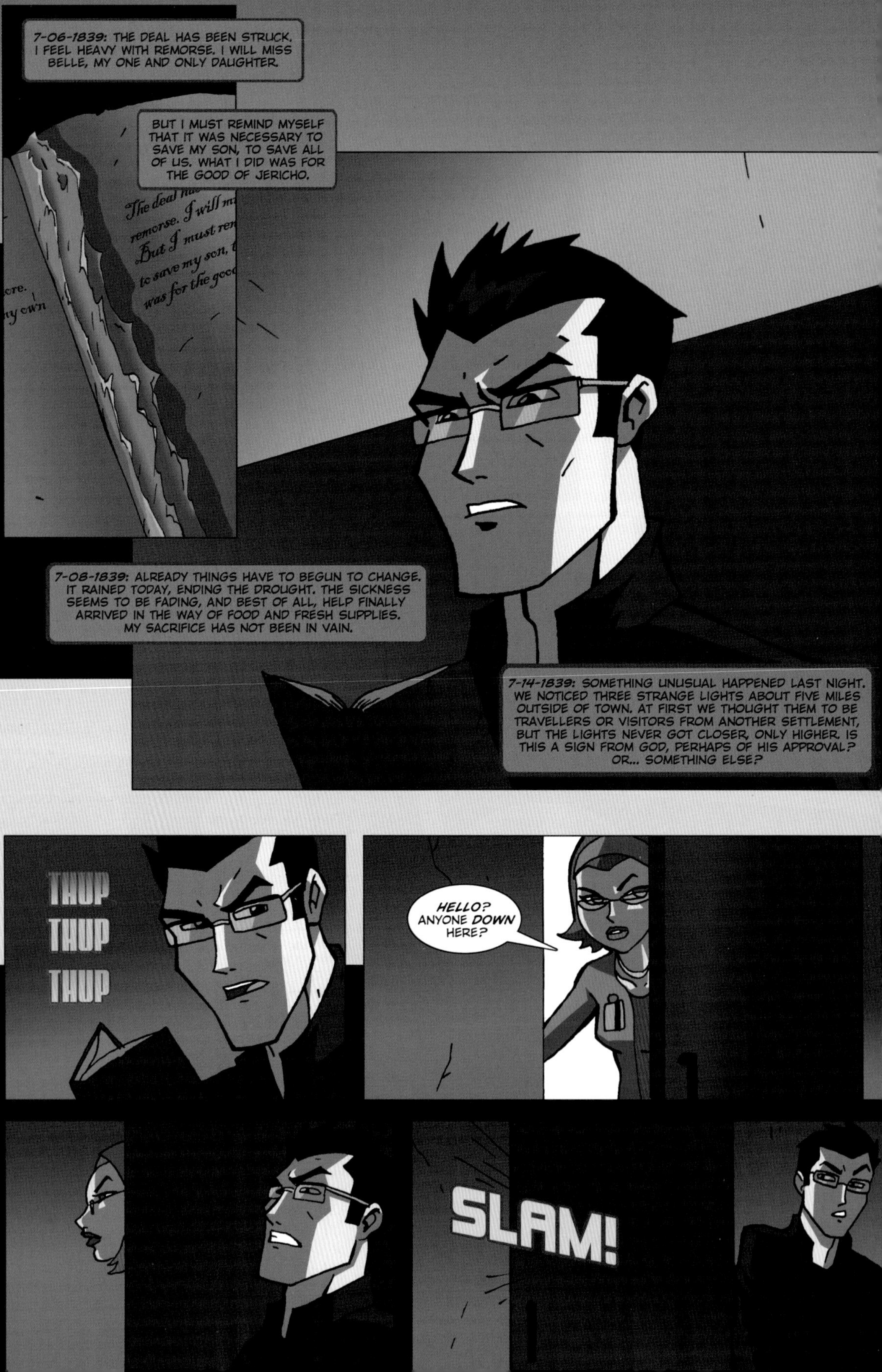
7-06-1839: THE DEAL HAS BEEN STRUCK. I FEEL HEAVY WITH REMORSE. I WILL MISS BELLE, MY ONE AND ONLY DAUGHTER.
BUT I MUST REMIND MYSELF THAT IT WAS NECESSARY TO SAVE MY SON, TO SAVE ALL OF US. WHAT I DID WAS FOR THE GOOD OF JERICHO.
7-08-1839: ALREADY THINGS HAVE TO BEGUN TO CHANGE. IT RAINED TODAY, ENDING THE DROUGHT. THE SICKNESS SEEMS TO BE FADING, AND BEST OF ALL, HELP FINALLY ARRIVED IN THE WAY OF FOOD AND FRESH SUPPLIES. MY SACRIFICE HAS NOT BEEN IN VAIN.
7-14-1839: SOMETHING UNUSUAL HAPPENED LAST NIGHT. WE NOTICED THREE STRANGE LIGHTS ABOUT FIVE MILES OUTSIDE OF TOWN. AT FIRST WE THOUGHT THEM TO BE TRAVELLERS OR VISITORS FROM ANOTHER SETTLEMENT, BUT THE LIGHTS NEVER GOT CLOSER, ONLY HIGHER. IS THIS A SIGN FROM GOD, PERHAPS OF HIS APPROVAL? OR... SOMETHING ELSE?
THUP
THUP
THUP
HELLO? ANYONE DOWN HERE?
SLAM!

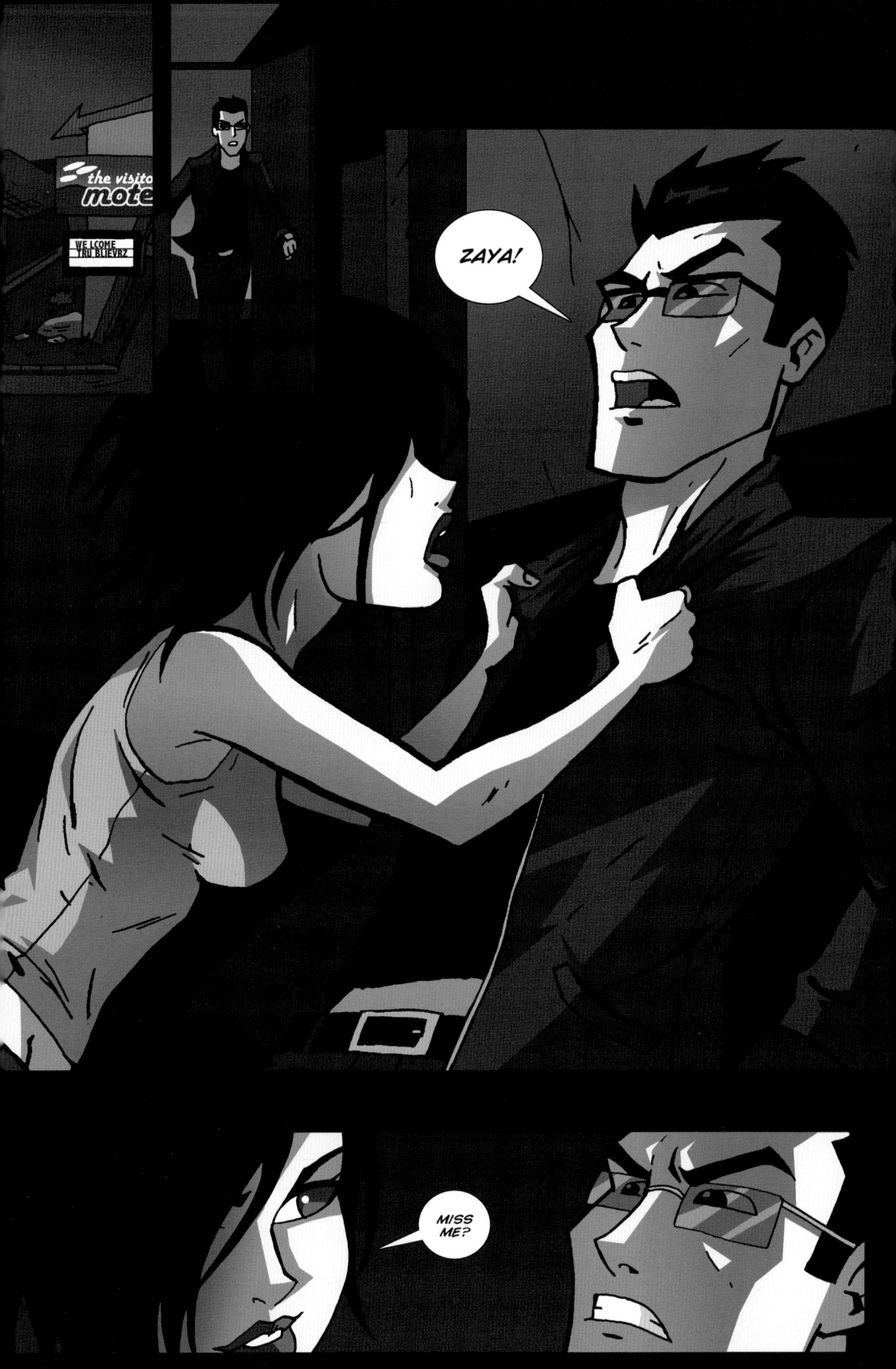
WE LCOME
TRU BLIEVRZ
ZAYA!
MISS ME?

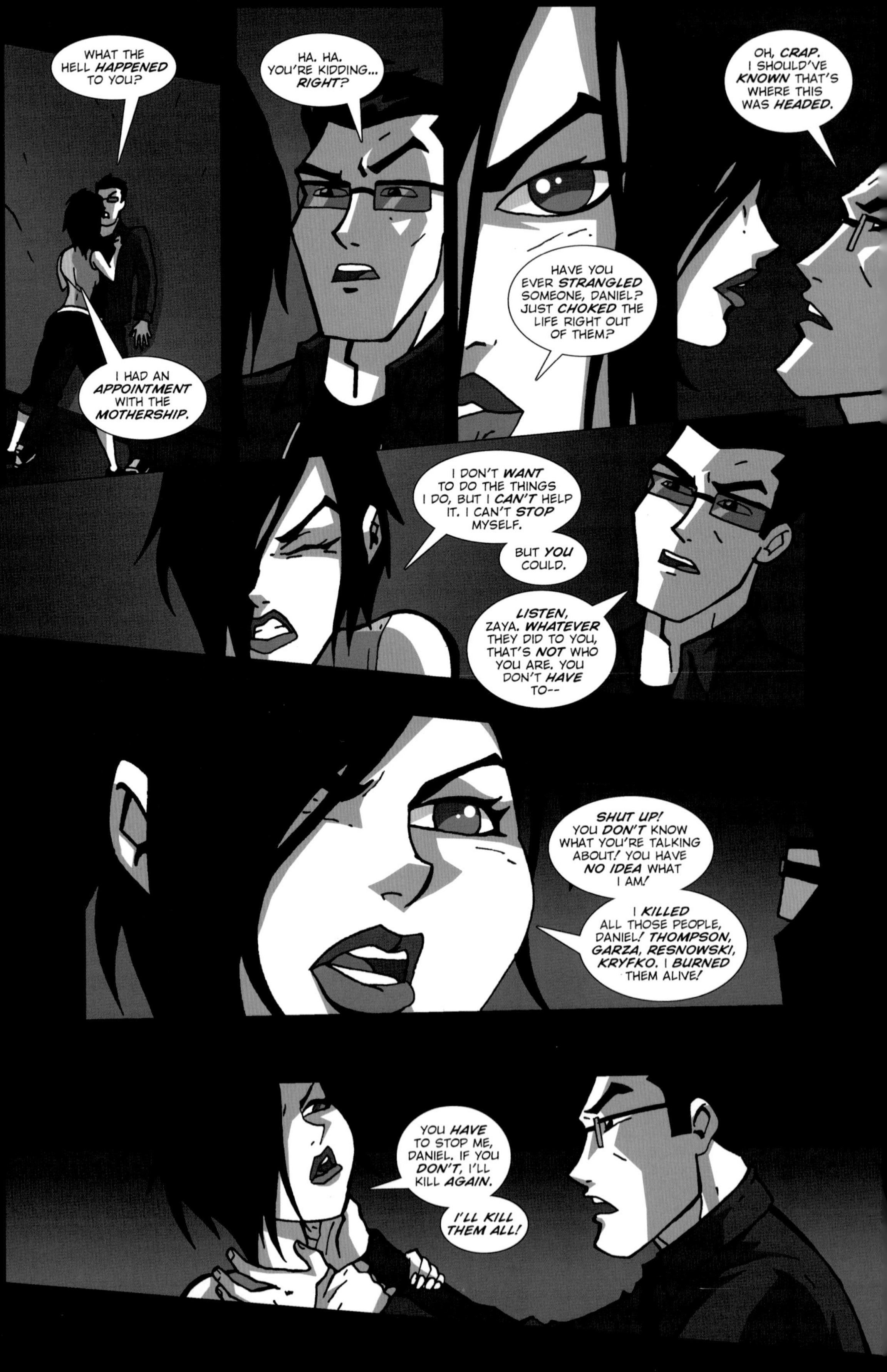
WHAT THE HELL HAPPENED TO YOU?
I HAD AN APPOINTMENT WITH THE MOTHERSHIP.
HA. HA. YOU'RE KIDDING... RIGHT?
HAVE YOU EVER STRANGLED SOMEONE, DANIEL? JUST CHOKED THE LIFE RIGHT OUT OF THEM?
OH, CRAP. I SHOULD'VE KNOWN THAT'S WHERE THIS WAS HEADED.
I DON'T WANT TO DO THE THINGS I DO, BUT I CAN'T HELP IT. I CAN'T STOP MYSELF.
BUT YOU COULD.
LISTEN, ZAYA. WHATEVER THEY DID TO YOU, THAT'S NOT WHO YOU ARE. YOU DON'T HAVE TO--
SHUT UP! YOU DON'T KNOW WHAT YOU'RE TALKING ABOUT! YOU HAVE NO IDEA WHAT I AM!
I KILLED ALL THOSE PEOPLE, DANIEL! THOMPSON, GARZA, RESNOWSKI, KRYFKO. I BURNED THEM ALIVE!
YOU HAVE TO STOP ME, DANIEL. IF YOU DON'T, I'LL KILL AGAIN.
I'LL KILL THEM ALL!

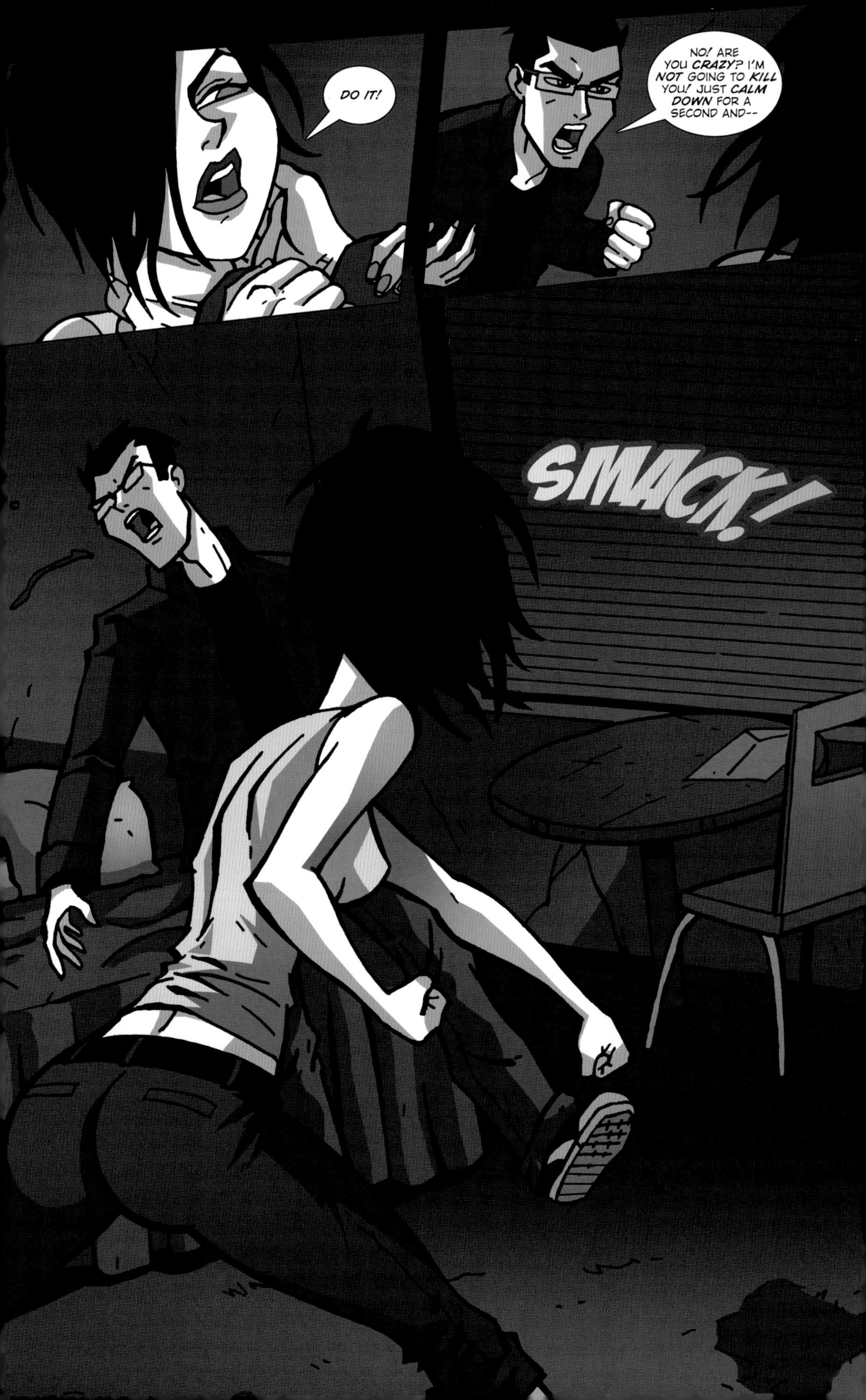
DO IT!
NO! ARE YOU CRAZY? I'M NOT GOING TO KILL YOU! JUST CALM DOWN FOR A SECOND AND--
SMACK!

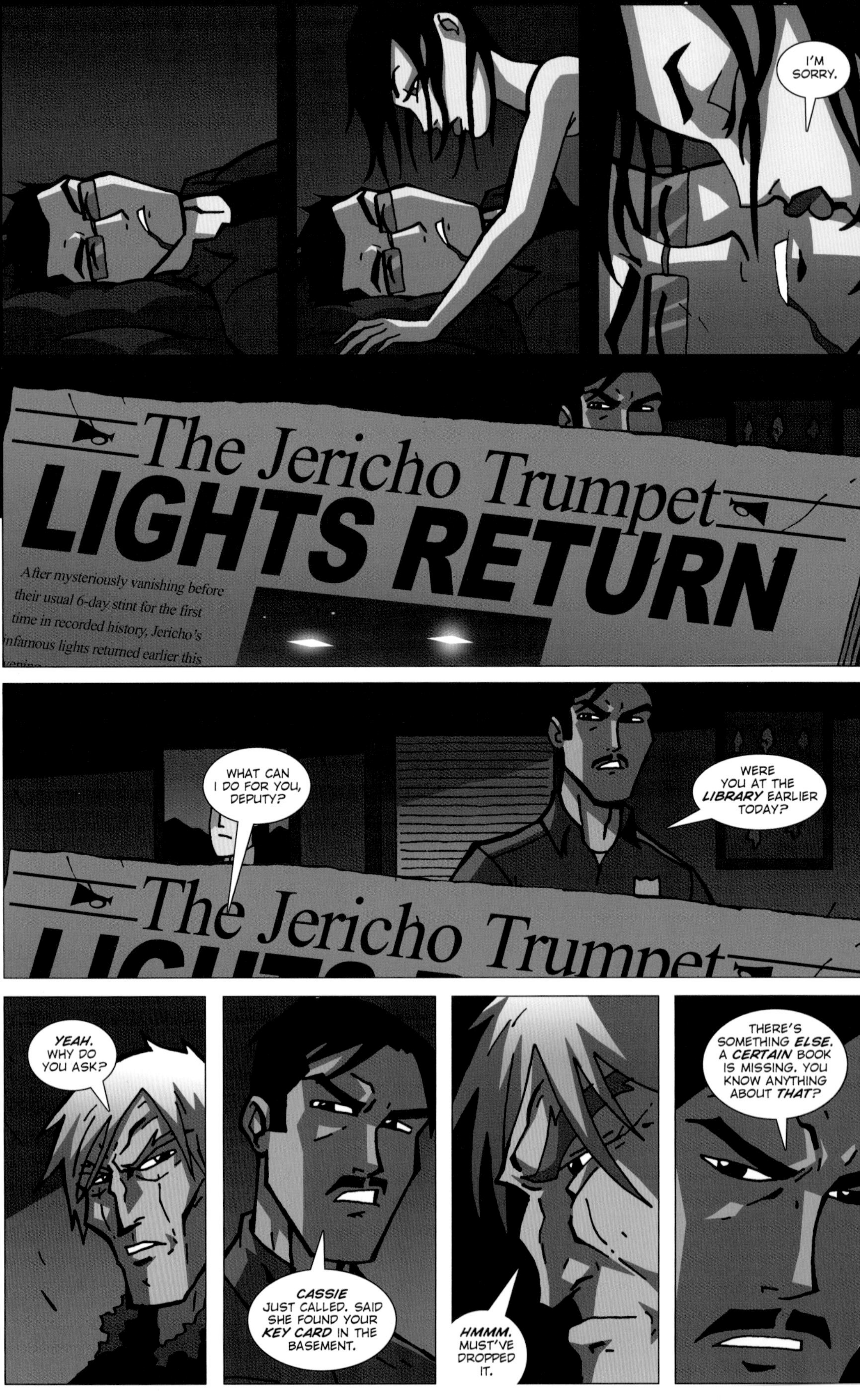
I'M SORRY.
The Jericho Trumpet
LIGHTS RETURN
After mysteriously vanishing before their usual 6-day stint for the first time in recorded history, Jericho's infamous lights returned earlier this
WHAT CAN I DO FOR YOU, DEPUTY?
WERE YOU AT THE LIBRARY EARLIER TODAY?
The Jericho Trumpet
YEAH. WHY DO YOU ASK?
CASSIE JUST CALLED. SAID SHE FOUND YOUR KEY CARD IN THE BASEMENT.
HMMM. MUST'VE DROPPED IT.
THERE'S SOMETHING ELSE. A CERTAIN BOOK IS MISSING. YOU KNOW ANYTHING ABOUT THAT?

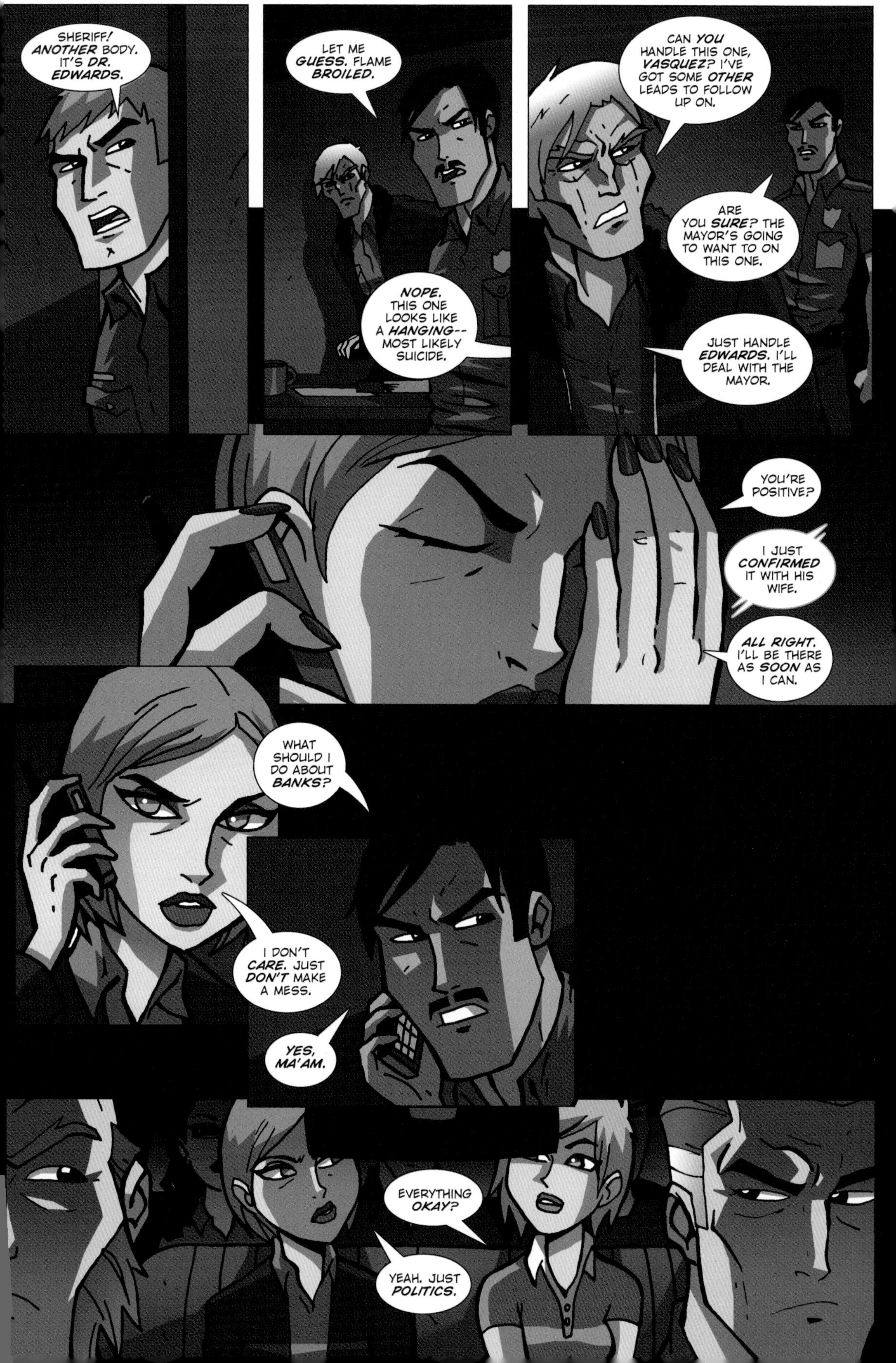
SHERIFF! ANOTHER BODY. IT'S DR. EDWARDS.
LET ME GUESS. FLAME BROILED.
NOPE. THIS ONE LOOKS LIKE A HANGING-- MOST LIKELY SUICIDE.
CAN YOU HANDLE THIS ONE, VASQUEZ? I'VE GOT SOME OTHER LEADS TO FOLLOW UP ON.
ARE YOU SURE? THE MAYOR'S GOING TO WANT TO ON THIS ONE.
JUST HANDLE EDWARDS. I'LL DEAL WITH THE MAYOR.
YOU'RE POSITIVE?
I JUST CONFIRMED IT WITH HIS WIFE.
ALL RIGHT. I'LL BE THERE AS SOON AS I CAN.
WHAT SHOULD I DO ABOUT BANKS?
I DON'T CARE. JUST DON'T MAKE A MESS.
YES, MA'AM.
EVERYTHING OKAY?
YEAH. JUST POLITICS.

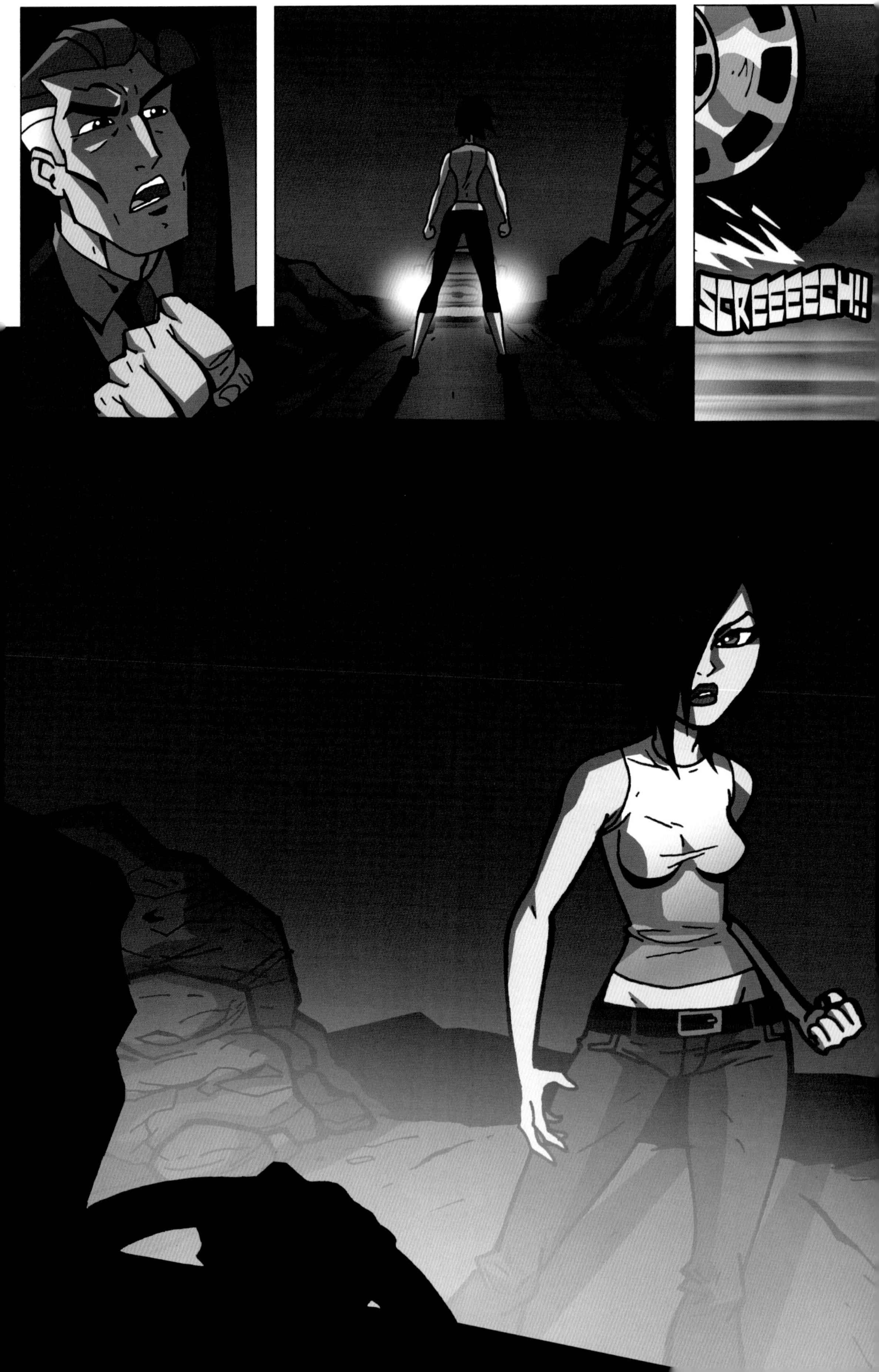
SCREEEEECH!!

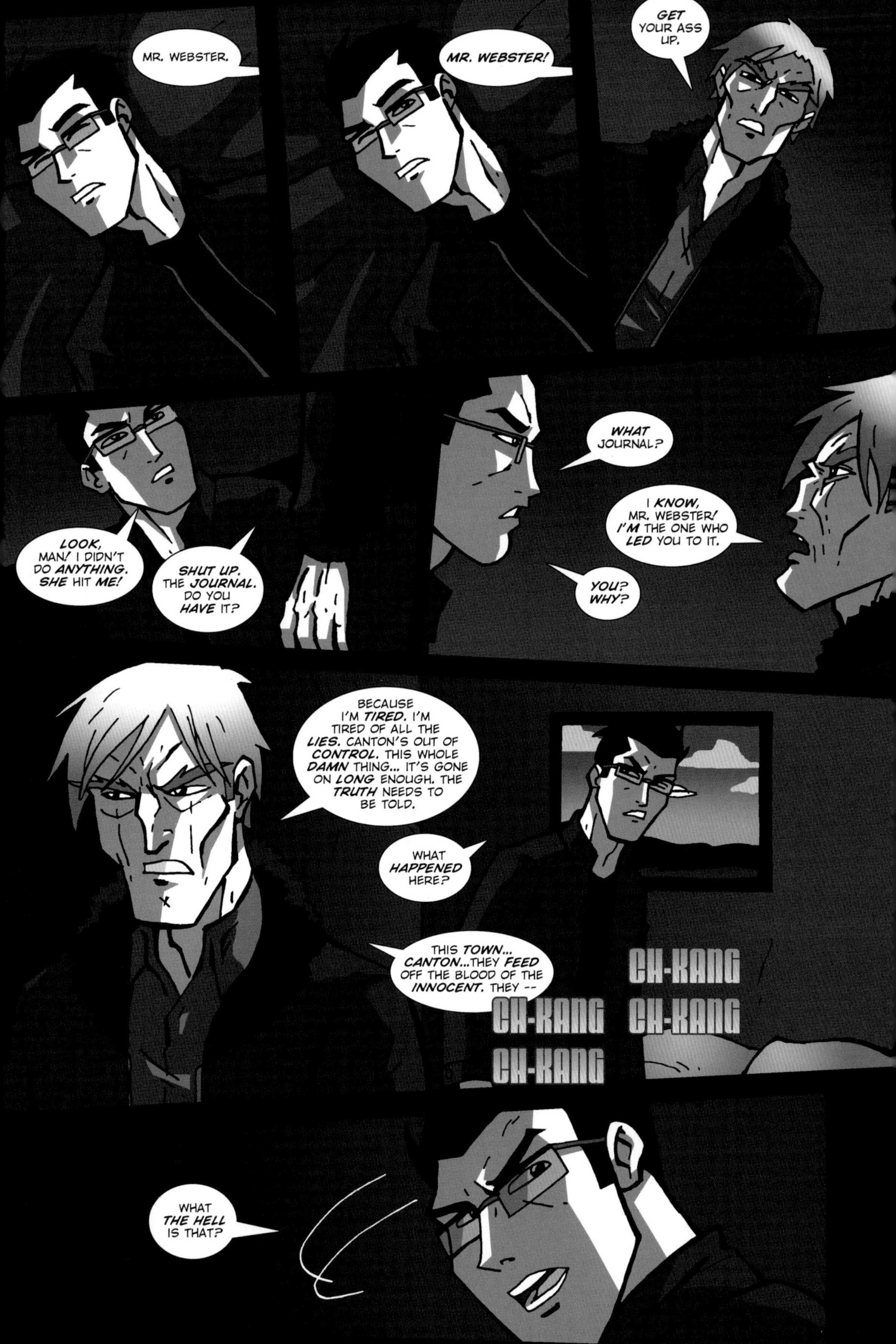
MR. WEBSTER.
MR. WEBSTER!
GET YOUR ASS UP.
LOOK, MAN! I DIDN'T DO ANYTHING. SHE HIT ME!
SHUT UP. THE JOURNAL. DO YOU HAVE IT?
WHAT JOURNAL?
I KNOW, MR. WEBSTER! I'M THE ONE WHO LED YOU TO IT.
YOU? WHY?
BECAUSE I'M TIRED. I'M TIRED OF ALL THE LIES. CANTON'S OUT OF CONTROL. THIS WHOLE DAMN THING... IT'S GONE ON LONG ENOUGH. THE TRUTH NEEDS TO BE TOLD.
WHAT HAPPENED HERE?
THIS TOWN... CANTON...THEY FEED OFF THE BLOOD OF THE INNOCENT. THEY --
CH-KANG
CH-KANG
CH-KANG
CH-KANG
WHAT THE HELL IS THAT?

CH-KANG
CH-KANG

CH-KANG
CH-KANG

CH-KANG
CH-KANG

YOU WANT TO GIVE ME A *HAND* WITH THIS?

WE DON'T HAVE *TIME* FOR THIS CRAP!

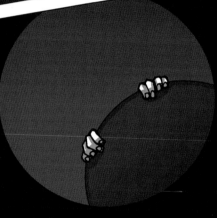

CH-KANG
CH-KANG

CH-KANG
CH-KANG

CH-KANG
CH-KANG

CH-KANG
CH-KANG

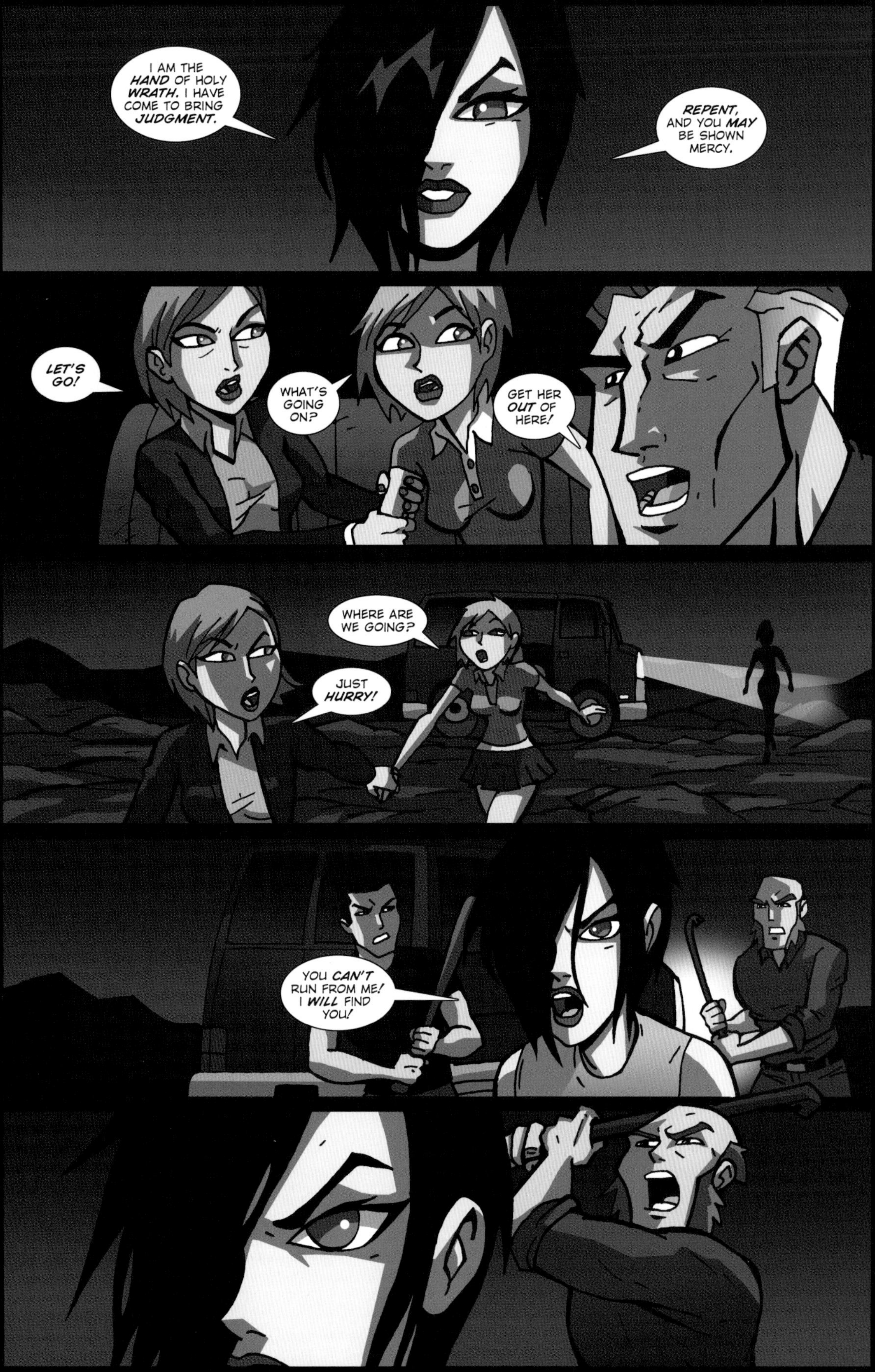
I AM THE **HAND** OF HOLY **WRATH**. I HAVE COME TO BRING **JUDGMENT**.
REPENT, AND YOU **MAY** BE SHOWN MERCY.
LET'S GO!
WHAT'S GOING ON?
GET HER *OUT* OF HERE!
WHERE ARE WE GOING?
JUST *HURRY!*
YOU *CAN'T* RUN FROM ME! I *WILL* FIND YOU!

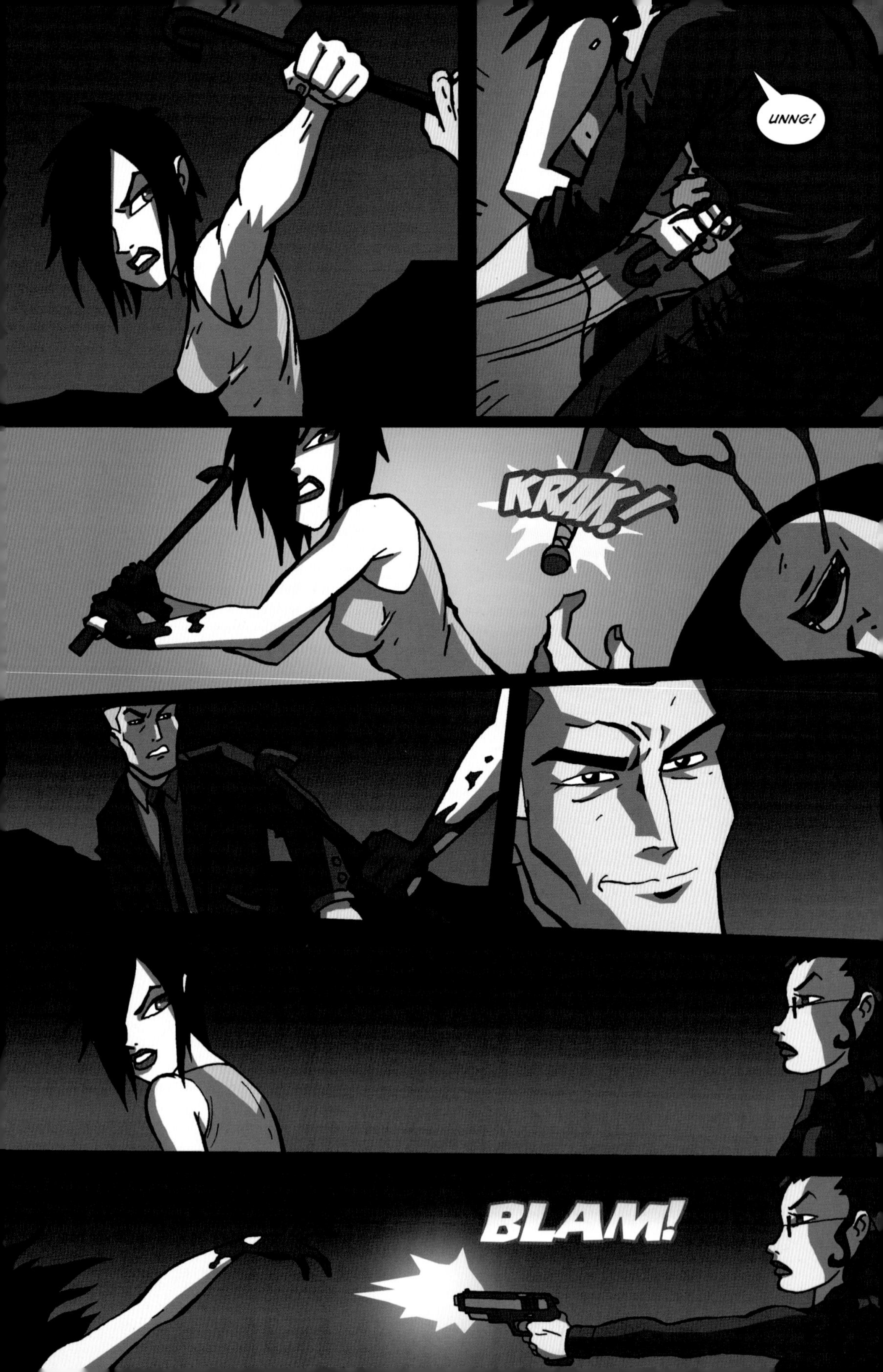
UNNG!
KRAK!
BLAM!

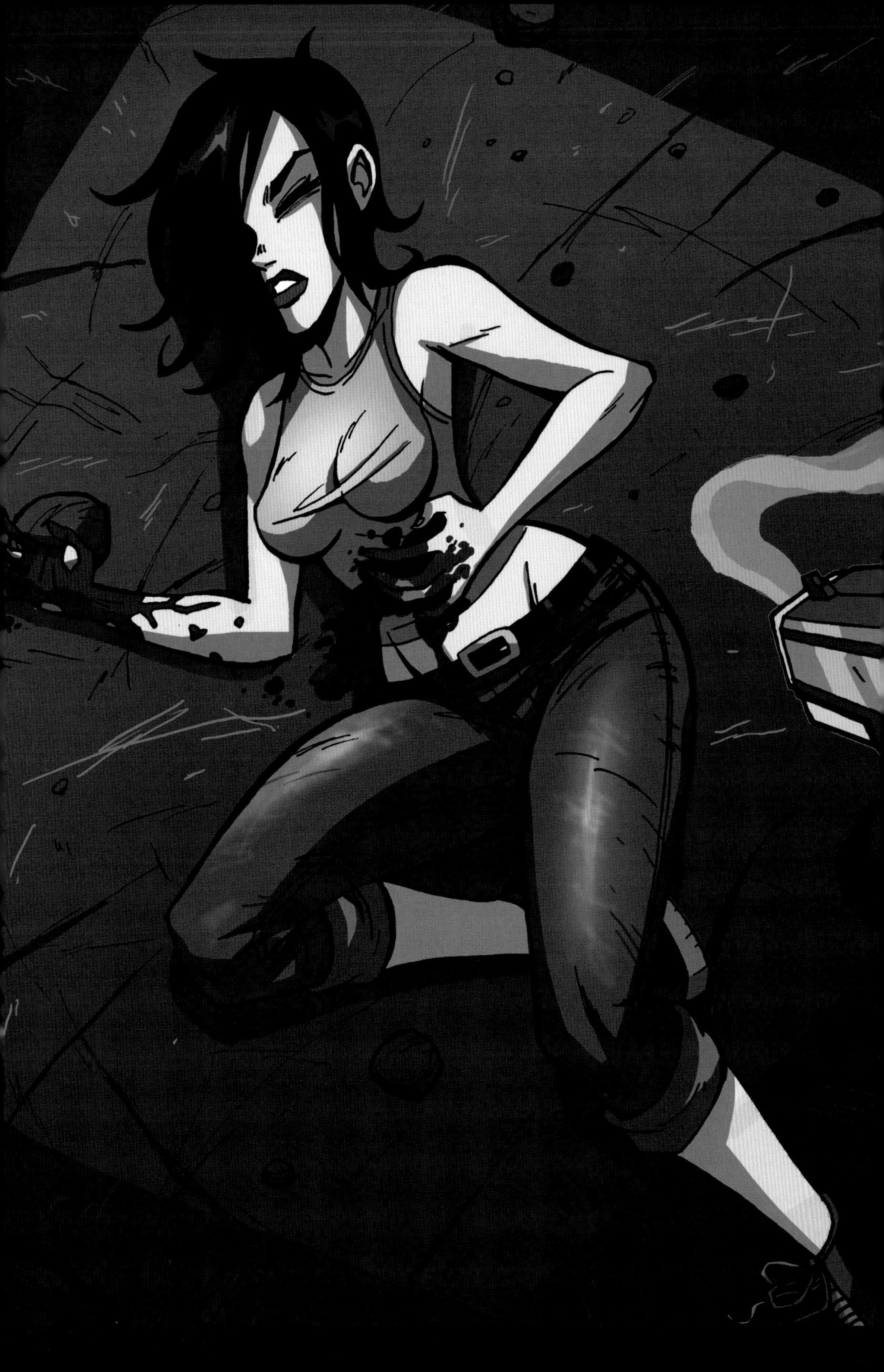

chapter 6

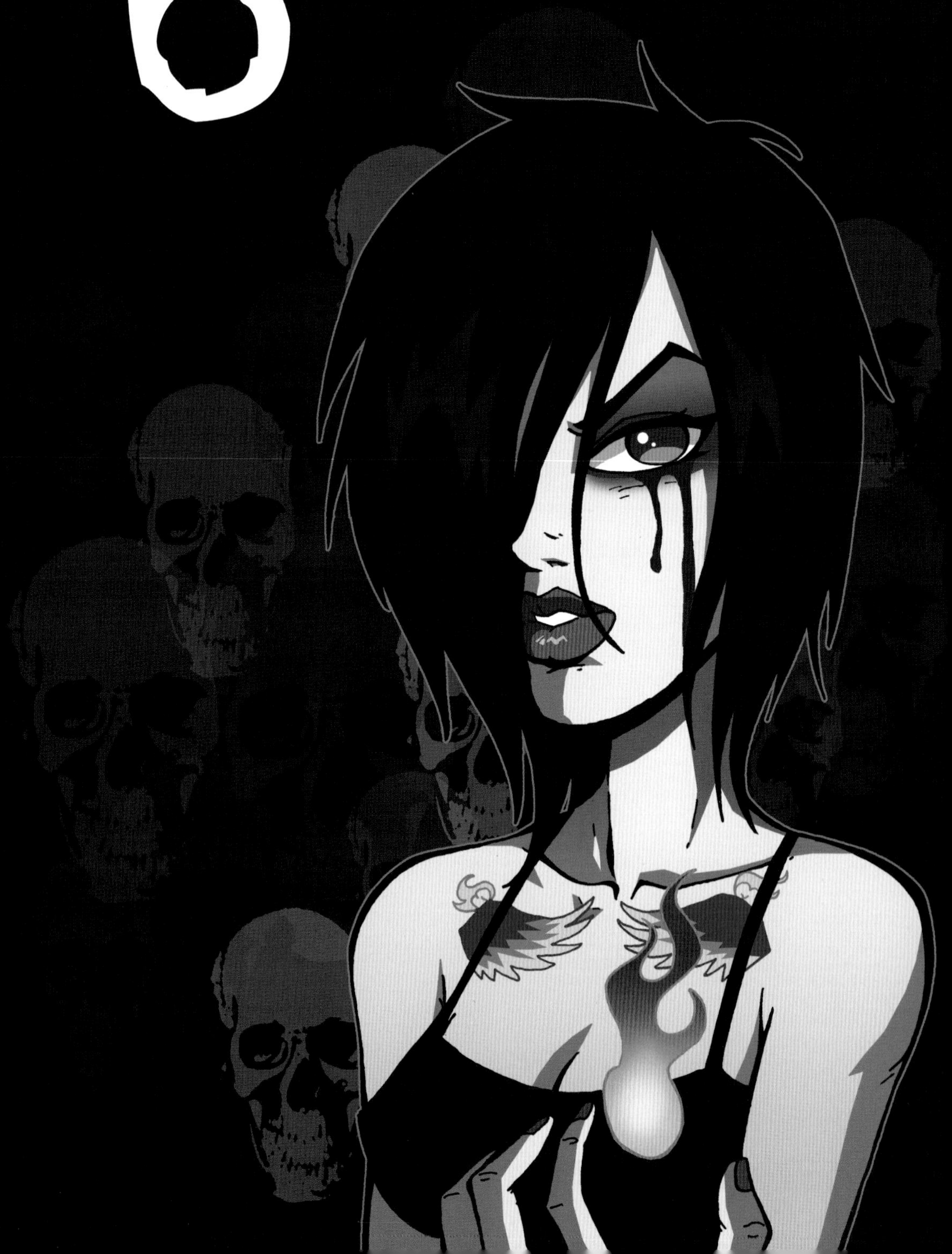

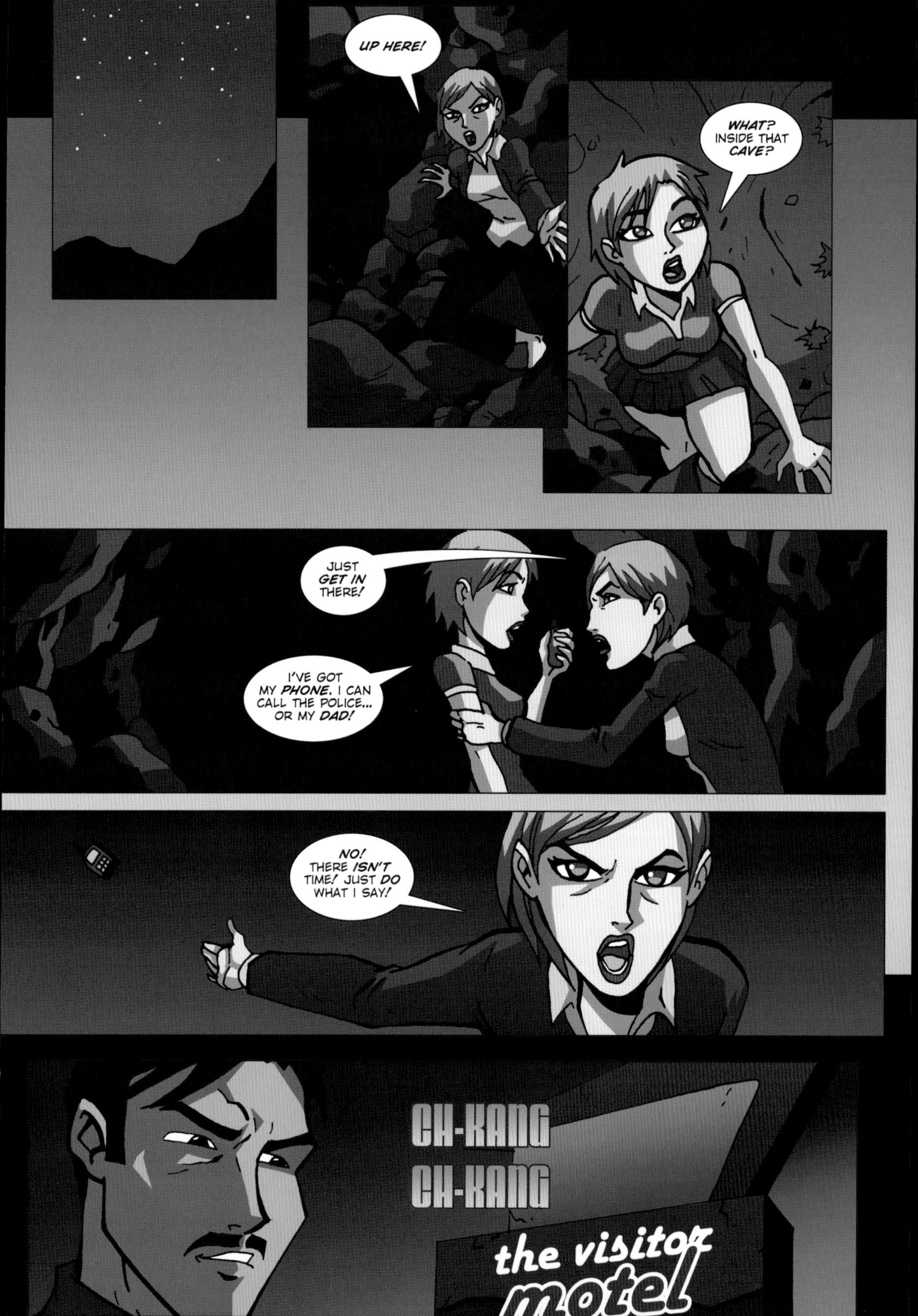
UP HERE!
WHAT? INSIDE THAT CAVE?
JUST GET IN THERE!
I'VE GOT MY PHONE. I CAN CALL THE POLICE... OR MY DAD!
NO! THERE ISN'T TIME! JUST DO WHAT I SAY!
CH-KANG
CH-KANG
the visitor motel

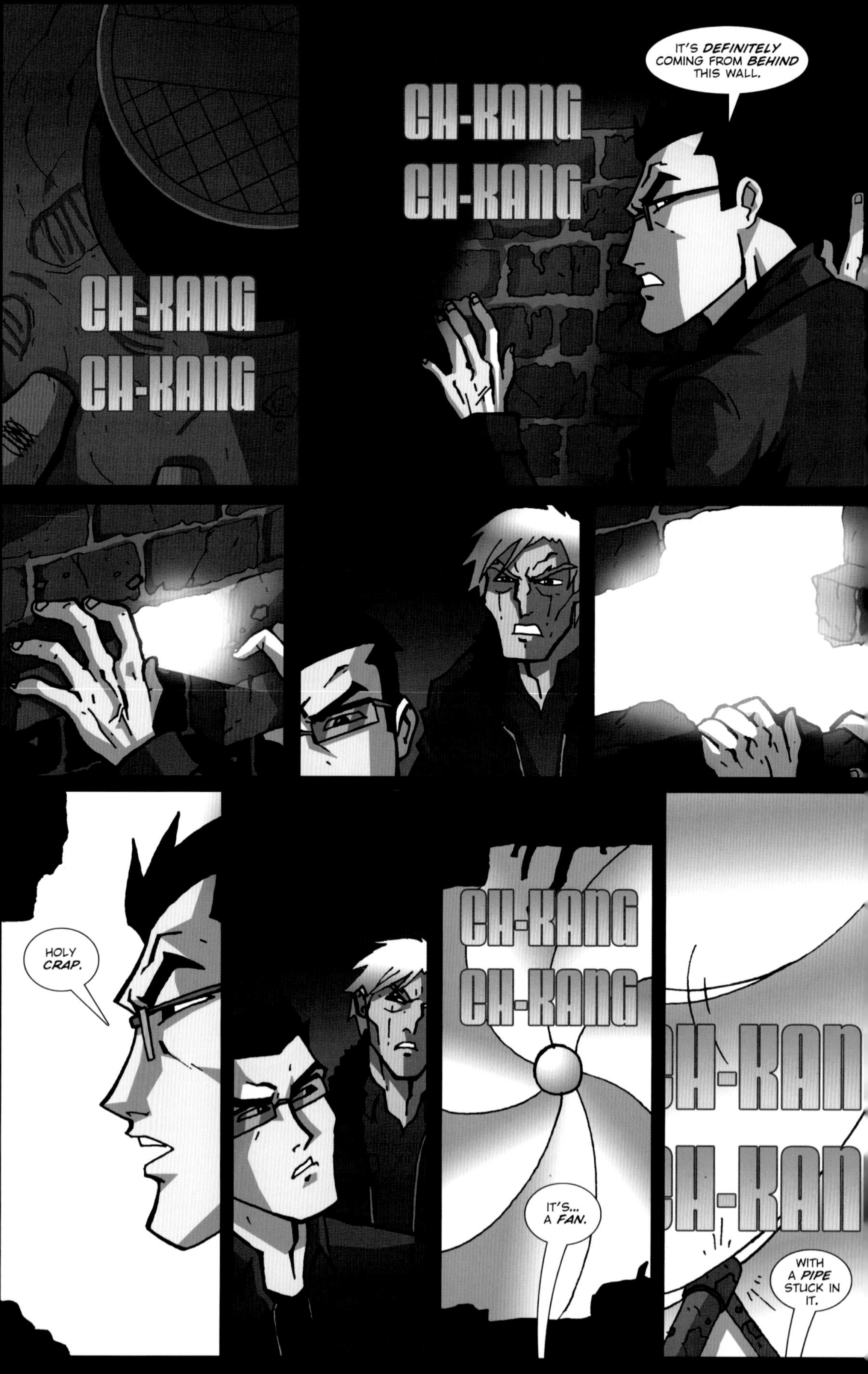
CH-KANG
CH-KANG
CH-KANG
CH-KANG
IT'S *DEFINITELY* COMING FROM *BEHIND* THIS WALL.
HOLY *CRAP.*
CH-KANG
CH-KANG
IT'S... A *FAN.*
CH-KAN
CH-KAN
WITH A *PIPE* STUCK IN IT.

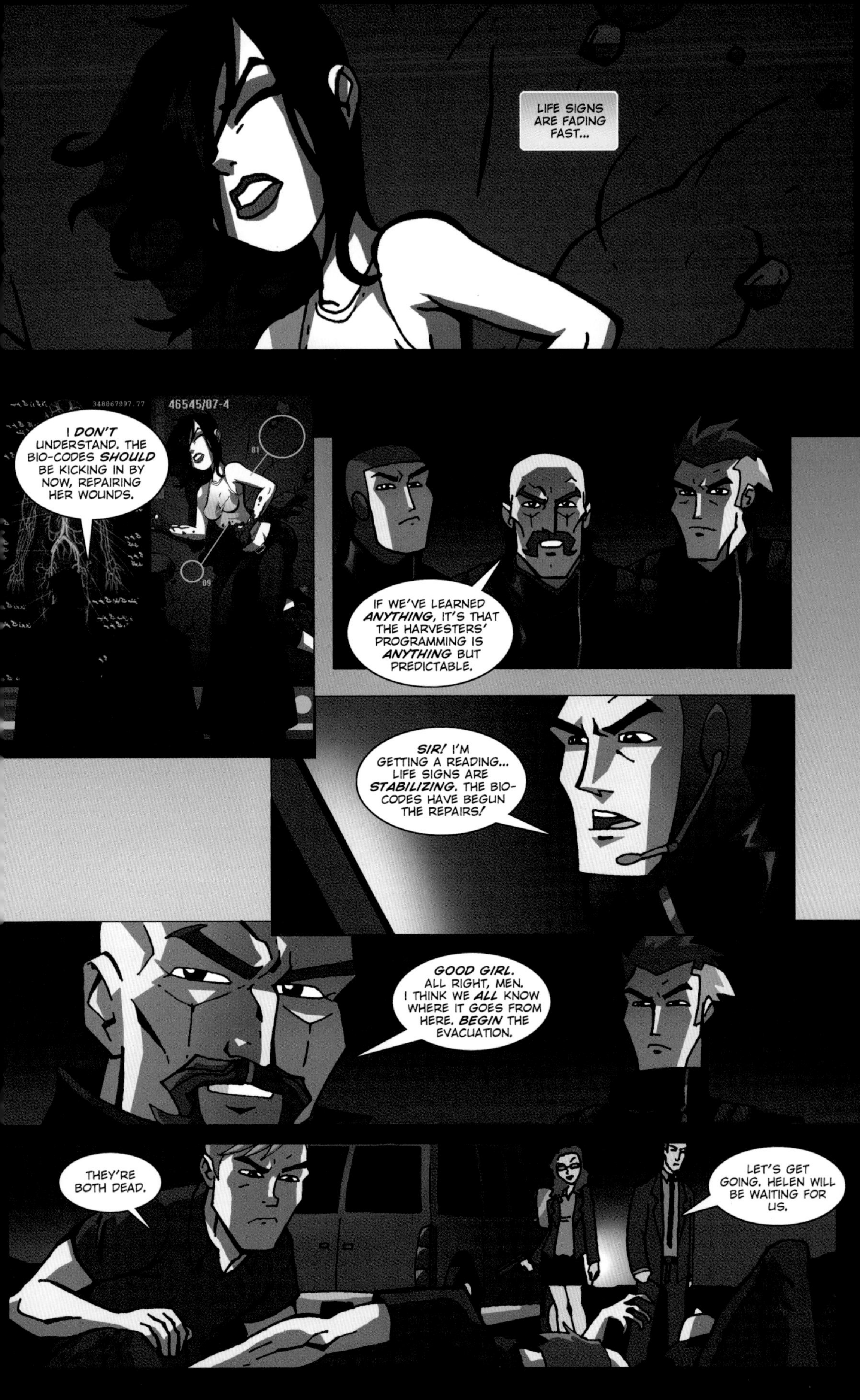
LIFE SIGNS ARE FADING FAST...
348867997.77
46545/07-4
I DON'T UNDERSTAND. THE BIO-CODES SHOULD BE KICKING IN BY NOW, REPAIRING HER WOUNDS.
IF WE'VE LEARNED ANYTHING, IT'S THAT THE HARVESTERS' PROGRAMMING IS ANYTHING BUT PREDICTABLE.
SIR! I'M GETTING A READING... LIFE SIGNS ARE STABILIZING. THE BIO-CODES HAVE BEGUN THE REPAIRS!
GOOD GIRL. ALL RIGHT, MEN. I THINK WE ALL KNOW WHERE IT GOES FROM HERE. BEGIN THE EVACUATION.
THEY'RE BOTH DEAD.
LET'S GET GOING. HELEN WILL BE WAITING FOR US.

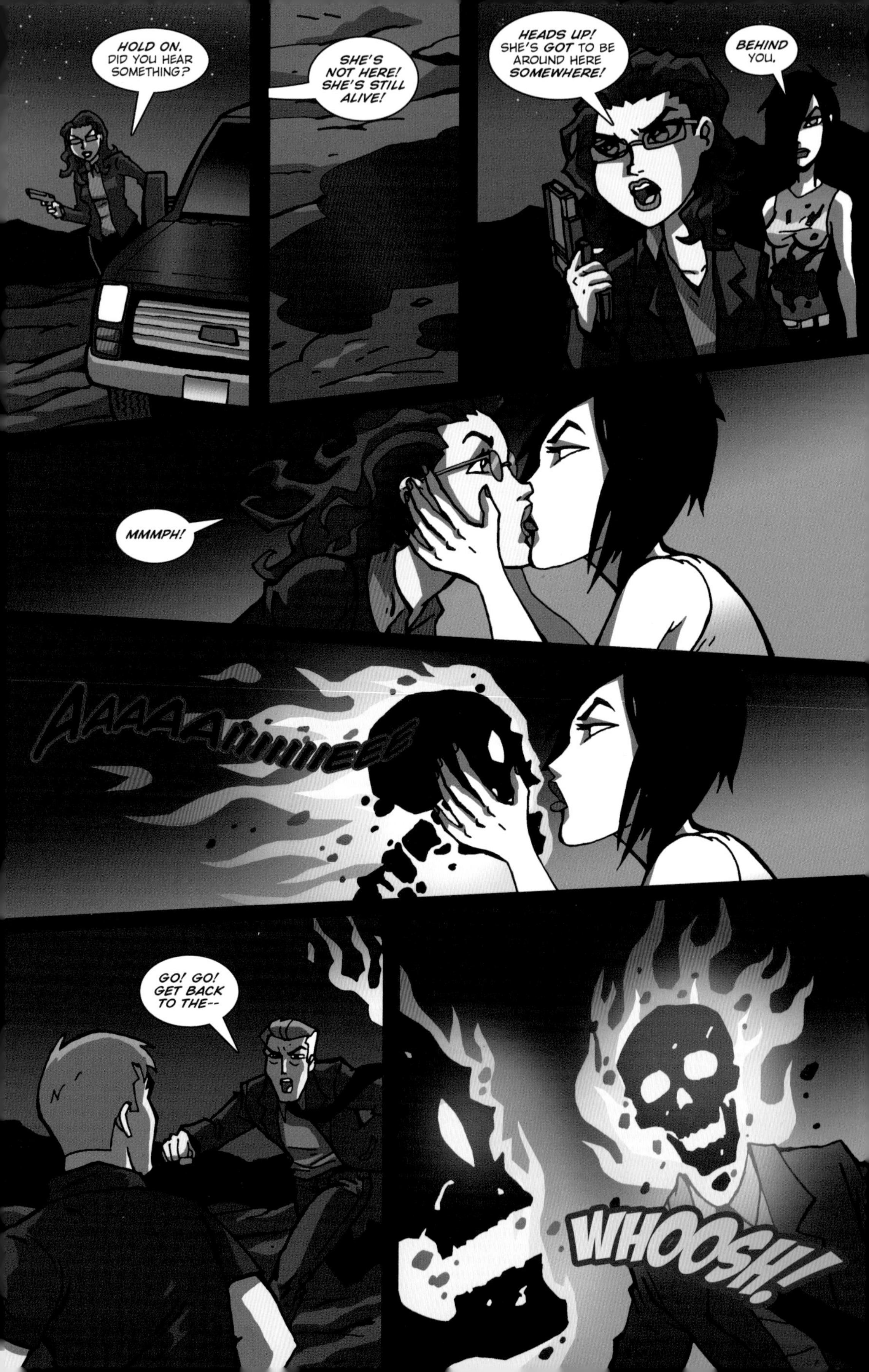
HOLD ON. DID YOU HEAR SOMETHING?
SHE'S NOT HERE! SHE'S STILL ALIVE!
HEADS UP! SHE'S GOT TO BE AROUND HERE SOMEWHERE!
BEHIND YOU.
MMMPH!
AAAAAIIIIIIIEEE
GO! GO! GET BACK TO THE--
WHOOSH!!

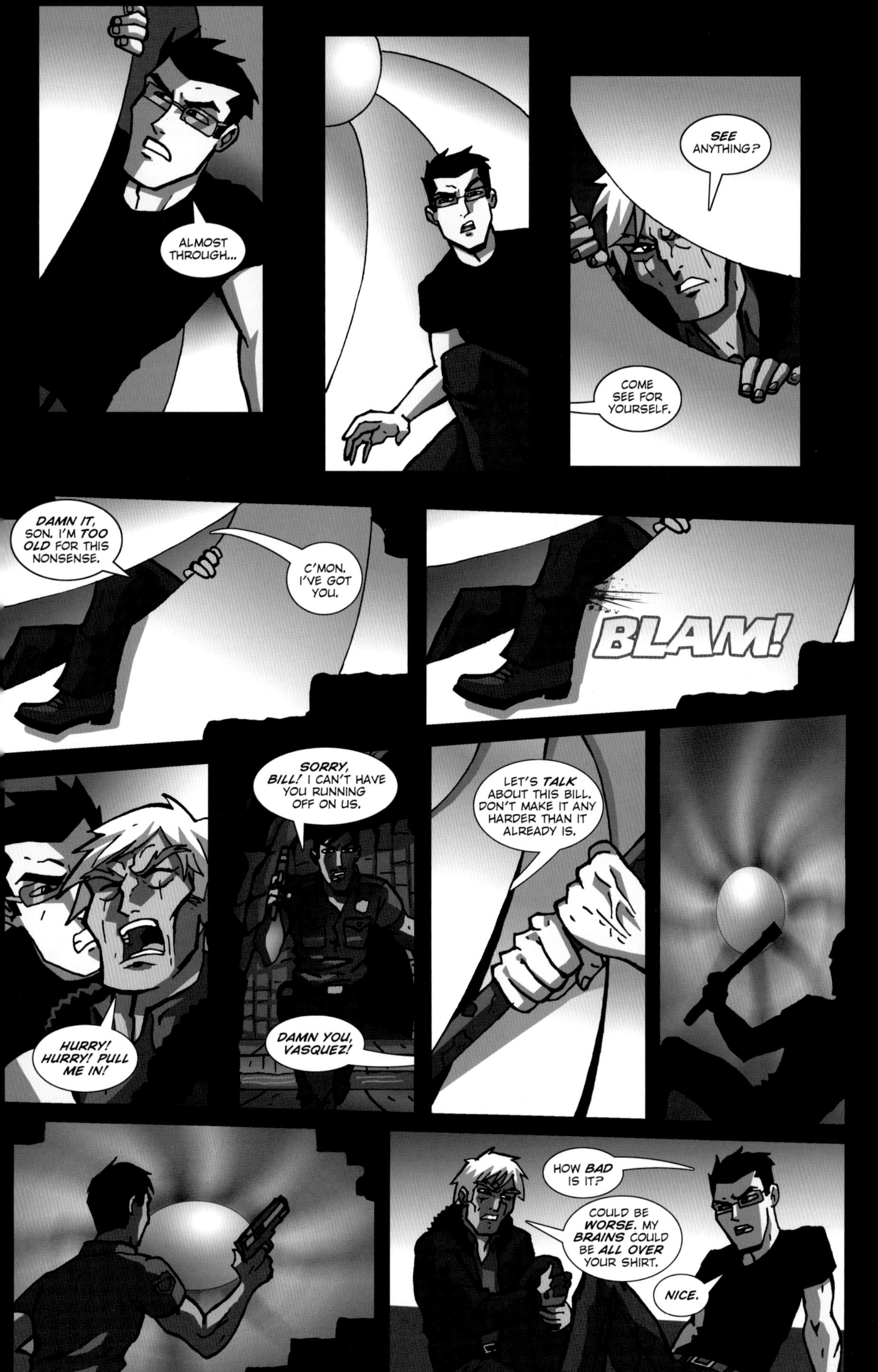
ALMOST THROUGH...
SEE ANYTHING?
COME SEE FOR YOURSELF.
DAMN IT, SON. I'M TOO OLD FOR THIS NONSENSE.
C'MON. I'VE GOT YOU.
BLAM!
HURRY! HURRY! PULL ME IN!
SORRY, BILL! I CAN'T HAVE YOU RUNNING OFF ON US.
DAMN YOU, VASQUEZ!
LET'S TALK ABOUT THIS BILL. DON'T MAKE IT ANY HARDER THAN IT ALREADY IS.
HOW BAD IS IT?
COULD BE WORSE. MY BRAINS COULD BE ALL OVER YOUR SHIRT.
NICE.

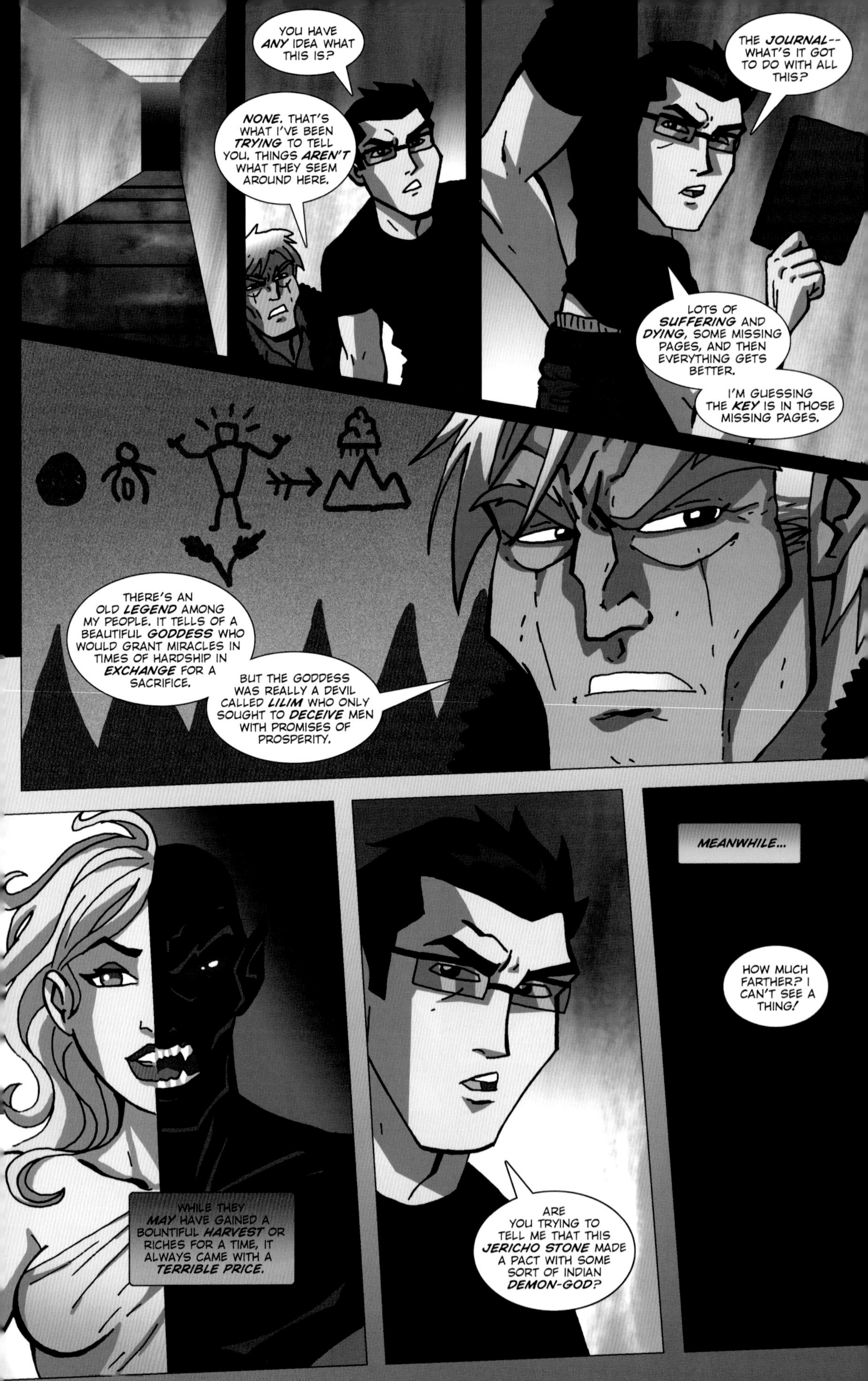
YOU HAVE ANY IDEA WHAT THIS IS?
NONE. THAT'S WHAT I'VE BEEN TRYING TO TELL YOU. THINGS AREN'T WHAT THEY SEEM AROUND HERE.
THE JOURNAL-- WHAT'S IT GOT TO DO WITH ALL THIS?
LOTS OF SUFFERING AND DYING, SOME MISSING PAGES, AND THEN EVERYTHING GETS BETTER.
I'M GUESSING THE KEY IS IN THOSE MISSING PAGES.
THERE'S AN OLD LEGEND AMONG MY PEOPLE. IT TELLS OF A BEAUTIFUL GODDESS WHO WOULD GRANT MIRACLES IN TIMES OF HARDSHIP IN EXCHANGE FOR A SACRIFICE.
BUT THE GODDESS WAS REALLY A DEVIL CALLED LILIM WHO ONLY SOUGHT TO DECEIVE MEN WITH PROMISES OF PROSPERITY.
WHILE THEY MAY HAVE GAINED A BOUNTIFUL HARVEST OR RICHES FOR A TIME, IT ALWAYS CAME WITH A TERRIBLE PRICE.
ARE YOU TRYING TO TELL ME THAT THIS JERICHO STONE MADE A PACT WITH SOME SORT OF INDIAN DEMON-GOD?
MEANWHILE...
HOW MUCH FARTHER? I CAN'T SEE A THING!

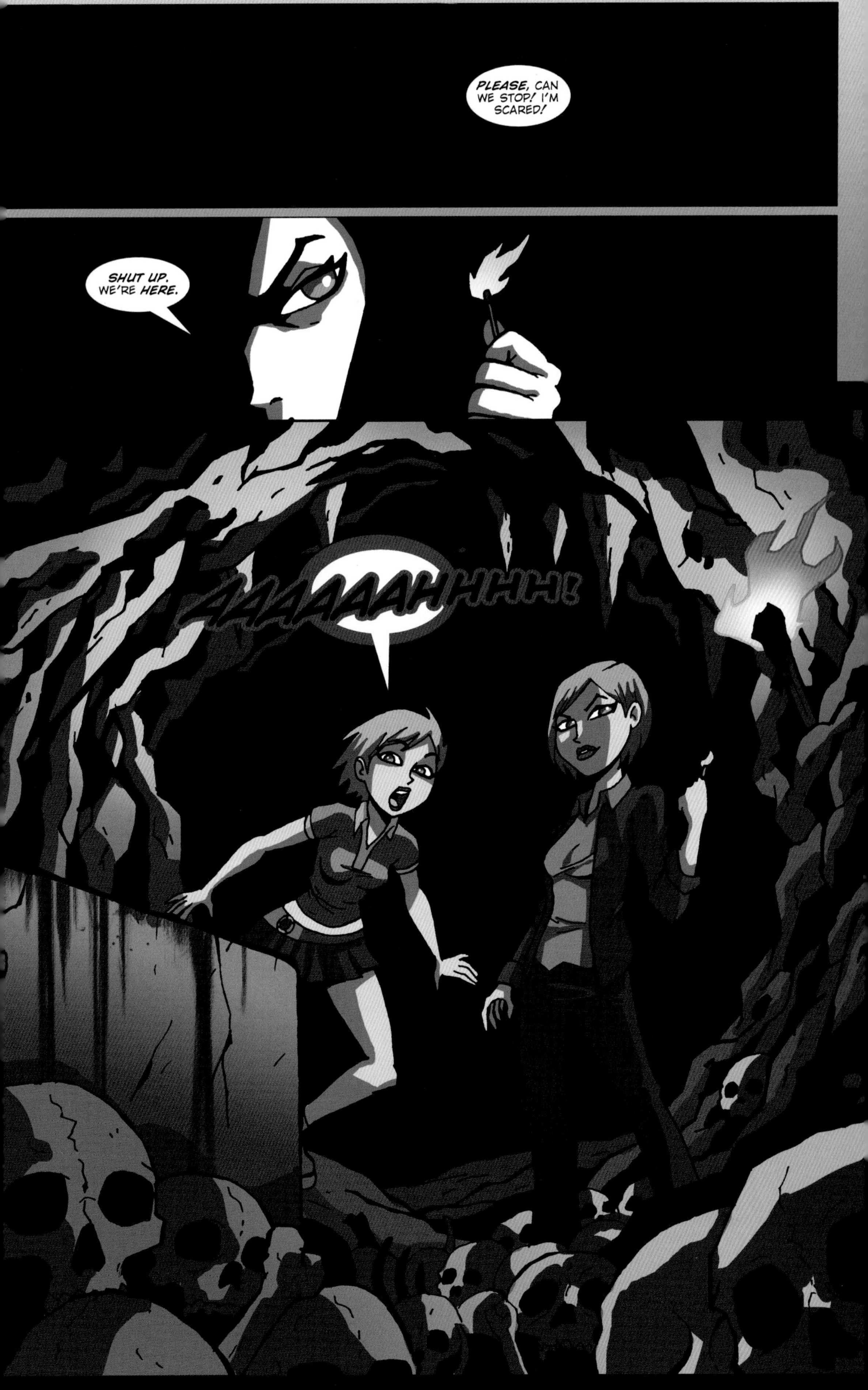
PLEASE, CAN WE STOP! I'M SCARED!
SHUT UP. WE'RE HERE.
AAAAAAHHHHH!

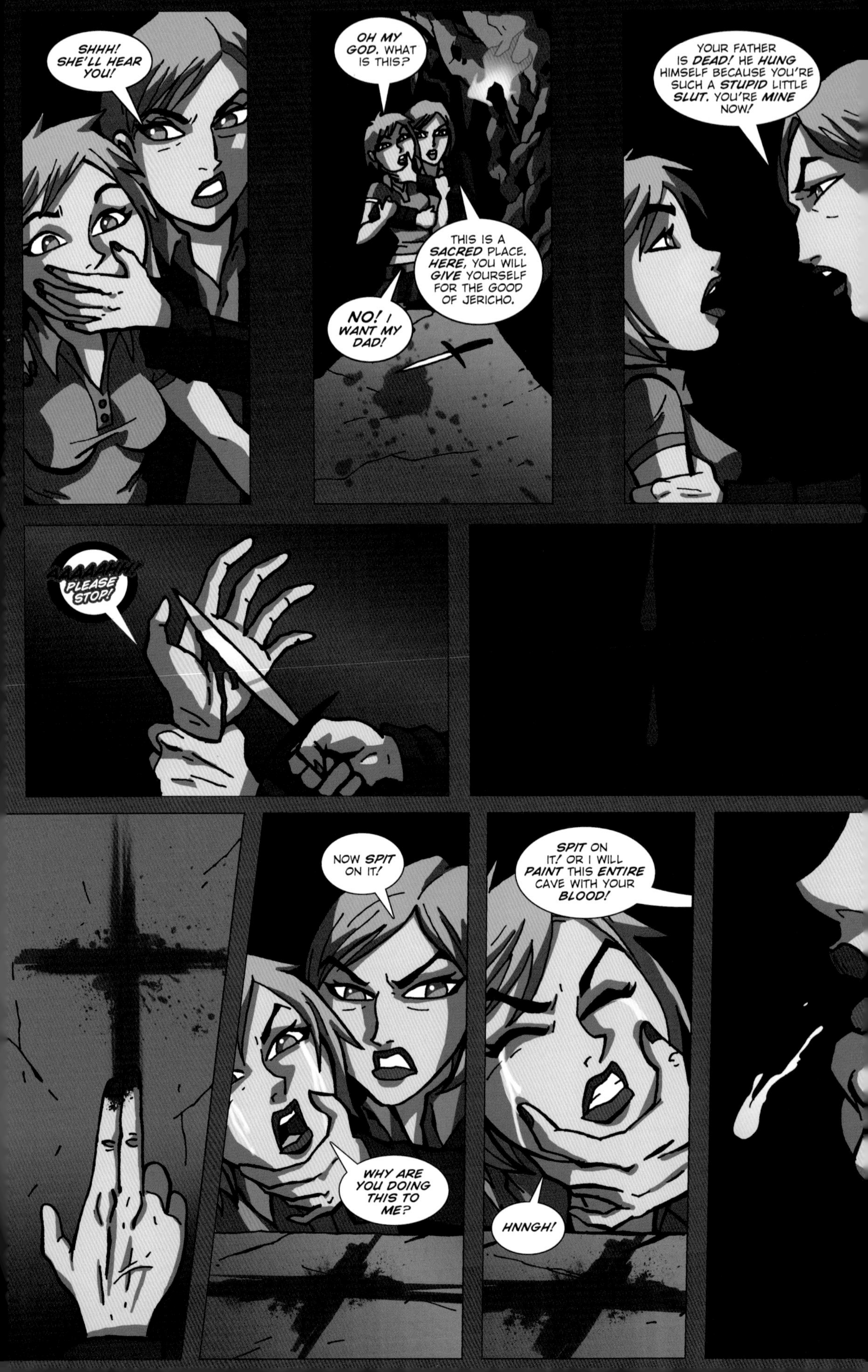
SHHH! SHE'LL HEAR YOU!
OH MY GOD. WHAT IS THIS?
THIS IS A SACRED PLACE. HERE, YOU WILL GIVE YOURSELF FOR THE GOOD OF JERICHO.
NO! I WANT MY DAD!
YOUR FATHER IS DEAD! HE HUNG HIMSELF BECAUSE YOU'RE SUCH A STUPID LITTLE SLUT. YOU'RE MINE NOW!
PLEASE STOP!
NOW SPIT ON IT!
WHY ARE YOU DOING THIS TO ME?
SPIT ON IT! OR I WILL PAINT THIS ENTIRE CAVE WITH YOUR BLOOD!
HNNGH!

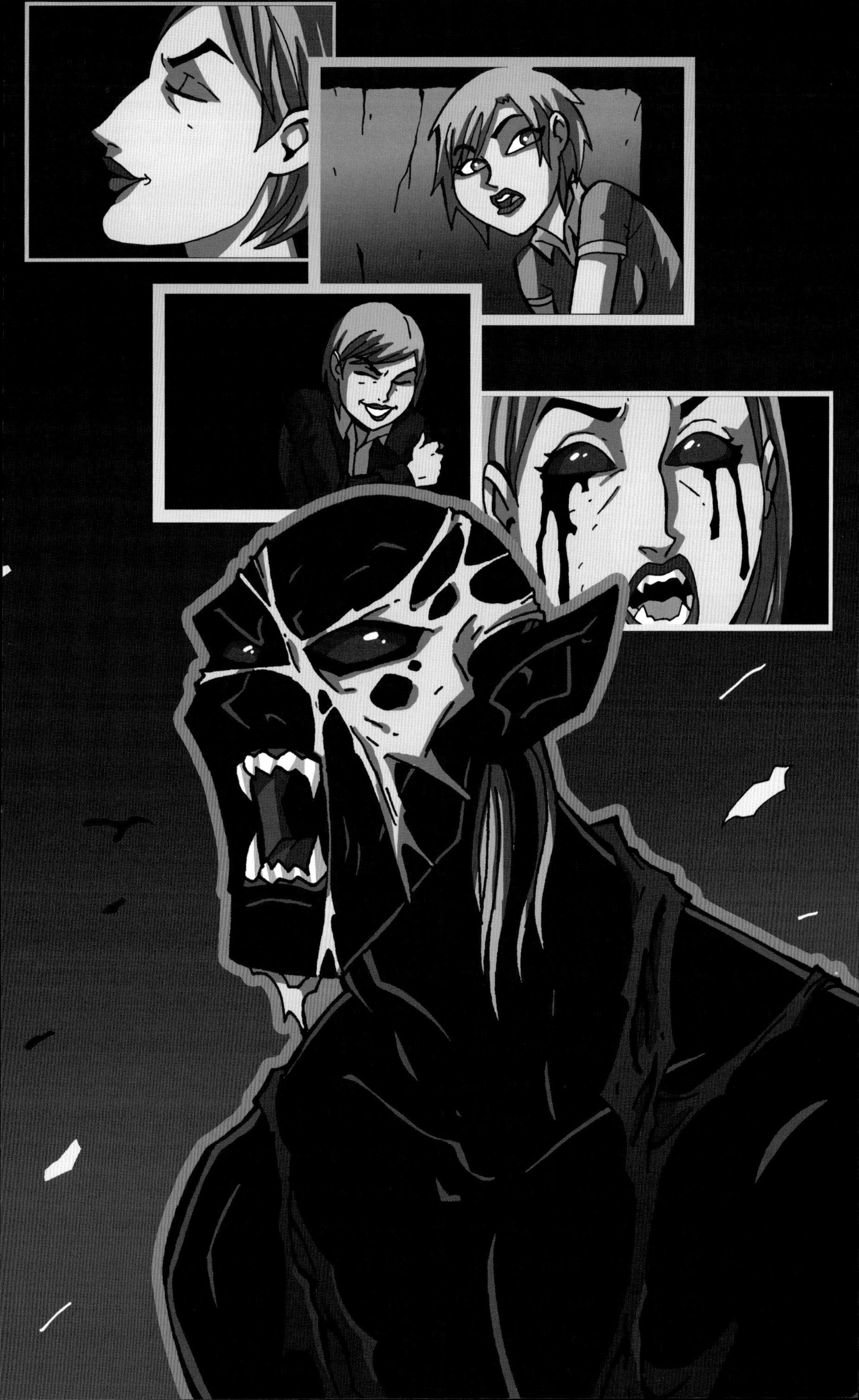

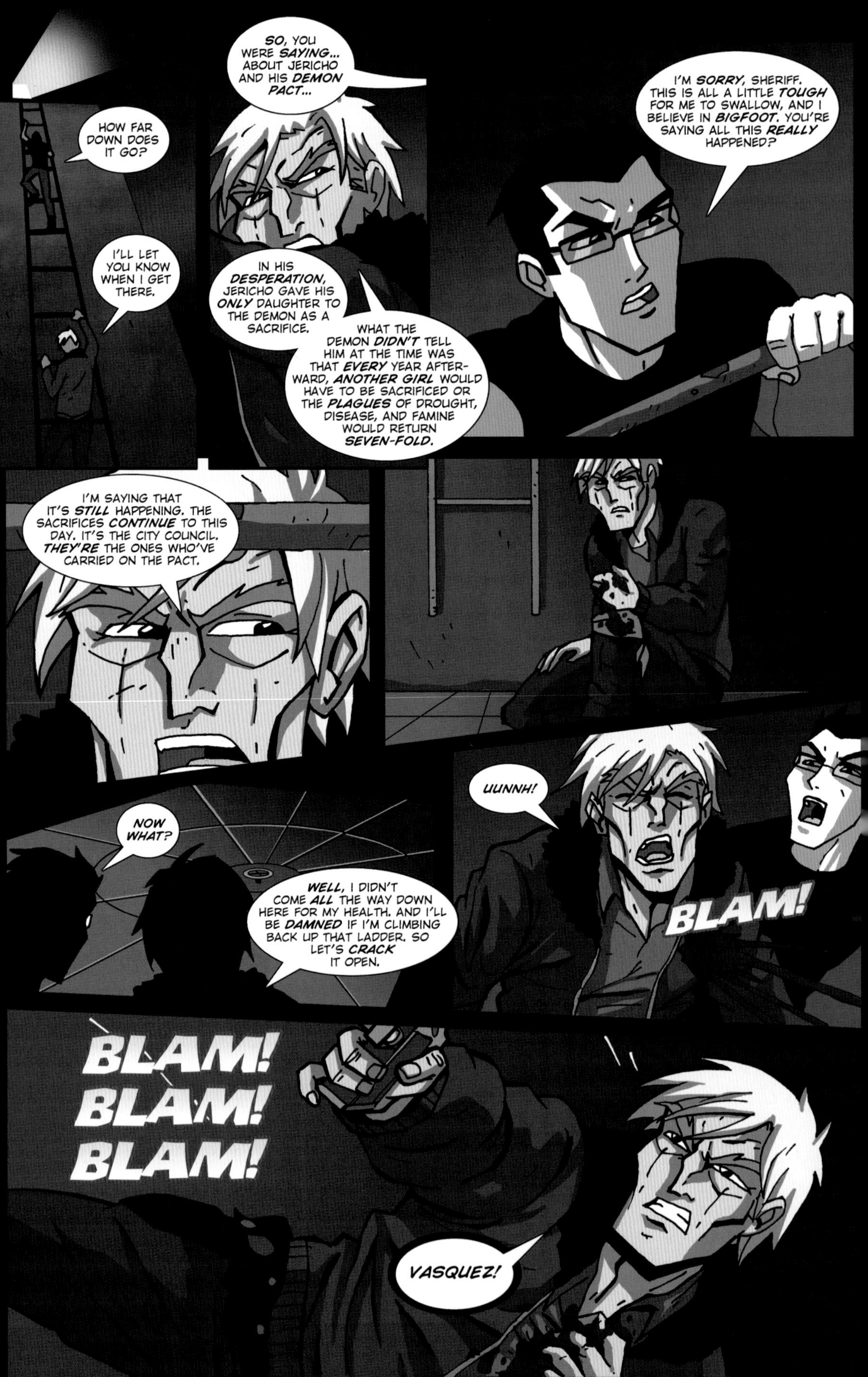
HOW FAR DOWN DOES IT GO?
I'LL LET YOU KNOW WHEN I GET THERE.
SO, YOU WERE SAYING... ABOUT JERICHO AND HIS DEMON PACT...
IN HIS DESPERATION, JERICHO GAVE HIS ONLY DAUGHTER TO THE DEMON AS A SACRIFICE.
WHAT THE DEMON DIDN'T TELL HIM AT THE TIME WAS THAT EVERY YEAR AFTER-WARD, ANOTHER GIRL WOULD HAVE TO BE SACRIFICED OR THE PLAGUES OF DROUGHT, DISEASE, AND FAMINE WOULD RETURN SEVEN-FOLD.
I'M SORRY, SHERIFF. THIS IS ALL A LITTLE TOUGH FOR ME TO SWALLOW, AND I BELIEVE IN BIGFOOT. YOU'RE SAYING ALL THIS REALLY HAPPENED?
I'M SAYING THAT IT'S STILL HAPPENING. THE SACRIFICES CONTINUE TO THIS DAY. IT'S THE CITY COUNCIL. THEY'RE THE ONES WHO'VE CARRIED ON THE PACT.
NOW WHAT?
WELL, I DIDN'T COME ALL THE WAY DOWN HERE FOR MY HEALTH. AND I'LL BE DAMNED IF I'M CLIMBING BACK UP THAT LADDER. SO LET'S CRACK IT OPEN.
UUNNH!
BLAM!
BLAM! BLAM! BLAM!
VASQUEZ!

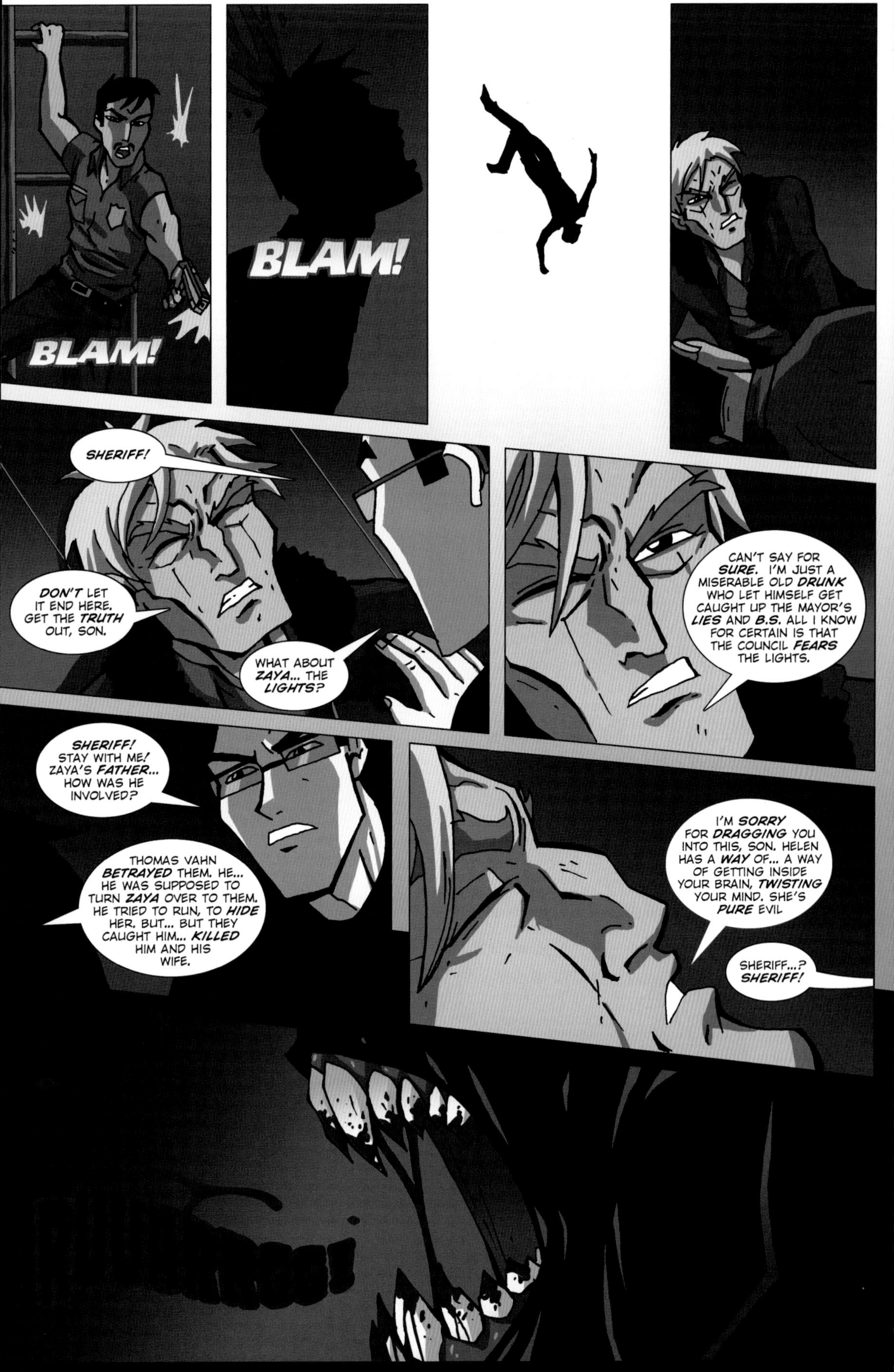
BLAM!
BLAM!
SHERIFF!
DON'T LET IT END HERE. GET THE TRUTH OUT, SON.
WHAT ABOUT ZAYA... THE LIGHTS?
CAN'T SAY FOR SURE. I'M JUST A MISERABLE OLD DRUNK WHO LET HIMSELF GET CAUGHT UP THE MAYOR'S LIES AND B.S. ALL I KNOW FOR CERTAIN IS THAT THE COUNCIL FEARS THE LIGHTS.
SHERIFF! STAY WITH ME! ZAYA'S FATHER... HOW WAS HE INVOLVED?
THOMAS VAHN BETRAYED THEM. HE... HE WAS SUPPOSED TO TURN ZAYA OVER TO THEM. HE TRIED TO RUN, TO HIDE HER. BUT... BUT THEY CAUGHT HIM... KILLED HIM AND HIS WIFE.
I'M SORRY FOR DRAGGING YOU INTO THIS, SON. HELEN HAS A WAY OF... A WAY OF GETTING INSIDE YOUR BRAIN, TWISTING YOUR MIND. SHE'S PURE EVIL
SHERIFF...? SHERIFF!

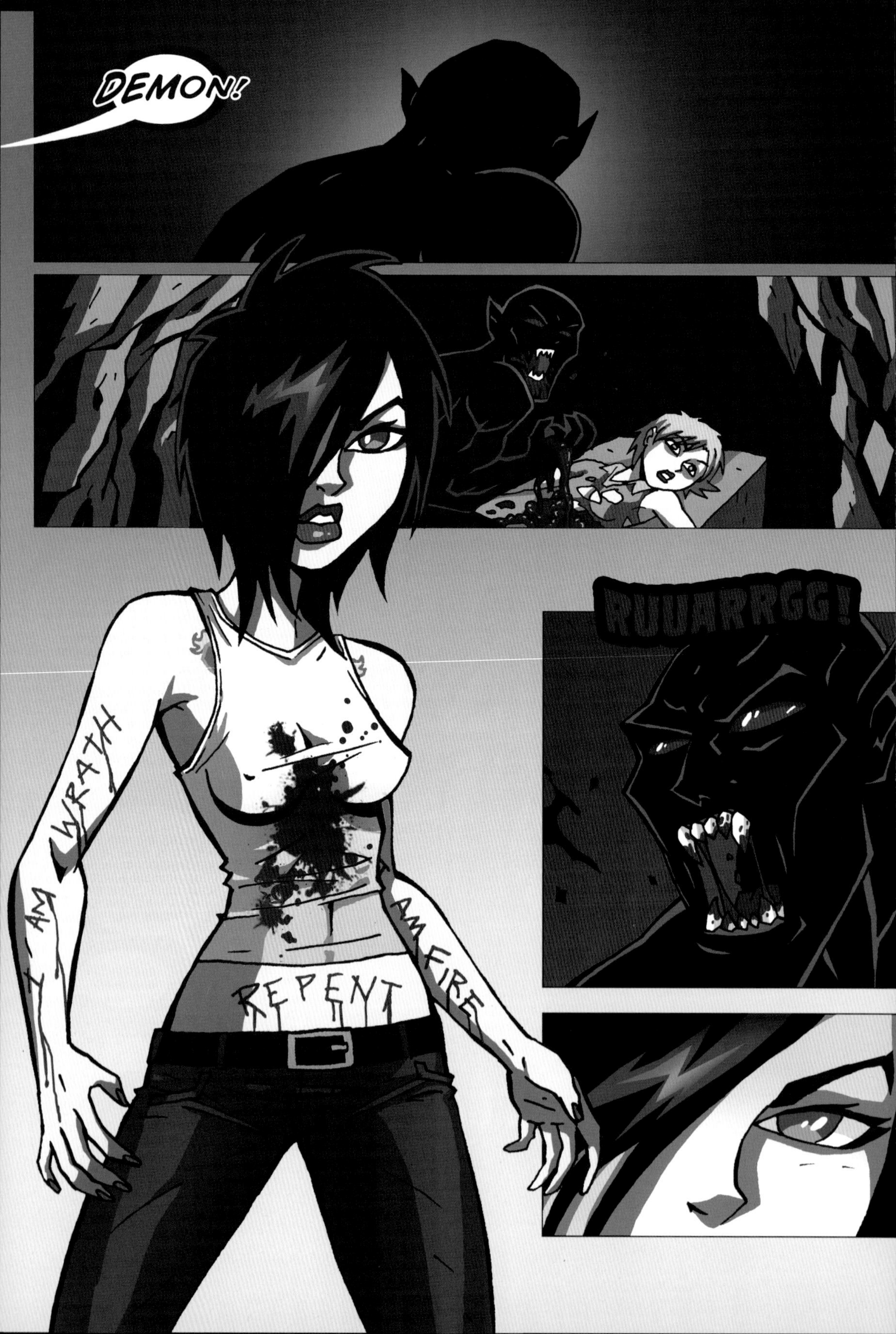
DEMON!
I AM WRATH
I AM FIRE
REPENT
RUUARRGG!

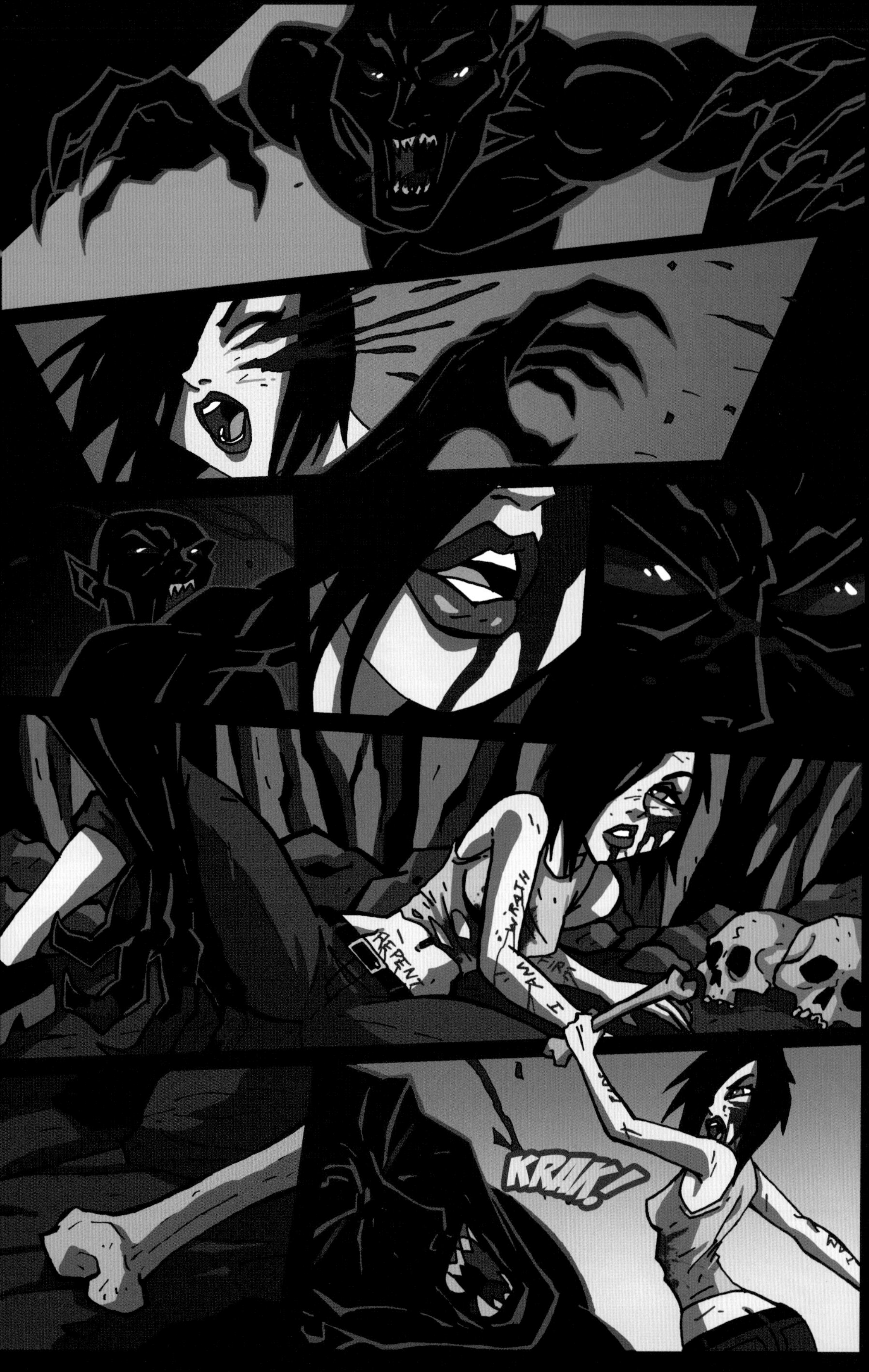
REPENT
WRATH
FIRE
KRAK!

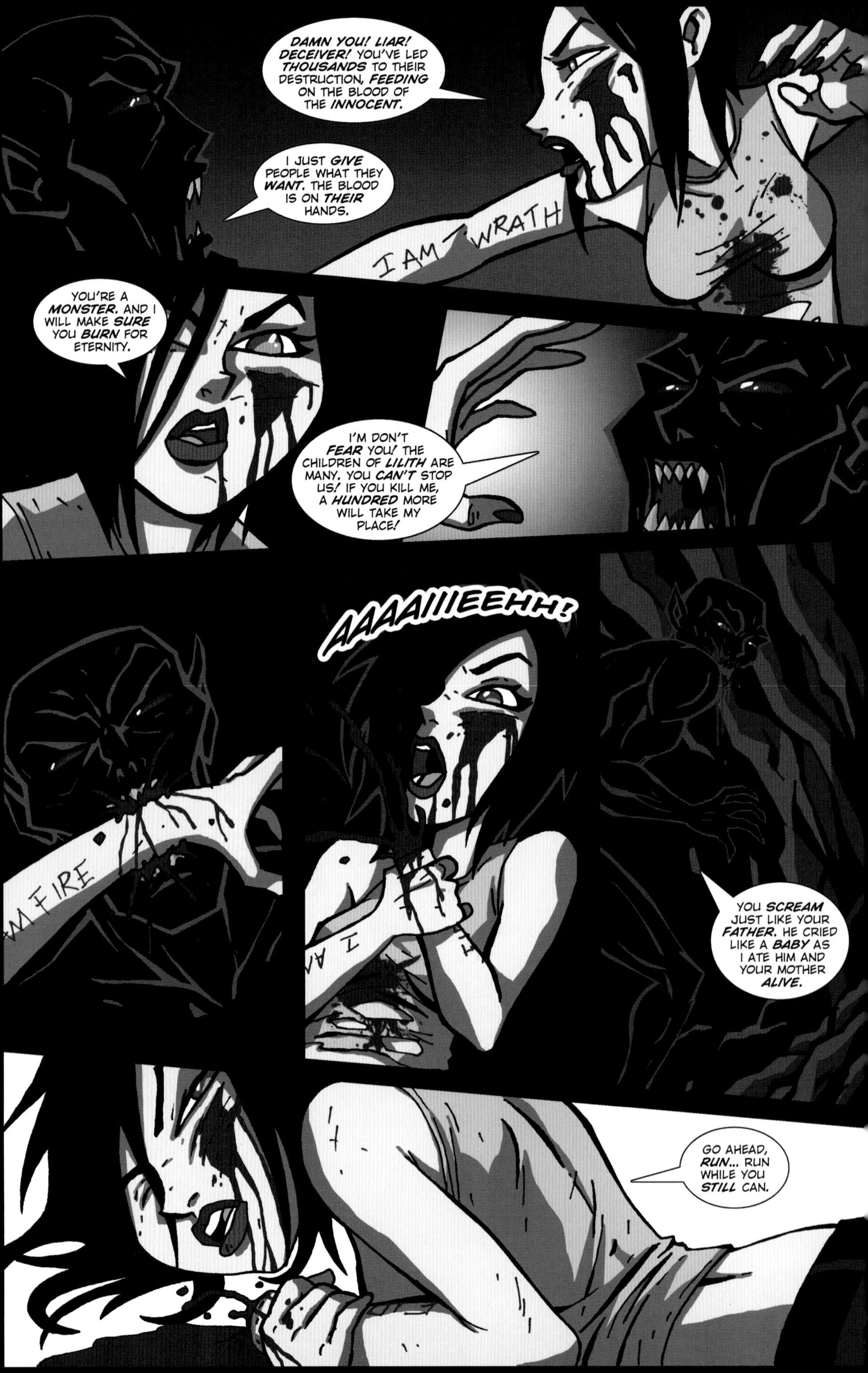
DAMN YOU! LIAR! DECEIVER! YOU'VE LED THOUSANDS TO THEIR DESTRUCTION, FEEDING ON THE BLOOD OF THE INNOCENT.
I JUST GIVE PEOPLE WHAT THEY WANT. THE BLOOD IS ON THEIR HANDS.
I AM WRATH
YOU'RE A MONSTER. AND I WILL MAKE SURE YOU BURN FOR ETERNITY.
I'M DON'T FEAR YOU! THE CHILDREN OF LILITH ARE MANY. YOU CAN'T STOP US! IF YOU KILL ME, A HUNDRED MORE WILL TAKE MY PLACE!
AAAAIIIEEHH!
M FIRE
YOU SCREAM JUST LIKE YOUR FATHER. HE CRIED LIKE A BABY AS I ATE HIM AND YOUR MOTHER ALIVE.
GO AHEAD, RUN... RUN WHILE YOU STILL CAN.

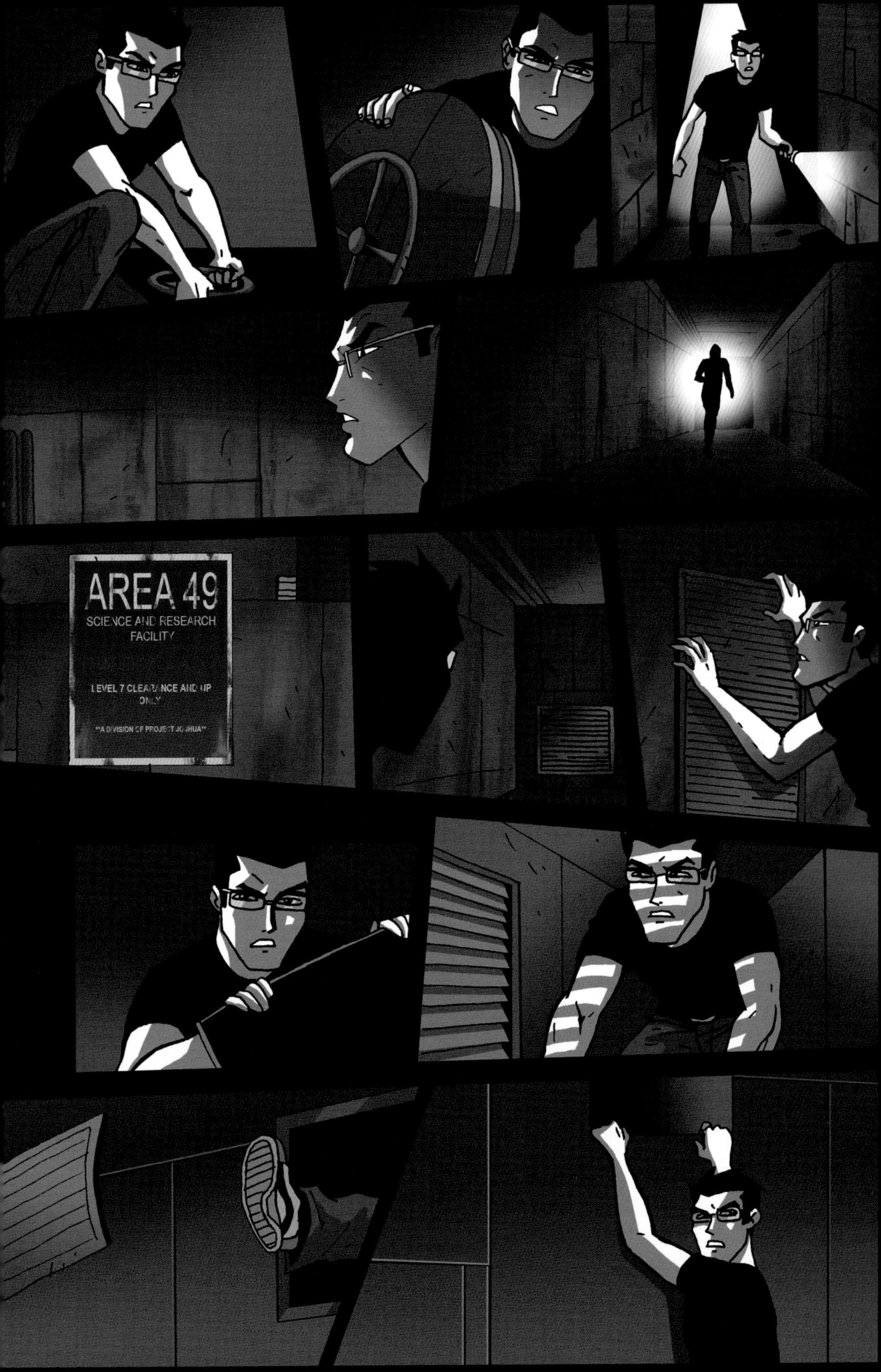
AREA 49
SCIENCE AND RESEARCH FACILITY
LEVEL 7 CLEARANCE AND UP ONLY
A DIVISION OF PROJECT JOSHUA

SUBJECT -
00170048900212000-001
0018924
6546869
0017-X-COVENANT
3900212000-001
LEVELS
0018924
OH, GOD... ZAYA!
I AM WRATH
WRATH

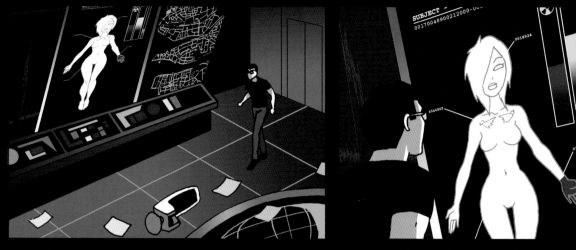

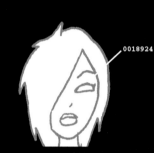

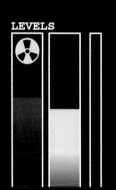

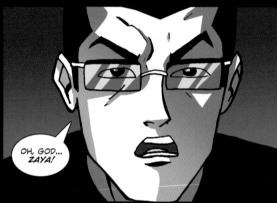

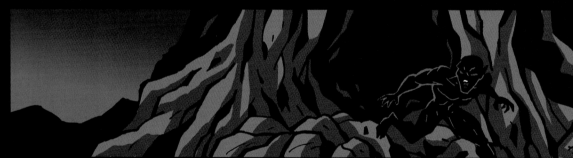

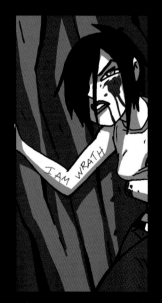

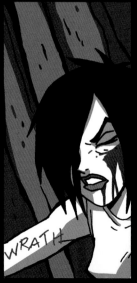

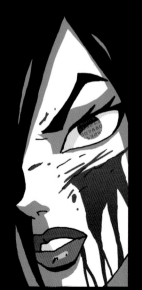

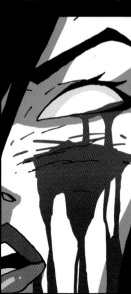

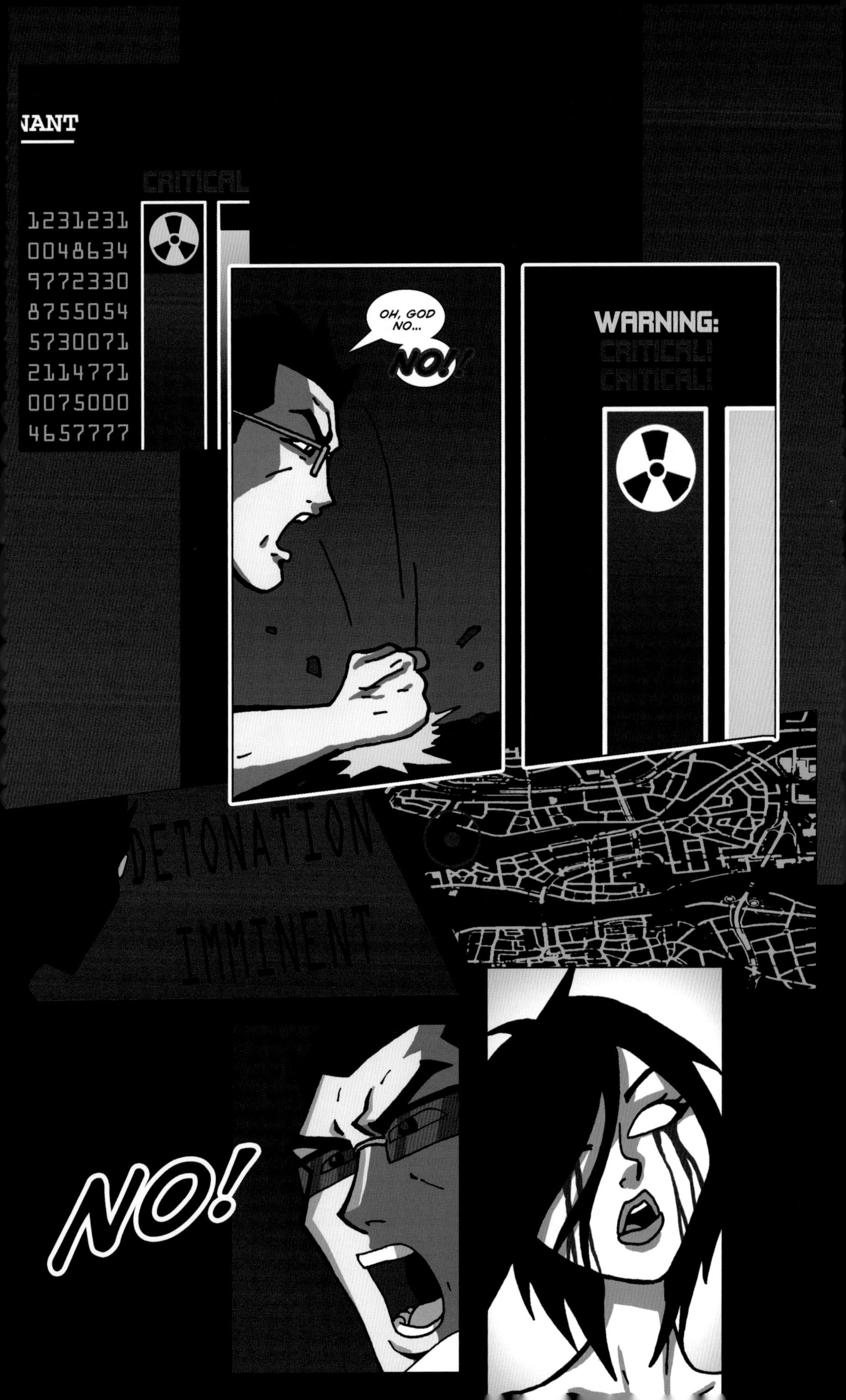
NANT
CRITICAL
1231231
0048634
9772330
8755054
5730071
2114771
0075000
4657777
OH, GOD NO...
NO!!
WARNING:
CRITICAL!
CRITICAL!
DETONATION
IMMINENT
NO!

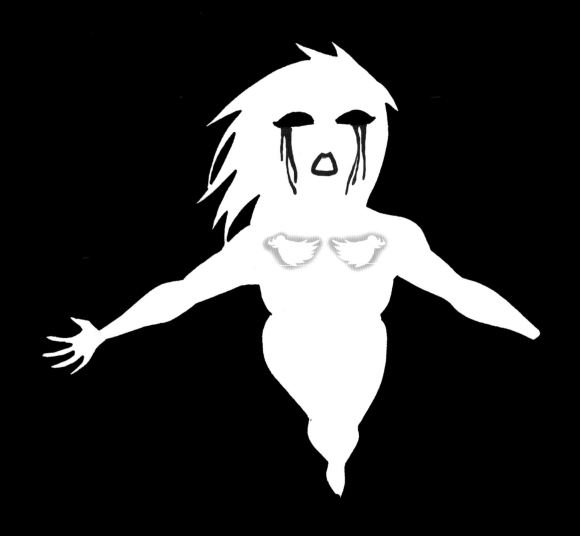

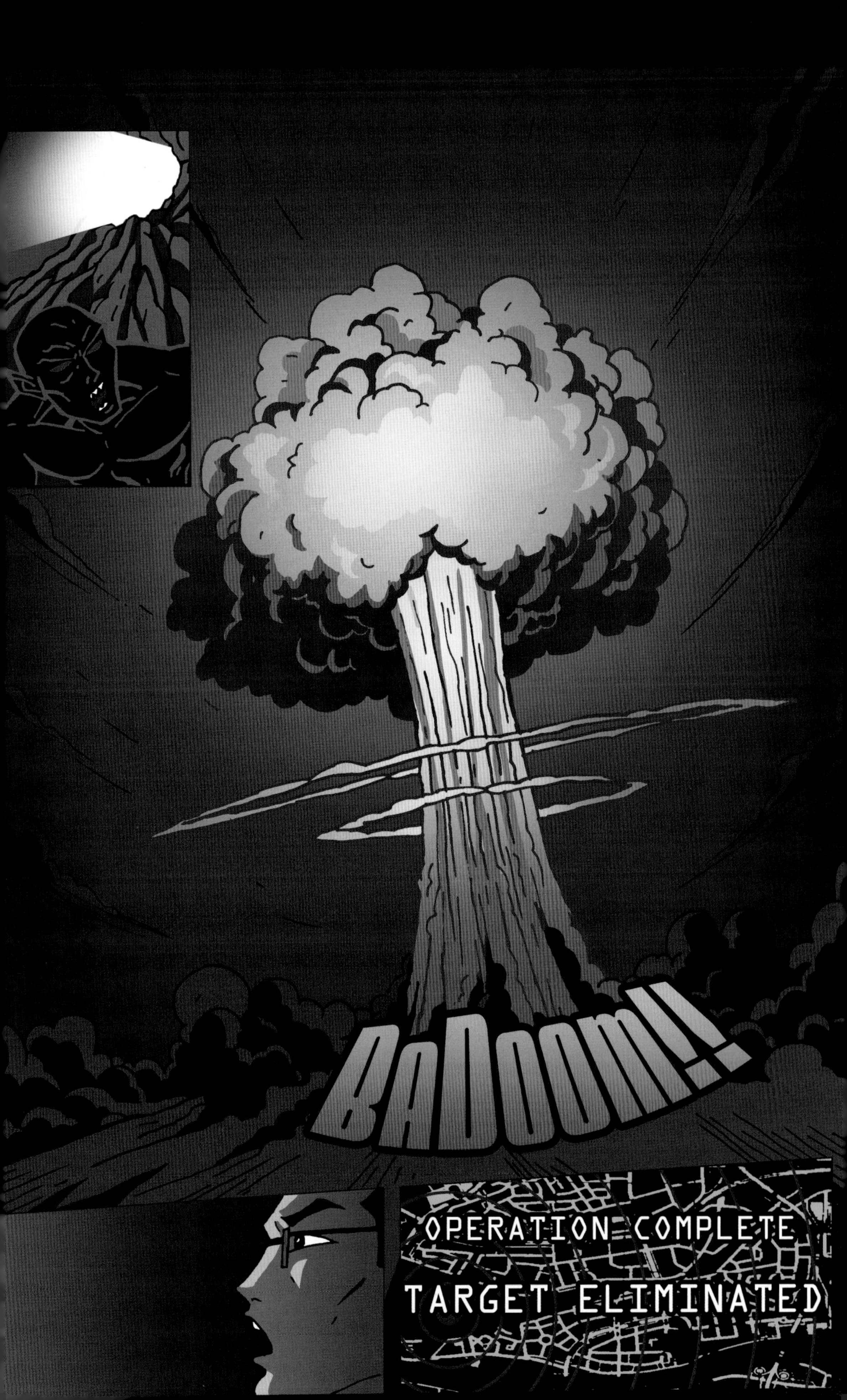
BADOOM!!
OPERATION COMPLETE
TARGET ELIMINATED

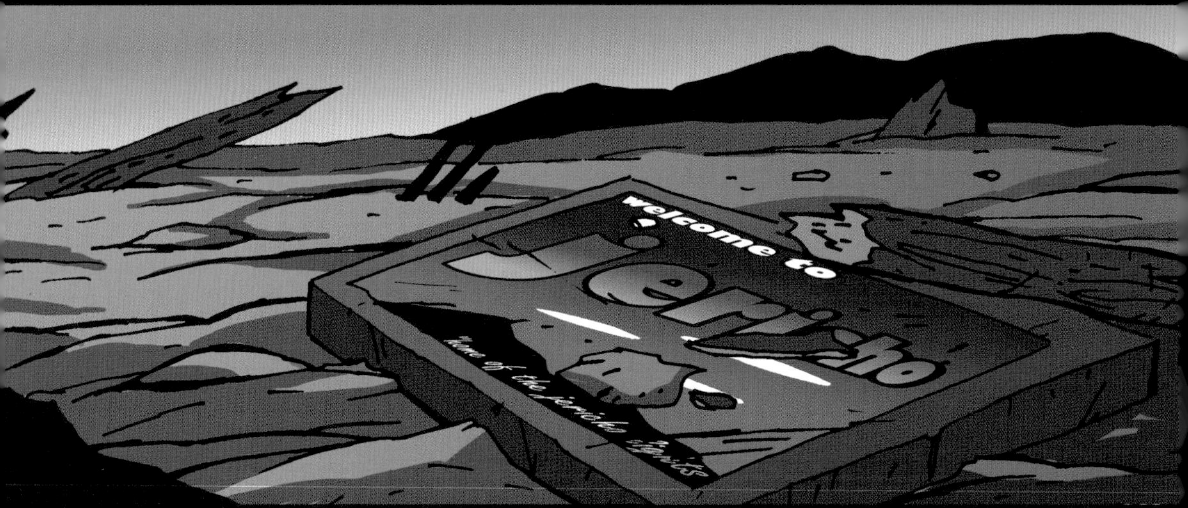
welcome to
home of the jericho spirits

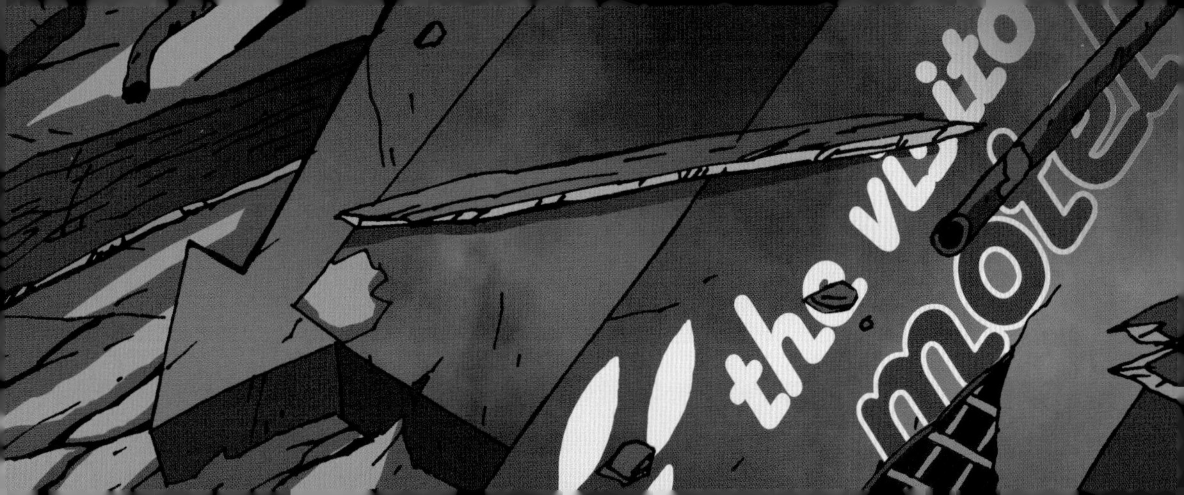
the

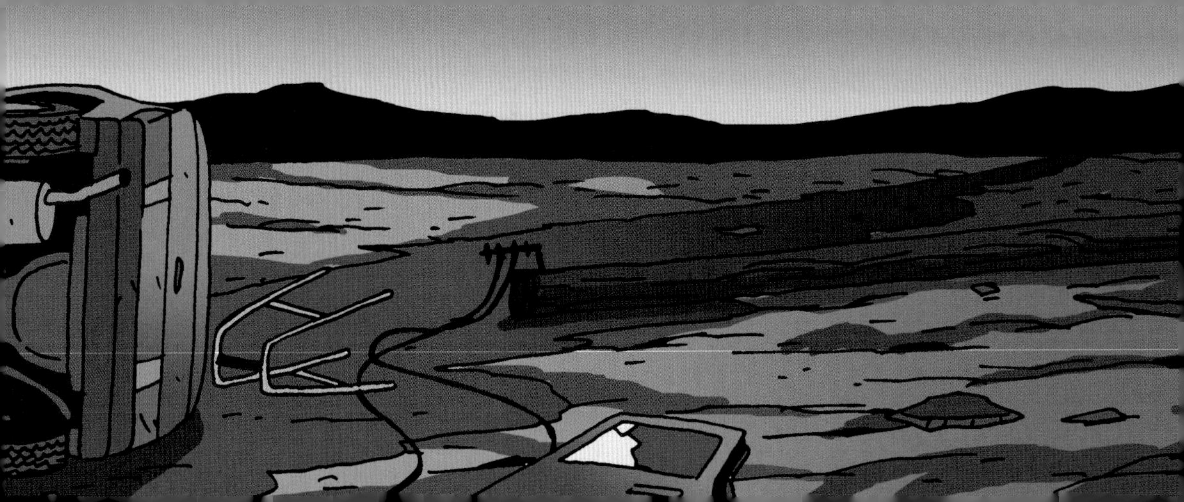

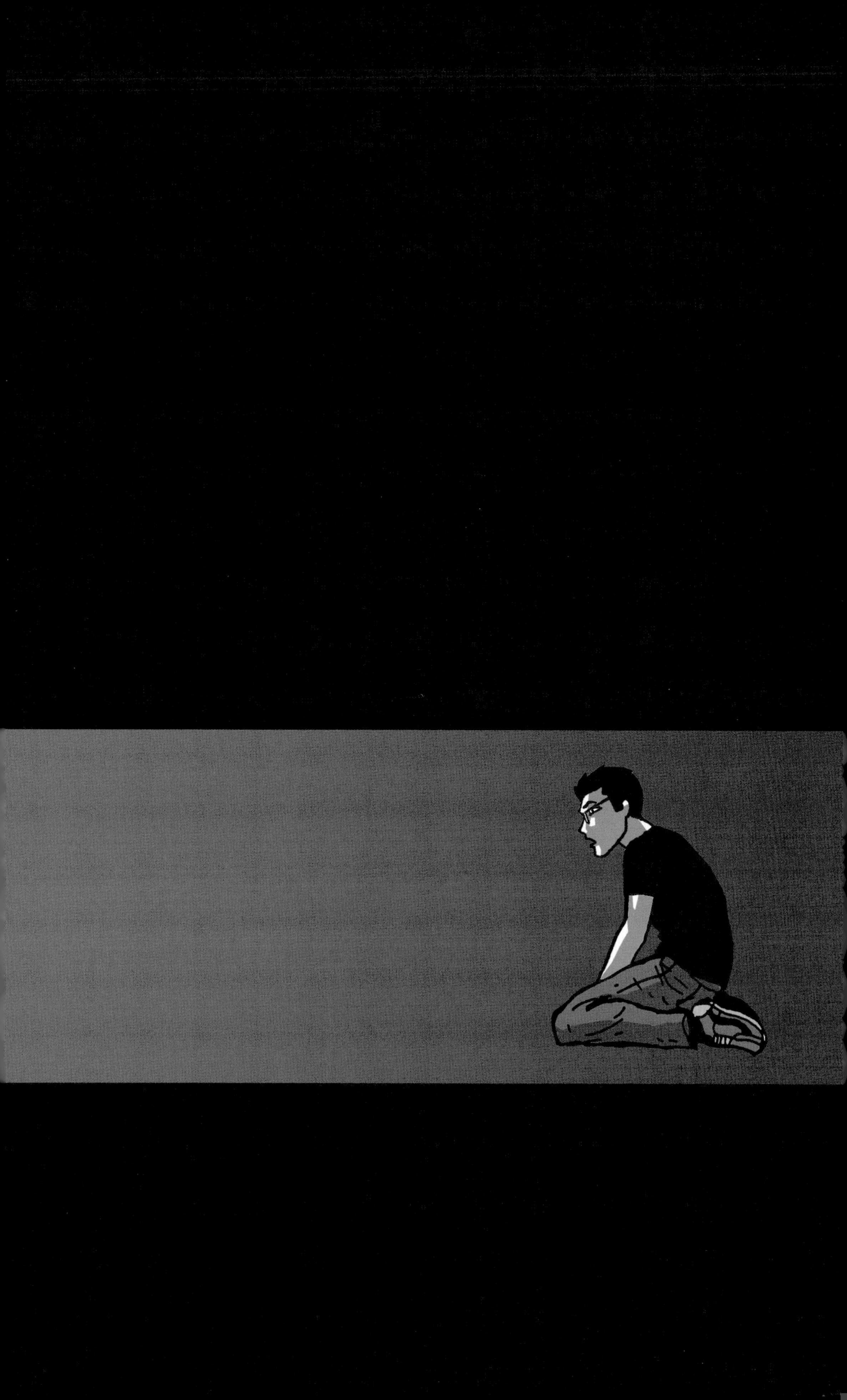

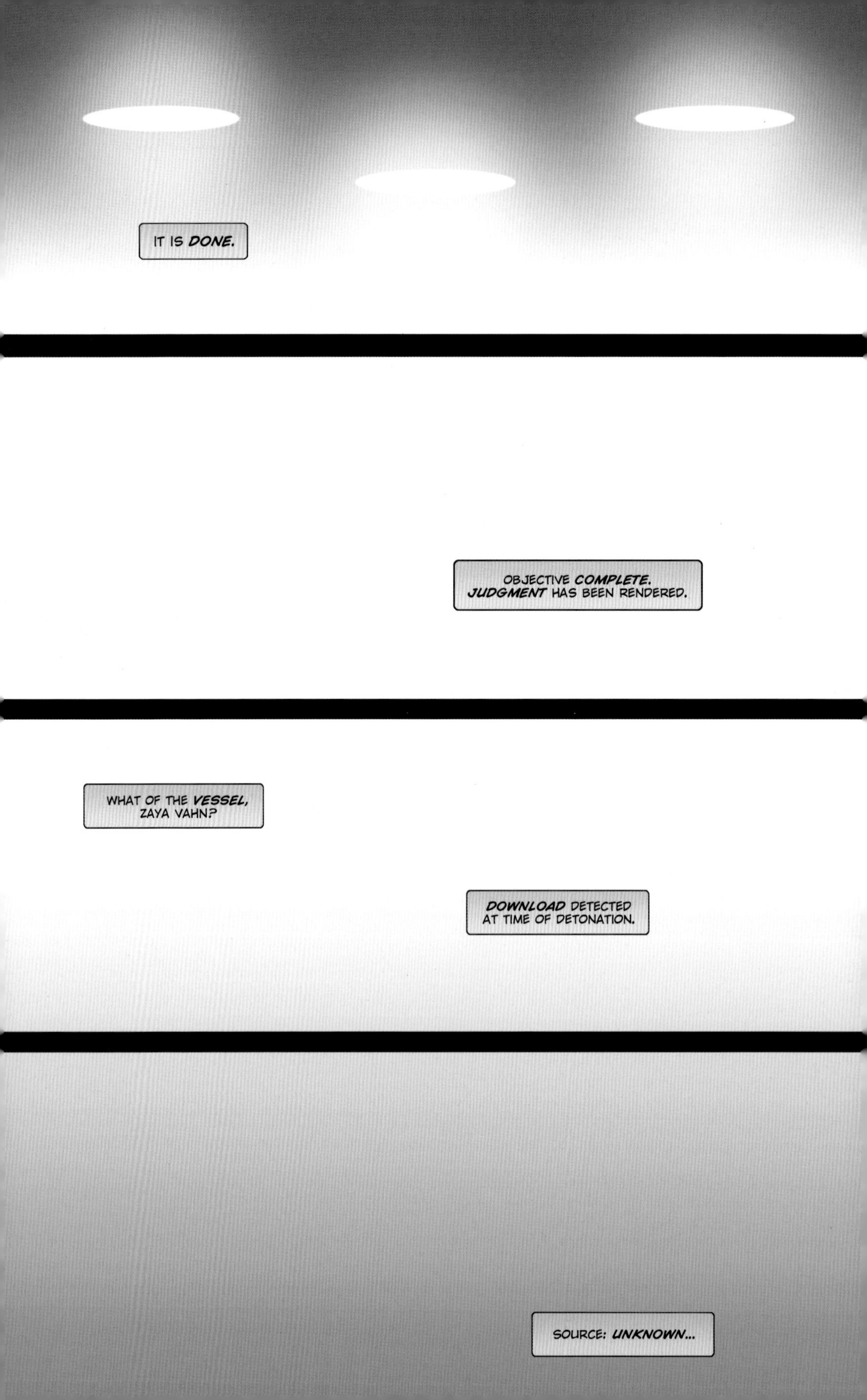
IT IS DONE.
OBJECTIVE COMPLETE. JUDGMENT HAS BEEN RENDERED.
WHAT OF THE VESSEL, ZAYA VAHN?
DOWNLOAD DETECTED AT TIME OF DETONATION.
SOURCE: UNKNOWN...

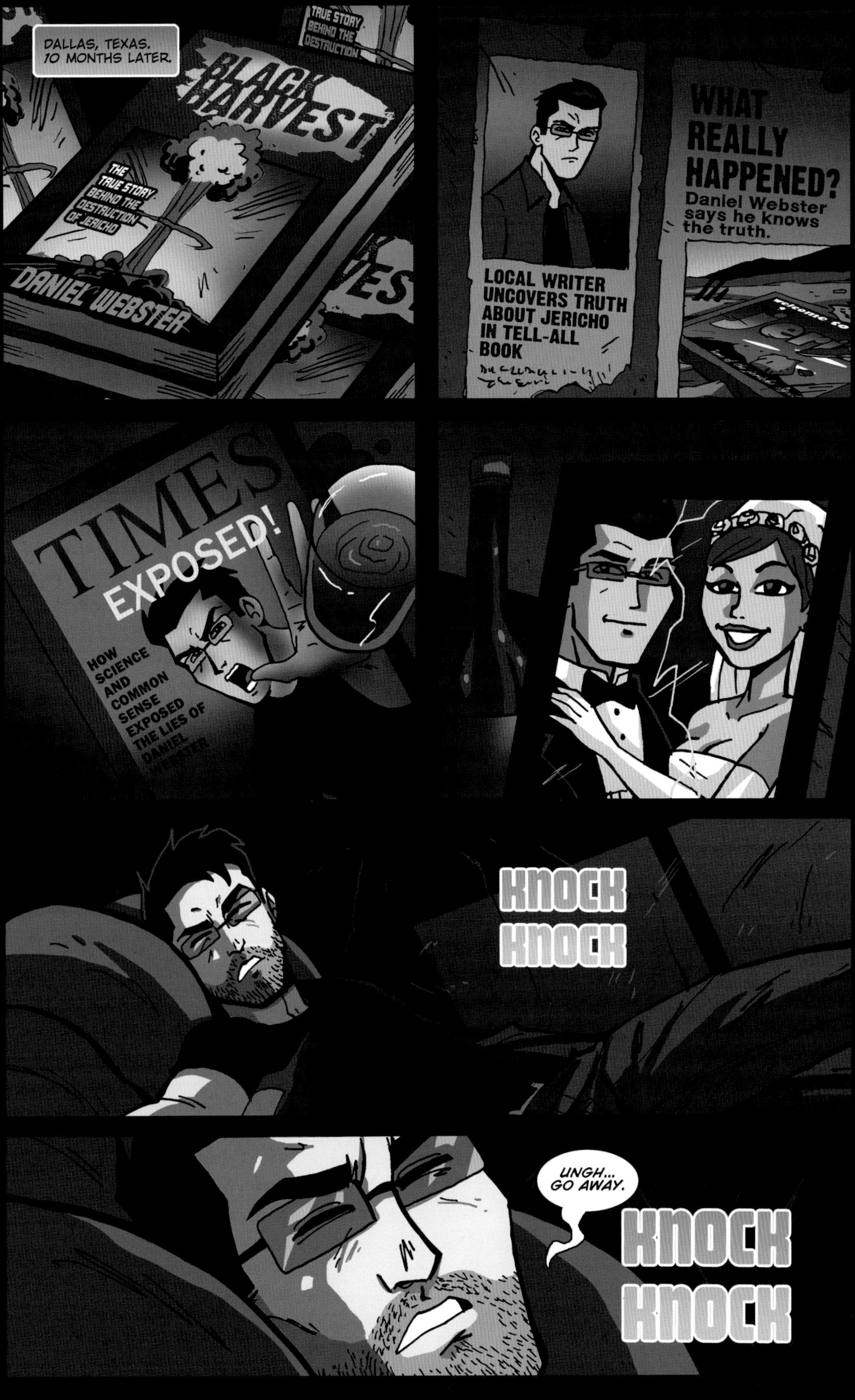
DALLAS, TEXAS.
10 MONTHS LATER.
TRUE STORY BEHIND THE DESTRUCTION
BLACK HARVEST
THE TRUE STORY BEHIND THE DESTRUCTION OF JERICHO
DANIEL WEBSTER
LOCAL WRITER UNCOVERS TRUTH ABOUT JERICHO IN TELL-ALL BOOK
WHAT REALLY HAPPENED?
Daniel Webster says he knows the truth.
TIMES
EXPOSED!
HOW SCIENCE AND COMMON SENSE EXPOSED THE LIES OF DANIEL WEBSTER
KNOCK
KNOCK
UNGH... GO AWAY.
KNOCK
KNOCK

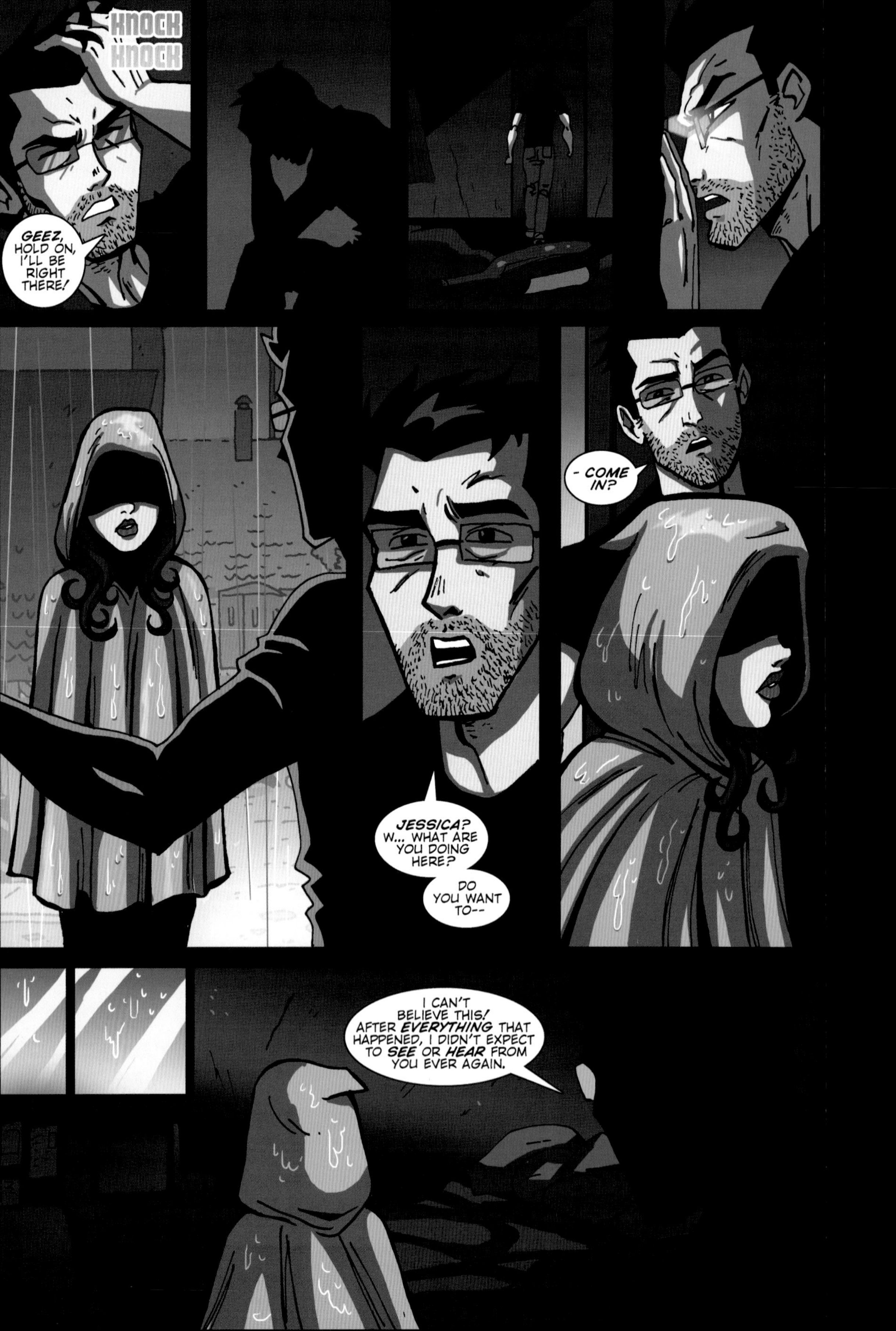
KNOCK KNOCK
GEEZ, HOLD ON, I'LL BE RIGHT THERE!
JESSICA? W... WHAT ARE YOU DOING HERE?
DO YOU WANT TO--
- COME IN?
I CAN'T BELIEVE THIS! AFTER EVERYTHING THAT HAPPENED, I DIDN'T EXPECT TO SEE OR HEAR FROM YOU EVER AGAIN.

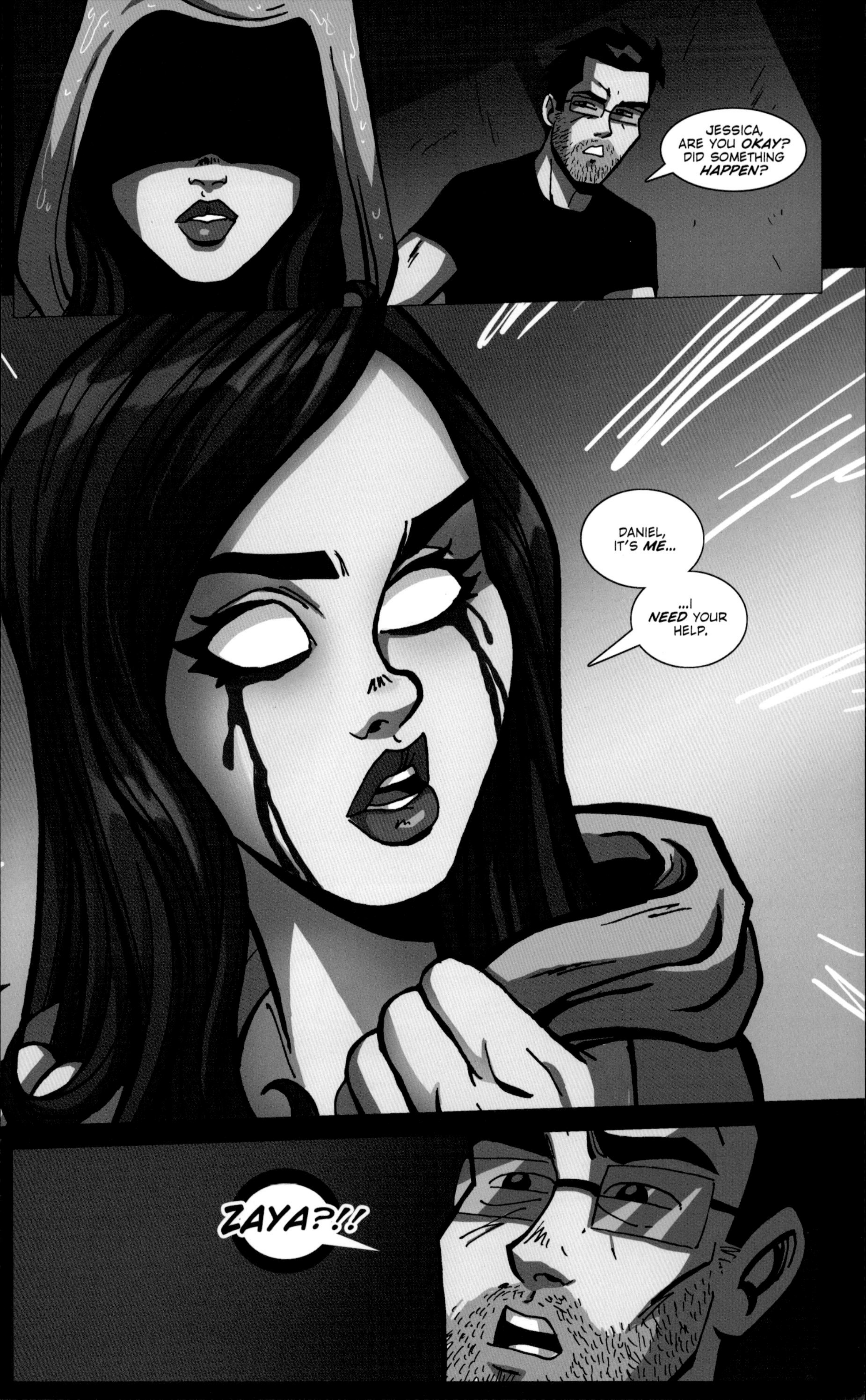
JESSICA, ARE YOU OKAY? DID SOMETHING HAPPEN?
DANIEL, IT'S ME...
...I NEED YOUR HELP.
ZAYA?!!

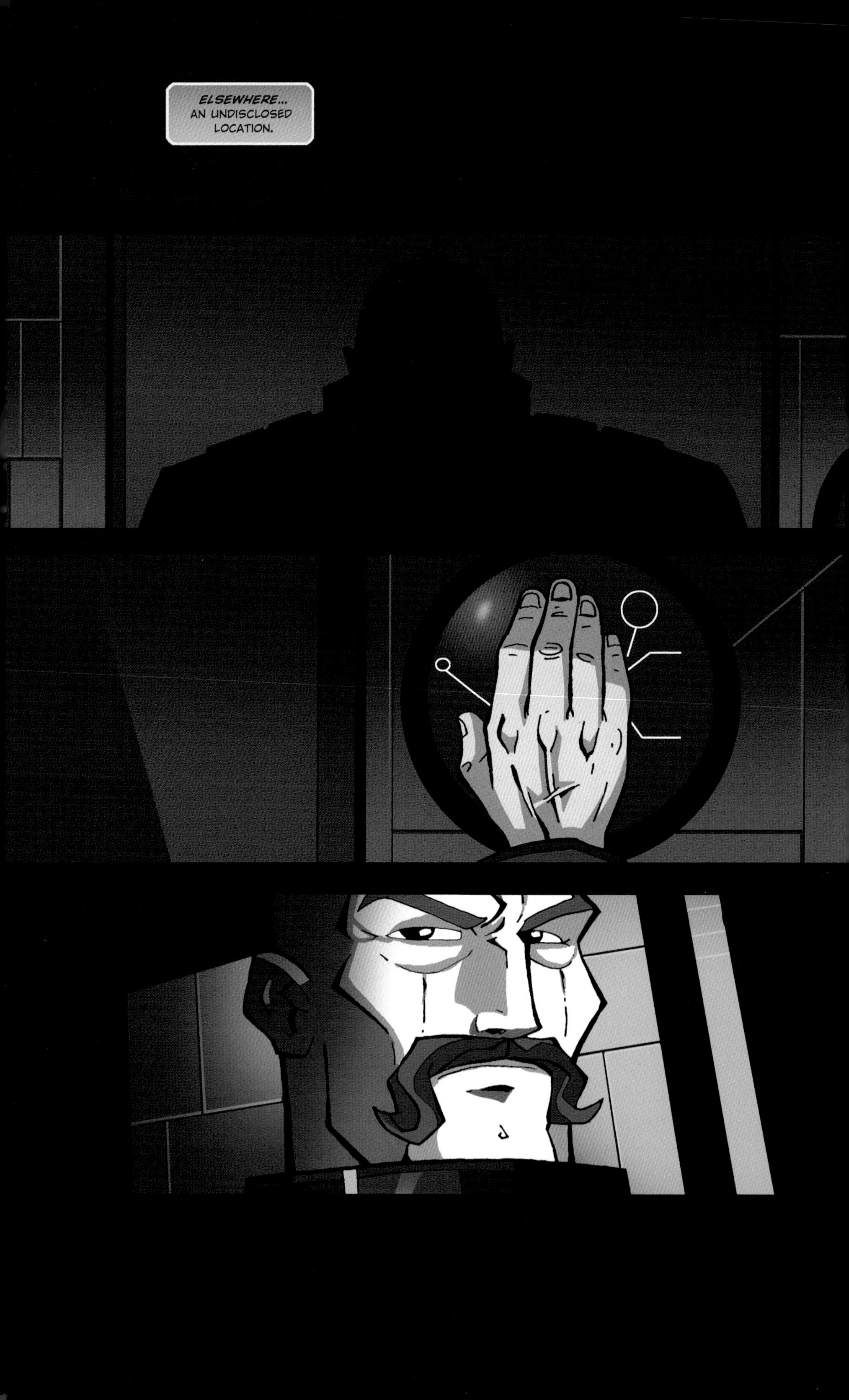
ELSEWHERE... AN UNDISCLOSED LOCATION.

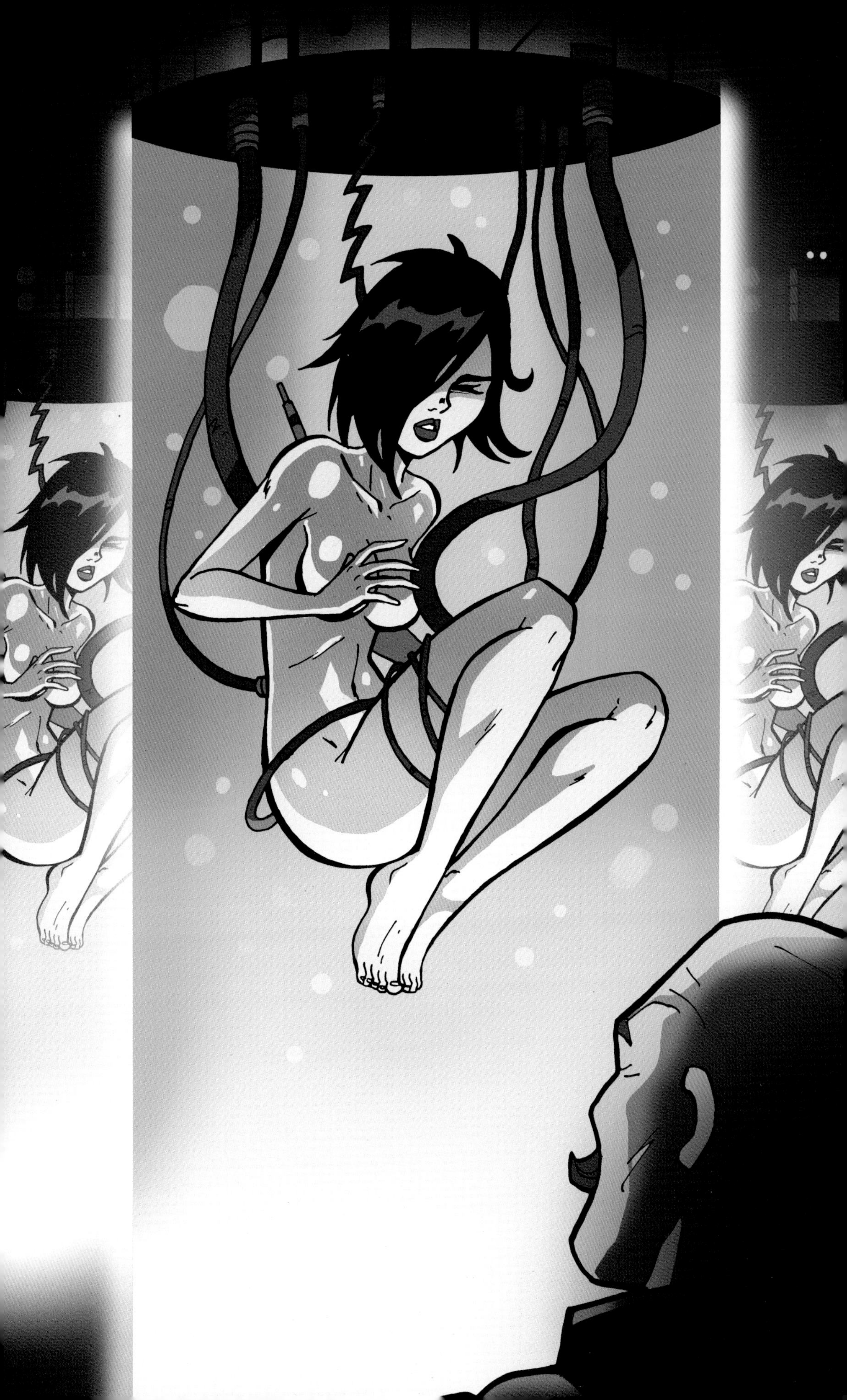

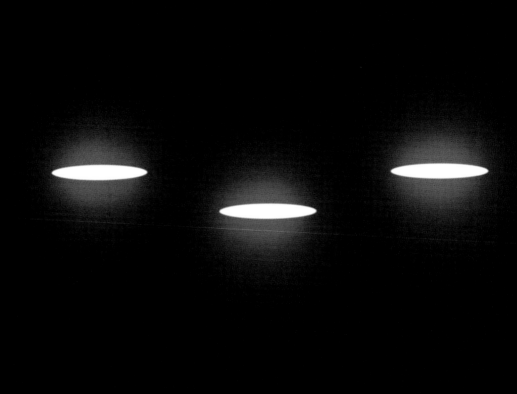

ABOUT THE CREATOR

Josh Howard's cult hit *Dead@17* was released in 2003 to rave reviews. It quickly made *Wizard Magazine's* top 10 hottest comics list and was ranked the #1 independent comic of 2005. It has also been featured in network TV shows and music videos and was recently optioned for film by Di Bonaventura Pictures.

Josh lives in Texas with his wife and two children. He is currently hard at work on the 7th and final chapter to the *Dead@17* saga.